THE

SKEENA

RIVER OF DESTINY

BY

R. GEDDES LARGE

F.R.G.S.

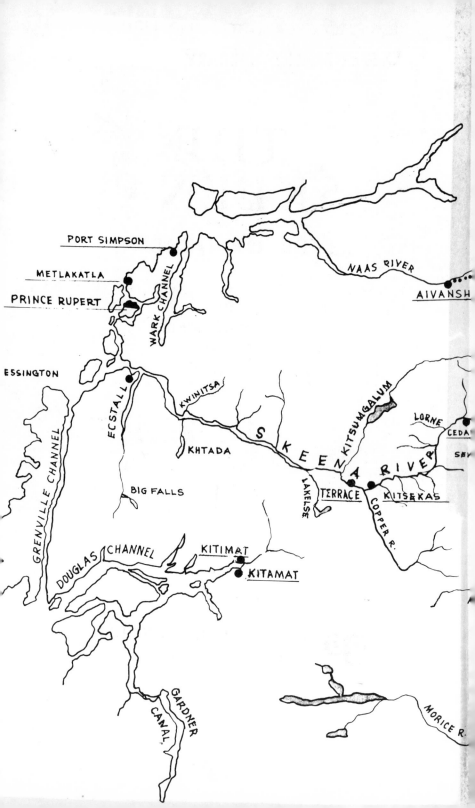

First Edition	1957
2nd Edition	1958
3rd Edition	1958
4th Edition	1962
This Edition	1981

Canadian Cataloguing in Publication Data

Large, R. Geddes, 1901 —
  The Skeena, river of destiny
  Originally published: Vancouver: Mitchell Press, 1957.
  Bibliography: p

Includes index.
ISBN 0-88826-091-1
1. Skeena Valley (b.c.) — History.

i. Title

FC3845.S594L37   1981   971.32   C81-09277-5
F1089.S5L37   1981

First published by Mitchell Press, Vancouver, B.C.
as part of a Prince Rupert, B.C. Centennial Project

Cover design this edition Nicholas Newbeck, Victoria, B.C.

Cover photos:

Top — Provincial Museum, Victoria, B.C.

Bottom left — Tourism B.C. Photo

        — Mrs. Vivian Comadina, Prince Rupert,
        B.C.

Bottom right — Mr. Fred Jessup, Sidney, B.C.

Printed in Canada

**TO
MY WIFE**

FOREWORD

This is an attempt to record the history of a portion of the Province of British Columbia which has been completely neglected by historians. It is almost too late to get first-hand information of the early days on the North Coast, but there are still a few "old-timers" who can go back a long way. When there are discrepancies in the reminiscences of these individuals, the lot of the historian is not a happy one. However, an attempt has been made to cross-check with written records wherever possible, and where there is reasonable doubt, both versions of an event have been recorded.

In the Bibliography will be found a record of the various books, papers and manuscripts consulted. In addition I am deeply indebted to Mr. Robert Tomlinson, the late Mrs. George Frizzell and Mr. Wiggs O'Neill for detailed accounts of their early experiences in the District; also to Mr. Frank Dockrill, Mrs. J. C. Spencer, Mr. T. P. Lyster (Barney) Mulvany, Mr. Charles Durham and the late Mr. George Little for personal stories. Some of the books and manuscripts were privately owned, and I wish to express my thanks to Bishop Anthony Jordan, O.M.I., Bishop H. G. Watts, Father G. Forbes, O.M.I., Major Poulton of the Salvation Army, Mrs. R. S. Sargent, Col. S. D. Johnston, Mr. Frank Anfield, Mr. John Morrison and Mr. and Mrs. T. Fraser for the loan of valuable documents. The courtesy of the management of the Prince Rupert Daily News in making available to me the early files of their own and other Prince Rupert papers was greatly appreciated.

Without the assistance and co-operation of the Provincial Archives at Victoria, this task could never have been accomplished, and a special "thank you" goes to Mr. Willard E. Ireland and his staff. I am also indebted to the Forestry and Mining Departments of the Provincial Government and to Dr. N. M.

Carter of the Dominion Fisheries Research Board for technical information.

Some of the data regarding the activities of the Hudson's Bay Company has been kindly supplied from their archives in Beaver House, London, and this information has been acknowledged in the Bibliography.

To mention all the friends who have assisted by suggestion or material would be an impossibility. Their help, nevertheless, was sincerely appreciated. The advice of Dr. W. N. Sage, until recently Professor of History at the University of British Columbia, was of great assistance in the final editing.

Finally, a large share of the credit for this effort is due my wife who first proposed the task and assisted me greatly in the work.

R. G. Large.

CONTENTS

ILLUSTRATIONS

Skeena Forks and Rocher de Boule

CHAPTER ONE

The River and The Land

Rivers are the high-roads to Civilization! From the Euphrates and the Nile of ancient days, to the Mississippi and the St. Lawrence of more modern times, they have been the gateways to continents, and the source of life for struggling man. Fortunate is the nation that is plentifully supplied with these natural highways, and much of a nation's history is recorded along their banks.

Canada is singularly blest in this respect, and the lakes and rivers, which cover the country like a net of silver thread from coast to coast, alone made it possible to explore and settle this vast domain. On the western coast three major rivers empty into the Pacific, while three more traverse Canadian territory before seeking their outlet in Alaska and the United States. Ranking second in importance amongst the three all-Canadian rivers is the Skeena, long a river of mystery, and now the road to the northern half of British Columbia.

The Indians called the river K-shian, literally, "water of the clouds". The name Skeena is commonly taken to be a derivative of the old Indian name, and certainly no other origin for it has been substantiated. Originally it was christened Ayton's River, and was so called by Capt. Charles Duncan who was in charge of the trading schooner "Princess Royal" in 1778. In his own words,[1] "on the 1st of June I got amongst Princess Royal's Isles, boomed the vessel off the rocks, and on the 2nd of June in the evening anchored in the mouth of Ayton's River about 15 leagues northeast of where I had stopt the night before". The name did not stick, however, for we find no further reference to it. For a short period it was also known as Simpson's or Babine River, and is so recorded on Arrowsmith's Map of the Province of British Columbia and Vancouver's Island, published in 1862. However, on Anderson's Map of British Columbia in 1867, it appears under its present name.

The Skeena, approximately 350 miles long, and draining an area of 15,000 square miles[2] in the northwestern portion of the Province, is the second largest river of British Columbia—

excluding the Columbia which empties south of the border. It rises in the Gunanoot Mountains, in close proximity to the headwaters of the Stikine and Naas Rivers, and flows in a southerly direction through the mountains of the Coast Range for 200 miles to its junction with its chief tributary, the Bulkley River. From that point it swings westward, to reach the sea at the 54th parallel. Essentially a mountain river, its waters are swift-flowing and treacherous. Its tributaries, with the exception of the Bulkley, Babine and Sustut, are short mountain streams, plentifully supplied by the heavy rainfall of the area; hence, the Indian name, "water of the clouds". Towards the east, however, its drainage basin encroaches on the central plateau with its myriads of lakes. The Sustut River drains Bear Lake. Babine Lake, one hundred miles long, the largest in British Columbia, empties its waters through the Babine River, which flows northward to enter the Skeena thirty-five miles above the Bulkley. The latter rises in two main branches from Morice Lake and Bulkley Lake, and flows for one hundred and twenty miles in a wide valley, before piercing the Coast Range through a narrow gap, to join the Skeena, one hundred and fifty miles from the sea. Morice Lake lies on the east side of the Coast Range, but is separated by only a few miles of mountains from salt water in Gardner Canal. Its water, therefore, makes a huge circle of nearly three hundred miles before reaching the sea, only a few miles north of its origin.

Nothing could better serve to emphasise the impressive barrier presented by the coast mountains along the whole western boundary of British Columbia. Only three valleys of any size penetrate that wall of rock throughout its length—the Fraser, Skeena and Naas. Of these the Skeena is the widest. Nowhere does one find the deep narrow canyons so characteristic of the Fraser, except in two very short stretches of river; the Bulkley rushes through a narrow gorge around the foot of Rocher de Boule Mountain as it enters the Skeena Valley, and mid-way from there to the sea, the Skeena is momentarily squeezed by the rocky walls of the Kitselas Canyon, as it enters the wide Kitsumgalum Valley.

The upper reaches of the river are tortuous, and fall rapidly through the heavily forested mountain valleys. As the Sustut and Babine tributaries enter, the valley widens and bench land on either side of the river makes its appearance. Nevertheless, the flow is still rapid and the river confined, for the most part, to steep banks. The Bulkley contributes an almost equal volume to the Skeena, and from the forks of the two rivers, the flow is widened and the velocity increased. Numerous short mountain tributaries join the river below this point, and by the time the

2

Skeena reaches the Kitselas Canyon, it hurls an impressive mass of tumultuous water through this rocky barrier into the broad Kitsumgalum Valley.

After crossing this valley, the Skeena, from a raging torrent, becomes a fickle stream, and meanders amongst islands and sandbars, unable to make up its mind which course to follow. Nevertheless, the towering mountains inexorably force its brown waters to continue westward, and finally the ocean tide rushes to meet them, adding a pinch of salt to the muddy brew.

Even at this last moment of its existence, another stream hastens to join it—the Ecstall—which enters the Skeena estuary on the south shore. This stream is important from an industrial viewpoint, as we shall see later.

Like all mountain rivers, the Skeena is obstreperous in its behaviour, and in the early summer is subject to sudden, and sometimes severe, floods. Normally the melting snow of the mountain peaks is chilled by the cold nights, so the rate of run-off is controlled. In an occasional year the heat of the summer comes early and lasts throughout the night. Then the water rages down the Skeena Valley, eroding banks, tearing up trees in its path, inundating the land and generally wreaking havoc everywhere. Such a year was 1936, when whole villages were rendered homeless; roads, railroad tracks and bridges washed out, and telegraphic communications severed. Fortunately, such years are infrequent, and generally the river stays within its banks. However, owing to the numerous short branches direct from the mountain slopes, the river level is constantly rising or falling, and in the constricted waters of the Kitselas Canyon, this can be as much as seven feet in twenty-four hours.

Such is the Skeena—a river with a dirty brown face and a violent disposition, but destined to be the gateway for the march of civilization across the northern half of the Province.

And what of the country through which it passes? For the most part it is forbiddingly mountainous, and only in the immediate vicinity of the river is there any level land. Mountain slopes and valley floors are heavily timbered, and only on the central plateau of the eastern tributaries is there any open grazing country.

And yet, if you look at a relief map of the area, a remarkable picture meets the eye. Nestled amongst the sea of mountain peaks is a chain of valleys in the form of a gigantic letter A, which to an imaginative mind might stand for Agriculture. It lies in a vertical north and south position, across the Skeena and Naas Rivers, and encompasses all the agricultural land of the district. The westward leg of the A begins at the north in the

3

broad valley of the Naas and runs straight south through the Kitsumgalum and Lakelse Valleys to the Kitimat Valley. The eastern leg begins in the same Naas Valley and extends south through the Kispiox, Skeena and Bulkley Valleys. The cross arm of the A is made by the Skeena itself which turns westward and flows across the Kitsumgalum-Lakelse Valleys. This latter valley chain is particularly important in the history and development of the district, for it gives a second line of approach to the Skeena Valley from the sea, and facilitates the recent industrial development at Kitimat.

During the last ice age a huge glacier filled these valleys, pulverized the surfaces of the confining mountains, and deposited the resulting gravel in layers along the floor. The gravel may be found today in the terraces and bars throughout the area. One immense hill lying near the mouth of the Kitamat River has supplied all the gravel needed for the big Alcan project and its surface is only scratched. All sizes of rock are there, and screening is all that is necessary before trucking it away to the cement mixer.

The large deposits of gravel in the Kitamat Valley have led some geology students to suggest that at one time the Skeena River flowed this way to the sea. It is an intriguing thought, and in some remote age may indeed have been true. Detailed geological study has not yet been carried out in the Skeena district, but it is conceded by those who should know that ever since the last ice age the Skeena has occupied its present course; and the gravel and silt of the Kitamat Valley is the work of the great ice cap, not of the mighty Skeena.

CHAPTER TWO

The People

The first inhabitants of the country, of course, were the Indians. Where they came from is still a matter of debate by anthropologists, but it is fairly well agreed that they are of Asiatic origin. Probably they entered the country in successive waves of migration, and not necessarily from the same area, as there are marked tribal differences exhibited by the Indians in the several coastal and interior sections.

One may reasonably assume that the migrants were primarily concerned with a plentiful supply of food, and certainly those who settled around the mouth of the Skeena River found it in abundance. This particular tribal group was known as Tsimpseans—"the people at the mouth of K-shian". Some of them ascended the river and settled permanently along its upper reaches, and they were called the Gitekshan, or "people who lived up the K-shian". Along the Bulkley River we find the representatives of a separate migration—a division of the Carrier or Dene Indians, who probably travelled by land across northern Alaska and the Yukon. In far smaller numbers than those who travelled by water, they were by nature a nomadic people and their villages were fewer and less well developed. Only two small settlements of these on the Bulkley and two on Babine Lake remain, and as far as historical record goes, ever existed, with the exception of a small group on Bear Lake. This statement, of course, applies only to the Skeena and its tributaries. The same tribe was settled widely along the Fraser watershed.

It can be summarily stated that the Tsimpsean civilization depended on cedar and salmon. The main body of this people settled on the islands in close proximity to the mouth of the river. There they built their permanent villages, collections of community houses constructed from the large cedar trees which abounded along the coast. They lived by, and on, the sea. Their food was, in large part, obtained from it, although berries and roots were used in season. Deer and other animals were plentiful, but the forest was dense and it was much easier to obtain the products of the sea.

They were skilled seamen and journeyed about in large canoes hollowed out of logs from the same bounteous cedar. Their utensils and even their clothing and bedding were made from it. Although they made some canoes themselves, the largest were obtained by trade with the Haida Indians of the Queen Charlotte Islands, who were the foremost canoe men of the coast.

As already intimated, their food was taken mainly from the sea. Halibut, cod, and shell fish were found everywhere in coastal waters the year round. However, the chief fish was the salmon, which came in schooling millions each summer, to ascend the streams and rivers of the coast. In this region, the greatest run was up the Skeena, and the presence of these fish and their pursuit was the dominant factor in the secondary migration of the Tsimpseans up the river. Summer villages or camps were established as far inland as the Kitselas Canyon, and when the salmon run was over, the people returned to their permanent homes on the coast. At Kitselas, a permanent village was built and some of them remained there throughout the year. They were still considered Tsimpsean, however, as distinct from the Gitekshan who lived further up the river.

The Gitekshan villages were situated along a fairly short stretch of the river around the mouths of some of the principal tributaries. Thus, where the Kitwancool River joins the Skeena was found the first village, Kitwanga, "the place of the rapids". About ten miles up the Kitwancool River was the village of the same name, which means, literally, "the narrow place". Further up the Skeena, at the entrance of the Kitseguecla River, was a third village. It took its name, Kitseguecla, from a prominent mountain peak in the vicinity. Ten miles above this point was the entrance of the Bulkley River, and the village of Gitenmaks was located on the bank of the Skeena nearby. The name was derived from the custom of the natives thereabouts to fish for steelhead salmon by spearing the fish in torch light. The village of Kispiox was another ten miles up the Skeena at the mouth of the tributary of that name, which means "loud talkers".

These were the main Gitekshan villages and they remain to this day; but there were two smaller villages some considerable distance above, at the confluence of the Skeena and Babine Rivers—the village of Kuldaw, "back in the woods", on the former, and Kisgegas on the latter. Both these sites have been long deserted, the villagers joining the settlements down the river.

The Carrier Indians, known as Babines, had one large village located near the lower end of Babine Lake. Another small group lived on Bear Lake which empties into the Sustut River, a branch

Fort Simpson from early painting

A portion of early Metlakatla

—Courtesy of Wrathalls Photo Finishing
Bulkley River at Moricetown

—Courtesy of Wrathalls Photo Finishing
Indian Bridge at Hagwilget

of the Skeena near its source. This group figures in the early trading history of the area and will be referred to again. On the Bulkley River two villages were strategically placed for gathering the annual supply of salmon. The largest, at the lower end of the Bulkley Canyon, was known as Hagwilget—"the gentle men or quiet people"—in contrast to the Kispiox. This was also the site of the great gatherings of coast and interior Indians in the fall of the year which will be described later. The second village was only a short distance further up the river beside a waterfall, where the salmon were easily obtained during their struggles to surmount the obstacle. This village now bears the name of Moricetown, in memory of the famous Father Morice.

It is not my intention to write a lengthy treatise on the Skeena Indians. Much has been written on the subject. But it is necessary that we know something of the habits and customs of these people, in order that we may be able to appreciate the problems that confronted the early settlers and explorers. They were a primitive people. With the exception of the gathering of the annual salmon run, which they preserved by smoking and drying, they were generally improvident, living from day to day, and suffering, in consequence, periods of near starvation. Their clothing was of the simplest kind. On the coast, the majority went naked during the milder seasons. In the winter, they wore robes woven from cedar bark and the skins of animals. In the interior, where the cold was more intense, cariboo and moose hides supplied their clothing and the moccasins for their feet.

Their social life was based on clans or phratries which extended beyond villages, and even tribes. They were ruled by chiefs of the various clans, great rivalry developing for supremacy in the respective villages. While hunting and fishing occupied the summer season the winters found them gathered together in their villages, feasting, dancing and enacting elaborate rites in connection with numerous secret societies. Strangely enough, the Indian had no fermented drink, and the winter orgies were free from drunkenness until the coming of the white man.

While not directly connected with the Skeena, one other activity should be mentioned because of its wide significance in the economy of these people. This was the annual run of a small fish known as the oolichan. It never appeared on the Skeena in significant numbers, but in the spring of the year, visited the Naas River, a short distance to the north, in teeming millions. To this point, therefore, in the month of March, came the natives from the whole north coast and even the interior. Hundreds of canoes filled with people made the journey, and all were engaged for the next month or so in the oolichan fishery.

The oolichan, a member of the smelt family, is exceedingly rich in oil. While some fish were eaten fresh and others dried and smoked, the chief industry was the extraction of the oil. The fish were allowed to partially decay before the extraction took place, and the resultant oil or grease had a very distinctive, strongly rancid odor. It was highly prized as a food and a source of energy, and was used as a sauce with nearly all their articles of diet. Such a valuable commodity placed the Indians of the area in an enviable position, and they used the oolichan grease as an article of trade with other tribes less fortunate. While most of the grease was transported by canoe, the interior Indians had to pack theirs over trails to their distant homes. Two such routes were in regular use from the upper limits of navigation on the Naas River. One crossed over into the Kitwancool Valley and thence to the Skeena, while the other went farther inland to descend the Kispiox River to the villages in that area. This latter route crossed the Cranberry River and was known as the Cranberry Trail, and both routes were familiarly known as the Grease Trails. Other than the arduous canoe trip up the Skeena, they were the only means of access to the upper country.

This was the Skeena district before the coming of the white man—a mountainous, heavily wooded land, traversed by a swift-flowing treacherous river. Guarded to the westward by numerous islands and sunken reefs against approach by sea, it was vulnerable only to the east of the coast mountains, where the open park land of the central plateau and the numerous lakes and streams awaited the coming of the explorer's canoe.

CHAPTER THREE

Early Explorations

The earliest European visitors to the shores of British Columbia were content to touch only the fringe of the outer islands. Their objective was the discovery of the elusive Northwest Passage, but the abundance of furs which could be obtained from the natives soon changed the nature of the voyages. Spanish, English and Russian ships came in increasing numbers to trade for the sea otter skins, which were then sold in China and the goods of the Orient purchased for the homeward journey.

The chief points of call for these traders were Nootka, on Vancouver Island, the northern end of the Queen Charlotte Islands, and King William Sound in what is now Alaska. Apparently no attempt was made to penetrate the numerous islands along the coast, and one can easily understand that with the ships of that day, the narrow channels and strong tides presented a formidable problem in navigation. They were content to let the Indians come to them with the furs, and nothing was known of the mainland north of the Straits of Juan de Fuca.

In 1792 Captain Vancouver undertook the first survey of the coast. Beginning in the south, he entered the same Straits and in the first year worked up the coast as far as Burke Channel. The following year he returned, and continuing north, completed his survey to include Dixon Entrance and southeastern Alaska. In due course he sailed up Grenville Channel, and entered what is now known as the mouth of the Skeena. On July 9th and 10th in 1793, his first officer, Mr. Whidby, conducted a survey of this area, and in Vancouver's diary we read—"they found themselves opposed by a very rapid stream against which the boats could scarcely make any way. It was remarked that no part of this stream seemed to enter the passage which the boats had pursued (Grenville Channel), but was wholly directed towards the above SSW opening that appeared to divide the south western shore, and left little doubt of that passage communicating with the ocean, as the current was evidently the ebb tide."

Mr. Whidby proceeded up the mainland shore and rounded a point which Captain Vancouver named Point Lambert, after

Commissioner Lambert of the Navy. He continued up to Raspberry Island at the mouth of the Ecstall River, where he determined to stay until low water—"that a better judgement might be formed of their actual situations, since from the rapidity and regularity of the tides, he began to suspect it to be a river." This estuary was called Port Essington after Captain Essington of the Navy, and although the ebb tide was noted as running 5 knots, it was only recorded that "three small rivulets entered at its head".

Thus, Captain Vancouver missed both the Fraser and the Skeena Rivers in his survey—a remarkable coincidence when one considers the painstaking thoroughness which characterized his work. Nevertheless, whether he knew it or not, to Mr. Whidby must go the honor of being the first white man to breast the waters of the Skeena River.

With the increasing knowledge of the coastal waters following Vancouver's surveys, the trading ships ventured further inland, and contacts were made with the Tsimpsean natives. The fur seal was still the prize they sought, and as the demand for the skin increased, the slaughter of these animals by the natives kept pace, until finally they became almost extinct. To make the trips profitable other furs were taken, notably beaver. These animals, while occurring along the coast, were much more plentiful in the Interior and the colder climate produced a much better fur. It is not surprising, therefore, to find the Coast Indian bartering with the Interior people for the skins which they, in turn, passed on to the traders on board ship, at a profit to themselves. This traffic was exclusively in the hands of the Nisgas of the Naas River, and the Tsimpseans, particularly the latter, who, through their excursions up the Skeena, had ready access to the tribes of the Central Interior. Canoes, loaded with Indians, passed up the Skeena in the fall of the year, and gathered at the Forks, (the junction of the Skeena and Bulkley Rivers), where the Interior tribes came to meet them. Days of feasting, dancing and gambling followed and the exchange of trade goods and furs took place. So the Interior Indians had the white man's goods long before the first white man set foot in the country.

When Simon Fraser founded Fort McLeod, he came in contact with Indians from the region of Bear Lake who had "iron works and ornaments"[1]; and Father Morice in his history of the area says, "The source of their supply of implements of European manufacture was merely the tribes of Tsimpsean parentage stationed along the Skeena, who obtained them from their congeners on the Coast." This trade, controlled by the Tsimpseans, was jealously guarded as we shall see later on when the Yukon Telegraph crews attempted to ascend the river. It was undoubtedly responsible in some measure for the delay in opening up this part of the country. To quote Father Morice again—"Nay, the Skeena Valley, precisely on account of the monopoly claimed by the Tsimpsean adventurers, is one of the territories of any importance within British Columbia which has remained the longest free of any real white man."

Under these conditions we must go to the east to find the first white penetration of the Skeena watershed. It is beyond the scope of this narrative to record the development of the fur trade in the Interior of British Columbia, and the march of civilization down the tributaries of the Fraser River. However, a brief note is necessary to maintain chronological order. After the voyage of exploration of Sir Alexander McKenzie who reached the Pacific in 1793, no further journeying in northern British Columbia was attempted until Simon Fraser entered the country via the Parsnip River, and established Fort McLeod in 1805. The following year he pushed further westward, discovered Stuart Lake and Fraser Lake, and built Fort St. James or Nakasleh and Fort Fraser or Natleh, respectively. In 1807 he built Fort George at the confluence of the Fraser and Nechako Rivers, and then descended the Fraser the next spring, to finally establish its identity as distinct from the Columbia further south.

After Fraser's departure, D. W. Harmon arrived in 1810 to assist John Stuart, Fraser's successor, and Harmon was placed in charge of the post at Stuart Lake. During the summer of 1811 a Babine Indian with his son had visited the fort; and in January 1812, while McDougall from Fort McLeod was visiting him for the New Year's festivities, the two friends decided to visit the Babine Indians. Travelling for seven days over frozen lakes, they finally met Indians who had never before seen white men, and journeying down the large lake they had now reached, they saw four separate villages. D. W. Harmon and James McDougall must therefore be credited with the first exploration of Skeena waters.[2]

No attempt was made to extend the forts in New Caledonia, as the area was called, until after the amalgamation of the Northwest Fur Company and Hudson's Bay Company which occurred in 1821. Trading excursions were made into the Babine each year, to compete with the traffic of the Tsimpseans to the west, and eventually, in 1822, a fort was built on the shore of Babine Lake. This fort was known as Kilmaurs, and the name was also spelt Killmars and Kilmers. In 1826 a second fort was erected on the Skeena tributaries at Bear Lake, and named Fort Connolly after the Chief Trader who was in charge of New Caledonia at the time.

The reason for building these two forts was twofold. Probably the primary reason was the extension of trading facilities and the hope of getting more furs. Another very important consideration was the need for food. The long and arduous trip across the Rockies made the transportation of sufficient food to supply the new posts an impossibility. Wild animals of the larger species were scarce in the western country, cariboo and deer being the only representatives of that family found, and they, not in large numbers. Fort Connolly alone had access to any considerable supply of fresh meat of this type, and Morice quotes the records of 1836 to show that 450 pounds were consumed in that Fort, while Fort St. James had only 32 pounds. The other articles of diet are of interest—67,510 salmon; 11,941 of the smaller fish plus 781 sturgeon and 346 trout; 2,160 rabbits; 153 ducks; 10 lynxes; eight marmots; three porcupines; one swan and 14 dogs. Horseflesh was also recognized as an article of diet, but the need for these animals in transportation made them too valuable to be used for food. Fish, therefore, became the chief article of diet, and a great deal of time and effort was expended in maintaining an adequate supply. It is interesting to note that even at that early date, the annual run of salmon up the Fraser River fluctuated between wide extremes. It is recorded[3] that "every second year the run was poor, and every fourth year a failure." And this, before there was any fishing by the white man! To tap the more reliable source of the Skeena River, it became necessary to have establishments on that river system—hence Forts Kilmaurs and Connolly.

No more beautiful location could be imagined for a post than the one chosen on Babine Lake. It was on a promontory on the east shore, not far from the outlet of the lake. The largest body of fresh water in the Province, Babine is also one of the most beautiful. It is long and narrow, with numerous islands, bays and sandy beaches throughout its length. The shores are heavily wooded, the eastern low and rolling, the western presenting a background of much higher hills which are called the Babine Mountains. The verdure is pine with cottonwood, birch and poplar along the water, giving rise to a veritable riot of color in the fall of the year.

The story of Fort Kilmaurs or Old Fort Babine, as it later became known, presents many names, some still widely known in the district—Messrs. Roussain, Brown, McBean, Morwick, Cameron, McLean, Thomas, Charles, etc. Father Morice, in his history, says—"Fort Babine was famous for the quantity of salmon it yielded. From the point of view of the trader, it was a place of but secondary importance, many of the Indians there taking their pelts to the Skeena River for barter with the native adventurers from the Coast. Another article which was derived from the Post was a sort of putrid salmon grease[4] to smell which is nowadays sufficient to disgust any civilized nostril. Yet in those days it was relished by aborigines and Hudson's Bay Company servants alike. Owing to the usual abundance of salmon at Babine, the sleigh dogs of the Stuart Lake establishment were generally sent to pass the summer there."

Life in all the early forts was strenuous, and threatened frequently by truculent natives; and Fort Kilmaurs was no exception. The natives here, as previously pointed out, were not particularly loyal to the Hudson's Bay Company, since they traded largely with the Coast, and their attitude to the various men who, in turn, took charge of the Fort was treacherous and oftentimes belligerent. This resulted in fatal consequences on one occasion, which does not reflect credit on the white man.[5] In 1842 the Fort was placed under the control of one William Morwick who held the rank of Postmaster. A Hagwilget Indian, Lekwe by name, brought a cariboo to the post for barter, and the negotiations for purchase became heated. No sale being accomplished, the Indian returned the next day, when Toin, the interpreter, provoked the Indian, and finally shot him in the arm with a load of rock salt which had been prepared the night before by Morwick. The Indian, in retaliation, stabbed the interpreter and was then restrained by Morwick and another employee. A rumour of Lekwe's death somehow got out amongst the Indians without the Fort, so the son-in-law, whose name is recorded as "Grand Visage", rushed up to the building, and fired a shot at Morwick, whom he could see within, through a window. Morwick was hit in the head and succumbed.

To restore order, and avenge the Postmaster's death, Peter Skene Ogden, who was then in charge of the District, sent William McBean and a party of about twelve men. Before they arrived at Fort Babine, the murderer had built a crude block house and taken refuge within. It was obvious to McBean that an open assault would be costly, so under promise of leniency, he persuaded Grand Visage to come out, when he was immediately shot. So went "justice" in those early days of Hudson's Bay Company rule!

CHAPTER FOUR

Port Simpson

We shall now leave the Interior for the time being and return to the Coast. The Hudson's Bay Company had extended their string of forts down the Columbia to their headquarters at Fort Vancouver near the mouth of the river. The director of this large area, known as the Western District, was Dr. John McLoughlin, an able and benevolent administrator. Through his efforts, the Hudson's Bay Company became supreme in the region around the Columbia, American traders being repeatedly unsuccessful in opposition. On the north coast, however, the going was not so easy. Here the Yankee ships penetrated the coastal waters unhindered and vied with the Russians in procuring the bulk of the lucrative fur trade.

To meet this competition, it was decided to establish a series of forts along the coast, the first of which was built at Langley on the Fraser River. After a preliminary reconnaissance by Peter Skene Ogden in the summer of 1830, Captain Aemilius Simpson who was Superintendent of the Marine Department of the Hudson's Bay Company, journeyed to the Naas River in the "Dryad" the following year, and there he established Fort Naas near the large Indian village of Ewen Naas.[1] The site was on what is now known as Fort Point, just below Mill Bay. Captain Simpson survived the founding of the fort by only a couple of months, for he took ill on a trading trip to Skidegate on the Queen Charlotte Islands and died. He was buried in the fort he had founded and the name was changed to Fort Simpson in his honor.

Bancroft in his Northwest Coast II has this to say of Captain Simpson: "For a British tar and a brave man on duty, dealing rum, molasses, beads and blankets to savages for wild beasts' skins, Simpson was excessively the gentleman. Though an efficient officer, he was somewhat eccentric. For example, his hands must be incased in kid before he could give an order on his own deck in the daylight, and if the occasion was perilous or peculiar, his gloves must be white kid. Form was nine-tenths of the law with him and the other tenth was conformity.

"It is believed that Captain Simpson was the means of bringing the first apple trees to this coast. At a dinner party in England, just before sailing, a lady laughingly slipped some apple pips into his waistcoat pocket and told him to carry them out to his far-off destination and then plant them. The incident was forgotten by Simpson 'til he arrived at Fort Vancouver, when, wearing the same waistcoat at a formal dinner at the Fort, the pips were found, duly planted, and produced apple trees."[2]

The fort on the Naas proved very unsatisfactory, as the distance from the open sea made its approach extremely difficult, and the winters were very severe. In 1834, Captain Alexander Duncan, the new commander of the "Dryad", in company with Messrs. James Birnie, Alexander C. Anderson and Dr. William F. Tolmie selected a new site for the fort in McLoughlin's Bay, a point about midway between the Naas and Skeena Rivers. The work of clearing was immediately begun and on August 30, 1834, the original fort was abandoned and Fort Simpson, or as it is now known, Port Simpson, came into being. The establishment had been under the charge of Dr. John Frederick Kennedy, who should be remembered as the first medical man on the Naas River and at Fort Simpson. He spent most of his years of service with the Hudson's Bay Company as the factor in charge at Fort Simpson, was made a Chief Trader in 1847 and retired to Victoria in 1856.

Anyone who is familiar with the vegetation of the coast can appreciate what a task confronted the builders of the new fort. John Wark, who visited Fort Simpson the following year, describes their labors in his diary[3]—"In pursuance of instructions, some ground is being cleared for a garden and a most tedious, laborious, and difficult job it will be. The ground is so thickly wooded and so full of stumps, fallen timber and roots, and though it is on the declivity of a rising ground it is so wet that it will require a good deal of draining. The soil on the surface is composed of black peat and moss with decayed roots, wood and other vegetable substance and does not appear well adapted for tillage, but may answer this purpose well when mixed with the under strata which is composed of sandy gravel and some shells. But stirring this up and mixing it will require much time and labor." And again, "the men employed clearing ground for potatoes, and a most tedious and laborious job it is. When the trees are cleared away with their branches, the stumps that remain are mostly of a large size and so close together that there is no means of making the ground of any use but by entirely removing them, which from their great weight is very difficult. Indeed the ground is mixed with a complete mass of roots intertwined and in order to get rid of them the ground has to be all turned over from one to two and a half or three feet in depth; moreover it is so wet that a considerable part of it is a complete quagmire." To make matters worse, the climate was hard on the men, with a quarter to a third of them constantly laid up. The Indians were an additional hazard, as they were of a thieving disposition. Wark records the incident of one man laying down his axe to light his pipe and when he stooped to retrieve his axe it had been stolen. As a matter of fact, this occurrence built up into a serious crisis in a very few minutes. A group of Massett Indians, on their return from the oolichan fishing on the Naas, had stopped in for a visit at Fort Simpson. It was one of these men who pilfered the axe. Dr. Kennedy immediately ordered the chief to have it returned, which he agreed to do. He asked Dr. Kennedy to accompany him and Kennedy was prepared to go when Wark dissuaded him—a fortunate thing as it turned out. The chief was shot in the altercation which ensued between him and the thief. This precipitated a pitched battle between the two families concerned. The marksmanship was poor, and although the contest continued throughout the day, only one woman was killed and the contestants finally settled the dispute by a property exchange. However, there is no record of the axe being returned to its owner.

In spite of the difficulties of construction, the new fort was admirably located. The harbor was of uniform depth for anchoring, reasonably well protected from the prevailing winds, and easily accessible for a sailing ship from the open ocean. The surroundings were beautiful, and while the land was similar in character to that found generally along the north coast, it was more level than in most places and provided ample space for future gardens and an expanding community.

There were no Indians encamped in McLoughlin Bay. Large settlements were located five miles south at a creek called Lakou, and again twenty miles further south in what was later to become the harbor of Prince Rupert. With the building of the Fort, the natives rapidly congregated in its vicinity, erecting their large community houses along the beach on either side until over two thousand were permanently living there.

The Fort itself was typical of those built throughout the Province by the Hudson's Bay Company. An area 240 feet square was surrounded by a stockade 22 feet high with block houses at each corner. On the inside of the stockade walls a platform extended around all four sides about four feet below the top, which enabled a sentry to see clearly around the surrounding country, and also permitted the defenders to fire over the top of the walls in case of attack. Six and nine pounder guns were mounted in two of the corner blockhouses, diagonally opposed, so that the guns commanded the approaches to all four sides of the fort. Within the enclosure, separate buildings were provided for the senior employees and the laborers. There was also a large building for storing trade goods and furs, and another one for the trading. Eventually, smaller buildings housed the blacksmith shop and carpenter shop. In the center were the bell tower and flag pole.

The stockade walls were very heavy, one writer reporting them as constructed of tree trunks two feet in diameter.[4] Certainly, the gate in the front wall, facing on the beach, was massive and would have required cannon to demolish it. In spite of all this precaution, or perhaps because of it, the Fort was never put to the test and Morrison[5], when he visited it in 1866, commented on the fact that the gate was wide open and the Indians free to pass in and out at will. It is doubtful, however, if such freedom was permitted in the early years, as the Indians were considered to be treacherous, and it was the usual practice to restrict the trading to one man at a time.

It was the policy of the Hudson's Bay Company that their establishments should be self-supporting as far as possible, and it was not long before land was cleared around the Fort and a large garden planted in potatoes and assorted vegetables. The season was late, but the ground, once it had been turned over and properly fertilized, often by seaweed, was productive. However, it never met the entire needs of the Fort, and additional potatoes were purchased from the Queen Charlotte Island natives; other supplies were requisitioned from the farms at Fort Vancouver on the Columbia.

Fort Simpson immediately became the headquarters of the fur trade on the Canadian side of the north coast. The Company ships visited in northern waters each year, and for several months worked out of the harbor on short trips to the neighbouring tribes, even invading Russian territory to the north. In the intervals between these visits the Indians came in by canoe and traded their furs and produce—chiefly deer and fish, but also some wild fowl.

The first clerk in charge was John Kennedy, and he was superseded by John Wark in 1835. The latter's name and that of Finlayson, a later employee, are commemorated in the names of two well known channels on the coast, Wark Channel near Fort Simpson and Finlayson Channel near Millbank Sound.[6]

CHAPTER FIVE

Duncan and Metlakatla

The opening up of this small corner of Canada was in sharp contrast to the history of the development of the rest of the country. The usual sequence of the entrance of explorers, followed by exploiters, then settlers, and finally the Church, was in the main reversed. Except for the explorers who journeyed along the fringes of the territory, as already recounted, and the men in the isolated trading posts at Fort Simpson and the central interior, the first white settlers in most of the Skeena area were the emissaries of the Church. Indeed, the development of this northern country for the next fifty years is dominated by the personalities of two men, William Duncan and Robert Cunningham, both of whom came out from the Old Land to British Columbia in the employ of the Church Missionary Society.

Until 1850 all commerce centered around Fort Simpson, and it was a point of call for all ships entering these waters. Among them were ships of Her Majesty's Navy, and the commanding officer of one of them, Captain Prevost of H.M.S. "Virago", was deeply impressed by the debauchery of the native population surrounding the Fort. On his return to England he communicated with the Church Missionary Society and urged them to send out a missionary to minister to the needs of the Pacific Coast Indians. William Duncan, a young man who was just completing his studies at the Church College, was chosen. Duncan was born in 1832 and began life as a clerk and salesman for a tannery.[1] He was deeply religious and finally applied for training for the ministry. The call for a missionary to the natives at Fort Simpson came just before he graduated, and as the ship on which he must sail was due to leave in a few days, he was commissioned without graduation, but, on the understanding that after he had learned the language and his health had proven adaptable to the Coast climate, he would be ordained.

He took passage with Captain Prevost on his new ship the H.M.S. "Satellite" and after an uneventful voyage arrived at the port of Victoria. Such was the reputation of the Indians of the north coast, that Governor Douglas and other prominent people in the community tried to dissuade Duncan from proceeding to his northern post, and urged him to undertake work in the vicinity of Victoria. The young man was resolute, however, and occupied his time in Victoria by beginning a study of the language of the Tsimpseans, his teacher being one of the Tsimpsean Indians camped on the outskirts of the settlement. Eventually he was able to secure passage up the coast on the Hudson's Bay Company ship "Otter", on one of her periodic trading voyages, and with letters of introduction from Governor Douglas, he landed at Fort Simpson on October 1st, 1857, and was given quarters in the Fort.

Word of his impending arrival had preceded him and the Indians awaited him with mingled curiosity and hostility. However, he was in no hurry to gratify the former, nor face the latter, but spent the first months amongst his future parishioners behind the walls of the Fort. Anyone knowing the later history of his life would protest any suggestion that this was due to a lack of courage. On the contrary, it was a deliberate course of action, built on a determination to make his first contact with the native through his own language. He secured the services of a young man, Clah by name, as his instructor and spent the long winter preparing and mastering a vocabulary and grammar of the Tsimpsean tongue. Since Clah knew very little English it was a difficult task, but by the 13th of June of the following year Duncan felt he was sufficiently familiar with the language to make his first attempt at preaching. He did not lack an audience for the Indians' curiosity had been greatly stimulated by the delay, and the first day he preached to large gatherings in seven different houses. Contrary to the rosy stories of many missionaries, he did not make any immediate converts. Indeed he immediately aroused very definite hostility from powerful chiefs and leading medicine men. Nevertheless he persevered and soon, with the help of some sympathisers, was able to erect a small log building to serve as a school and meeting house.

The story of his mission at Fort Simpson was one of slow but steady progress, particularly among the women and children. On occasion the hostility of the established rulers broke out into open violence and on at least two occasions his life was in jeopardy. The best known of these stories deals with the visit of the leading Chief Legaic, who came to order him to close his school while the winter festival was in progress. Duncan refused, and Legaic, brandishing a knife, threatened to kill him. There seems little doubt that he would have carried out his threat, had not Clah, the interpreter, sauntered in with a loaded pistol under his blanket and stood at Mr. Duncan's side. Not long after,

Chief Legaic became a Christian and an ardent supporter of Duncan.

As the number of converts increased, the problem of maintaining a Christian group in the midst of a large heathen community became acute and Duncan cast around for a solution. After lengthy discussions with the men of his little flock, he decided to establish a Christian village in a place remote from heathen influence. He finally set upon a site previously occupied by these same people in Venn Passage, about twenty miles to the south. On May 27th, 1862, Mr. Duncan with fifty Indians, men, women and children, made the voyage by canoe to the new site, and thus came into being the village of Metlakatla. This Indian name means a passage joining two bodies of salt water, and such was Venn Passage. It joined Tuck Inlet with the open sea, and the location chosen was the seaward end of the channel. It was a beautiful spot, surrounded by a number of small islands which perfectly protected the small harbor in any storm. The beach in front of the village was suited to drawing out canoes and the land had been partially cleared years before, when occupied by the ancestors of these same people. Within two weeks the population was increased by three hundred more who decided to make the break from their heathen life. Membership in the new community required the native to subscribe to a set of rules. They were simple, but all-embracing, and required a complete about-face for the Indian.[2]

In the village of Metlakatla, Duncan ruled with an iron hand. No hereditary chieftainship was recognized, Duncan being the sole person in authority. He appointed twelve constables to enforce the law, and later a village council to assist him in governing. He was undoubtedly a severe disciplinarian, and he has been criticized for the severity of his methods which, on occasion, included the use of the lash. However, those were primitive times and doubtless stern measures were required. In any event, the Indians were there voluntarily and, if they felt they were being unjustly dealt with, could always leave. The fact that the reverse was true, and that the population showed a steady increase, is the best answer to Duncan's critics.

One of the great obstacles to the advancement of the Indian was the liquor traffic which was rampant along the coast. All the traders used rum in greater or lesser degree in their dealings with the native, and Duncan soon found the problem facing him in his new village. To strengthen his hand, Governor Douglas appointed Duncan a Justice of the Peace, and he became the terror of the liquor traders in those parts. When a case came before "Judge Duncan", there was only one punishment for selling liquor—the maximum fine.

Much has been written of Father Duncan and his village of Metlakatla, and there are those who praise and others who condemn. None can deny, however, that he did a great work of Christianising and educating the Coast Indian, and instructing him in the intricacies of European civilization. He built a sawmill driven by a water wheel and cut lumber for houses, church and school. He made numerous trips back to England, and studied several trades which he then taught to his pupils. In this way blacksmithing, brick making, soap manufacture, weaving and other industries were introduced, some successfully and others which proved a failure. The two ventures which contributed most to the economic success of the village were the operation of their own trading post, and later a salmon cannery.

The population at Metlakatla increased steadily until it was approximately one thousand. From time to time, teachers and ministers were sent out from the Church Missionary Society to assist Duncan in the work, and from Metlakatla as a center the gospel message was sent up and down the coast and to the Queen Charlotte Islands. Mr. Duncan himself never accepted ordination, although it was offered him on more than one occasion and, as we noted earlier, was supposed to be conferred as soon as he had established his fitness for the work. This reluctance to accept priestly orders was the prime reason for the final tragedy which blighted his work. As the number of workers increased and the scope of the labors widened, the Church Missionary Society decided to appoint a Bishop to superintend the diocese. Had Duncan been ordained, he would undoubtedly have been the first Bishop of Caledonia, but he preferred to retain his lay status which left him free to pursue his economic activities. Consequently, November, 1879 saw the arrival in Metlakatla of William Ridley, the new Bishop of Caledonia.

Bishop Ridley was a man of headstrong will, who stopped at nothing to gain his end. In Duncan he met a man of equal determination, who was bitterly resentful of any authority which superseded his own in his beloved Metlakatla. The clash of these two personalities and the bitter struggle it produced is a black page in the history of the Church Missionary Society. It resulted in the division of the peaceful village into two armed camps, with threats and counterthreats, and finally the inevitable open violence.

The reasons given for the disagreement do not carry much conviction. Bishop Ridley undoubtedly wanted to be supreme and could not tolerate the opposition of Duncan. The Church at Metlakatla had been organized in a very simple manner, and the services conducted by Duncan were evangelical in type and free from ritual. Ridley introduced the Church of England ritual with all its vestments and sacraments. Duncan took exception to the use of priestly robes and particularly opposed the administration of the Sacrament of the Lord's Supper. While the reasons he gave seemed sound enough at the time, it is interesting to note that later, when Duncan was once more in complete charge in New Metlakatla, he himself instituted the celebration of Holy Communion. One is forced to conclude that this was fundamentally a clash of two dominating personalities, both of whom forgot their Christian teachings in the heat of the struggle.

Mr. Duncan finally approached the United States Government and was successful in obtaining a grant of land in Alaska. In 1887, with 823 Indians, he moved to a site on Annette Island and there founded New Metlakatla. It was virtually the end of the old village. In 1901 a disastrous fire destroyed all the old buildings — church, school, cannery and mission house. The church, school and mission house were rebuilt on a smaller scale, but the village never returned to its former importance, and has since been left far behind in the rapid development of the north coast.

Duncan duplicated his original efforts in the new village in Alaska. In many respects it was an improvement on the old Metlakatla. The progress of the people was steady, and to-day they are an outstanding example of the potentialities inherent in these Tsimpsean people. As the result of an enlightened policy on the part of the American Government, the community has thrived economically; and culturally they have made great strides. Their own teachers, ministers and nurses have been trained, and the fame of the town has been carried abroad by their musical organisations of choir and concert band. The town itself boasts a cathedral, town hall, and fully modern houses supplied by their own electric light plant.

It is perhaps too soon to pass final judgment on Duncan and his work. It would seem, however, that he early grasped the necessity of feeding the body as well as the soul. Prior to his arrival on the coast there was no attempt to do aught but exploit the native, who was rapidly becoming debauched with drunkenness and decimated by disease. Duncan stepped out with determination and courage, defied vested rights and dared to hold out a helping hand. By making the Indian economically independent, he gave him a chance to develop spiritually and culturally. In the light of his great achievements, one can afford to overlook his weaknesses.

CHAPTER SIX

Collins' Overland Telegraph

Although life on the north coast changed little during the first half of the century, it was far different in the southern part of the Province. The discovery of gold on the Fraser had brought a rush of settlers who spread up that river as far as Barkerville and Quesnel. After them came transportation in the shape of river boats, roads and pack trains; and it was only natural that, as the possibilities of that river became organized, some of the more adventurous should look for new fields.

It had long been known that gold was to be found on the Queen Charlotte Islands,[1] as the Haida Indians had the raw metal in fair quantity. So, in 1859, Governor Douglas commissioned an Englishman, Major Downie, to visit and search the Queen Charlotte Islands for the source of the metal.[2]

The Major spent some time enquiring from the Indians and examining likely spots, but without finding any commercial quantity, and by September he gave up in disgust and crossed over to Fort Simpson. There he disbanded his party but, in company with two other white men and two Indians, decided to extend his investigations up the Skeena River. Downie claims that he was commissioned by the Governor to search for a suitable valley for the proposed transcontinental railroad, and this was probably one of his reasons for continuing his trip. Inasmuch as he was to be paid for his services on presenting his report, he, no doubt, hoped to be able to make a better showing than the wasted summer on the Islands. The trip up the Skeena was made without serious incident, and the party arrived at the Forks in a little over two weeks. Somewhere in the neighbourhood of Copper Mountain they recorded being shown a tree on which had been carved PIONEER HBC.[3] This was reported as having been done by John Wark,[4] one of the first factors at Fort Simpson, and must serve as evidence of the first exploration of the lower Skeena by a white man. It is doubtful, however, if the Indians would have permitted him to ascend past the canyon as they were exceedingly jealous of their trading privileges on the river and would look on John Wark as their opposition. Downie visited the Indian village of Gitenmaks and then took to the forest. He visited the Carrier village of Hagwilget and, being impressed with the possibilities of the valley of the Bulkley and the river he had just ascended, put up a sign which read:

"Notice—September 22, 1859. I have this day located and claimed this pass as the route of the Great Canadian and Pacific Railroad—William Downie."

From there he pushed northward and again reached the Skeena at Naas Glee, probably Kisgegas, and followed it up to Babine Lake. On the lake he was fortunate in meeting a party from Fort St. James, on a salmon buying expedition, and received directions for the remainder of his trip to that Fort which he reached on October 9th. From there he followed the established trails to reach Victoria the end of November.

The trip was a tremendous undertaking and it is hard to believe it could be accomplished with such despatch and so little fuss. Major Downie, however, was a man of wide experience, having pioneered in the California gold fields, and he had a natural gift for dealing with primitive peoples. To travel through a country of hostile Indians without any serious altercations, and, in fact, with their cordial co-operation, was an amazing feat. The information he was able to give Governor Douglas on his return undoubtedly contributed greatly to the success of subsequent efforts to open up the country.

Soon after this the Skeena was featured in an international race. Cyrus Field had been trying for some years to lay a cable across the Atlantic Ocean to join Europe and America. His several attempts had ended in failure, and finally the newly formed Western Union Telegraph Co. decided to lay a telegraph line across the North American continent, up through Russian America and then via the Behring Sea to Asia and so across to Europe. The man who conceived this plan was Perry McDonough Collins. The route north in America was up the interior of British Columbia following the Fraser River to Fort George or Quesnel, then westward to the Skeena Forks and again northward to "Alaska". It was proposed to send supplies into the interior by the several northern rivers and in 1864 a Captain Tom Coffin bought the small river steamer "Union", a stern-wheeler, which had seen service on the Fraser, and proceeded up the coast to survey the problem. He successfully ascended the Skeena River for 90 miles and the Naas River for 30 miles, but was unable to buck the strong current of the Stikine. The next year he took supplies up the Skeena as far as he could go with the "Union" and completed the journey in two canoes to the Forks where the supplies were stored in a log cabin.

On the basis of his experience he drew plans for a boat to be used the following year, but the New York office of the Western Union rejected them, and submitted their own plans from which the steamer "Mumford" was built. Unfortunately eastern naval architects had little conception of the problems of navigation on western rivers and the small sternwheeler was totally inadequate for the task.

In July 1866 a party finally got under way from Victoria with supplies for the Skeena portion of the Telegraph line. It was headed by Captain James L. Butler and consisted of approximately forty men. The ship was under the command of Captain Coffin. Charles Morrison,[5] one of the members of the expedition, records the trip up the coast: "We had a fine trip up the coast, got through Seymour Narrows in flying style, called at Suquash, coal mine below Fort Rupert, since deserted; there was no Alert Cannery or Mission in those days, and arrived at Fort Rupert, then a flourishing Hudson's Bay Company Post in charge of Mr. Compton. We met him below the Fort returning from a hunting trip and towed his large canoe up to Fort Rupert; leaving Fort Rupert in the evening, we crossed Queen Charlotte Sound during the night; there was very little swell which was a good thing for us as stern wheelers are by no means adapted for sea work, as Captain Butler quaintly remarked, 'it was very like going to sea in a wheel barrow'. We got over all right and after passing Bella Bella struck a calm streak in Milbank Sound; we had to anchor several times to go ashore and cut wood as the steamer, heavily loaded, had very little room for fuel. The weather was fine and the scenery grand; the food was good, but the boat only had sleeping accommodation for the ship's company; we, the passengers, had to pick a soft plank every night to lay our blankets on, which also was not grand. Our fresh beef soon gave out with so many mouths to feed, and we fell back on bacon, salt horse and salt pork, but as they were all excellent of their kind we did not do so badly; steaming through Grenville Channel a deer was seen swimming across, Captain Coffin shot it from the pilot house and it proved a welcome addition to our fare, although one of our men would not touch it as the gentleman said venison was not fit for food for white men and only fit for Siwashes (Indians) to eat, we let him enjoy his salt horse in peace; at the end of the Grenville Channel we made a sharp turn to the right; we perceived that the water was becoming muddy and were told that we were in the Skeena River."

The ascent of the Skeena soon demonstrated the weaknesses of the little "Mumford". In spite of lightening the ship of half her cargo, they were unable to ascend further than the Kitsumgalum

River and there the cargo had to be transshipped to canoes. The same writer describes the final attempt to get the "Mumford" up the last rapids: "Captain Coffin wedged the safety valve down, we had all line out and heaving on the windlass, I was busy with a bucksaw sawing short lengths of wood to fill the furnace; they threw a five gallon tin of lard into the furnace, all the cook's slush and several sides of fat bacon, the steam gauge had gone to 'No man's land', the line parted and we gave up, dropped down a few yards and tied up, the Chief Engineer knocked away the lever, opened the valve, threw the fire overboard and we were at peace."

Butler first obtained the services of a group of Indians from Fort Simpson, but they deserted almost immediately and he then hired men and canoes from Metlakatla under the command of Chief Legaic. These men worked nobly and successfully transported all the freight to the Skeena Forks where it was stored in a warehouse built on a point of land later identified as Mission Point. Trouble threatened when the party tried to pass through Kitselas Canyon. The Indians at this point thronged the banks and refused to let Butler's party through. They were under the impression that this was a gigantic trading enterprise, and saw it as a threat to their trade monopoly. However, Butler was able to convince them otherwise, and finally obtained their co-operation by hiring them to assist in the work.

Shortly after the arrival at the Forks the advance party of the linemen working west from the Fraser made contact with Butler's men and the work went forward rapidly. The man in charge of the whole project was Colonel Charles S. Bulkley, and his name is perpetuated in that of the Bulkley River, the chief tributary of the Skeena. This river originally bore the Indian name "Watsonquah".

One of the big problems to be solved was the carrying of the supplies, including the cattle which were regularly butchered for meat, across the Bulkley River. At Hagwilget the Indians had constructed a bridge which was a marvel of primitive engineering. Made of timbers lashed with cedar withes, it hung suspended between the canyon walls, a hundred or more feet above the rushing waters below. The Indians would not allow a second bridge to be built as their medicine men said it would stop the run of salmon, but they finally consented to having their own bridge strengthened with wire. This was done by the Company's engineer, and men, animals and equipment were safely taken across.

The line followed the Skeena north from the Forks, and by September had reached forty miles beyond Kispiox. Then the news came through that the cable across the Atlantic was finally a success, and all work stopped. All the remaining supplies were stored in a block house erected near Kispiox, and called Fort Stager. This was also the end of the operating line.

The men, thus summarily thrown out of employment, scattered throughout the Province, some staying to prospect in the District. As a result of their efforts the mining area of Vital, Manson and Germansen Creeks in the Omineca District was opened up and some of these men returned to the Skeena Forks to winter. Here, on the hazel flats beside the river, a small community sprang up which was given the name of Hazelton.

CHAPTER SEVEN

Cunningham and Port Essington

Robert Cunningham was born in Tullyvally, Ireland, on January 1st, 1837. We know very little of his early life, but report has it that amongst other things, he was a pugilist. He certainly had the build for it, but apparently the life didn't appeal, for he volunteered for service with the Church Missionary Society, and he was sent out to assist Duncan.

On the long journey out, it is said that Robert Cunningham fell in with some disreputable acquaintances, and Duncan received an anonymous letter warning him against his new assistant.[1] This was certainly a poor start for anyone who aspired to work with the uncompromising chief of Metlakatla, and the association did not last long. He arrived at the mission the end of 1862 and left the service of the Society in 1864. We do not know what was the cause of the break with Duncan, and certainly Cunningham's character in later life would give the lie to any scandal, but, in any event, he left the mission and took a position with the Hudson's Bay Company. While at Metlakatla he met and married a native girl, Elizabeth Ryan, and this may have been one of the causes of the rift.

In 1868, Robert Cunningham was appointed in charge of the Fort at Port Simpson. The following year he was joined by Charles Morrison as book-keeper, and we are indebted to the latter for a description of the Cunningham family, "consisting of his wife, one of the best and kindest of women, and two fine boys". Of Cunningham, he says, "He was a most capable man, a great Indian Trader, and a most genial good-tempered man, a giant in stature and strength, but a kindly man who never used his strength unless forced, it being almost impossible to put him out of temper". Cunningham's term of service with the Hudson's Bay Company was short, for he left their employ and Port Simpson in November 1870.

The manner of his departure is not unanimously recorded. What might be called the "Duncan version" makes a good story but is probably not the real reason. As already related, Duncan was commissioned as a Justice of the Peace and was particularly zealous in his pursuit of those who trafficked in liquor with the Indian. Since this formed one of the chief articles of trade used by all the traders, he did not lack for victims. It seems, however, that he was going out of his way for trouble, when one of his constables journeyed to Port Simpson and offered a beaver skin for trade to Hans Brentzen, who was an employee of the Hudson's Bay Company at that Fort, and demanded a bottle of rum in exchange. Brentzen, who was general factotum under Cunningham, took the skin to the latter and he agreed to the transaction. The constable immediately took the bottle to Duncan, and the missionary issued a warrant for Cunningham's arrest. Cunningham appeared in court at Metlakatla and denied that he had given the Indian the rum. The fact that he had apprehended the wrong man bothered the judge not at all, and he sent his constables to arrest Brentzen. In order to take the latter by surprise, he kept court in session and Cunningham in attendance until the constables had departed in their canoe for Port Simpson, and then adjourned court.

To understand what then happened, it is necessary to realize that just west of the village of Metlakatla is a famous sand bar which, at low tide, closes the passage to Port Simpson. As soon as he was released, Cunningham jumped in his canoe, and with his crew set out after the constables. The tide was low and they caught up with the larger craft while the Indians were hauling it across the bar to the open sea beyond. With their lighter vessel, Cunningham's party gained the water first and hurried on their way. But luck was against them, for they immediately entered a dense fog which confused them completely. The constables were in no better straits; but being armed, their leader fired a shot, and from the echo was able to hold his course and proceed successfully to Port Simpson. Cunningham, hearing the shot, thought it was a hunter on the shore, and was thereby misled. He wandered in the fog for some time and only arrived at Simpson in time to see his employee, Brentzen, leaving in the custody of the other party. He was thus prevented from advising Brentzen, and at the subsequent trial Duncan found them both guilty. He fined Brentzen one hundred dollars and Cunningham five hundred dollars—judgements which were upheld on appeal. Duncan's supporters would have us believe that this so exasperated the Hudson's Bay Company that they let Cunningham go.

A more plausible account is given by Charles Morrison who was book-keeper at Port Simpson and succeeded Cunningham as Clerk in charge. He states that Cunningham had been asking for a raise in salary for some time, and when the Company ship made its last call in November, and brought word that the raise was not forthcoming, Cunningham peremptorily quit; and Morrison, being next in command, had to take over the stock without an inventory. The fact that Cunningham had been planning his move for some time is borne out by the records in Victoria of his application for land at the mouth of the Skeena. The application was made in April 1870, and was a joint application from Thomas Hankin and Robert Cunningham. In any event, Cunningham was now, at the end of 1870, on his own and, with several years of trading experience, well fitted for the years which lay ahead.

Now that the Skeena had been shown to be a navigable route to the Interior—particularly the northern portion—it became popular with miners heading for the new fields in the Omineca country. Some of these men wintered at the mouth of the Skeena River on the north bank near the present site of Inverness Cannery. A man by the name of Woodcock had built an inn at this point to accommodate the travellers, and the place was variously known as Skeenamouth, Skeena Bay or Woodcock's Landing. In the spring of 1871, it is recorded that twenty men spent the winter there.[2] The year 1871 was the beginning of the gold rush up the Skeena, and this was the reason for Robert Cunningham's application for land. He and Thomas Hankin built a large store on the river bank and Hankin was appointed the first postmaster.

Men began to congregate, waiting impatiently for the ice to leave the river so that freighting could commence. What a scene of confusion was there! Over a hundred miners had arrived and the Indians, scenting remunerative work, had congregated in large numbers. They were offering their services at one dollar a day with food, and canoes one dollar and a half per day. Some of the more independent miners had stopped at Fort Rupert on the way up the coast and purchased canoes from the natives there. One can well imagine that the new store of Cunningham and Hankin was doing a roaring business, and these two far-seeing gentlemen were quick to take advantage of the possibilities of the new trade route. Hankin made a rush trip up the Naas River and across by the old grease trail to Hazelton and there obtained buildings for a store.[3] On his return he reported the river still icebound, but four men, who could no longer control their impatience, started off on snowshoes over the ice.

Many stories could doubtless be told of that mad rush for the gold fields—a drama which had already been enacted twice before, in California and on the Fraser River, and would be repeated on a far larger scale on the Yukon. The "Klondike Mike"[4] of the Skeena was one, Captain Billy Moore. He was a

30

famous riverboat man from the Fraser and Stikine Rivers, and he now turned his attention to the Skeena. The route to the new goldfields led up the river to Hazelton, thence overland to Babine Lake, up the lake by boat, then on foot to Tahtla Lake and so on to the Omineca River. The Provincial Government gave Cunningham and Hankin a contract to build a trail from Hazelton to Babine and, with it, the right to levy tolls. Woodcock was placed in charge of the work of cutting the trail, and Billy Moore of the transportation. The latter was to take a pack train of mules to work on the trail.

Moore set out with the mules on a flat-bottomed barge called the "Minnie", accompanied by thirty men. He had nothing but grief, and when he reached the Canyon, his men deserted him, going on by foot. Moore was in desperate straits. His hay was gone, his food was low and only thirty sacks of grain left between the mules and starvation. The mules were tethered on the shore in two feet of snow.

He sent his son down river for a crew of Indians and tried again, but the "Minnie" wasn't meant for the Skeena shallows and he finally had to abandon her. They drove the mules along the bank for ninety miles and finally reached Hazelton, having lost only one animal in the trek. Surprisingly, the mules were in prime condition when they arrived and ready to pack on the trail to Babine. A Mr. Dewdney had already completed a survey of the trail and the work of cutting out the sixty miles to Babine was completed that summer. Moore freighted with the mules all season and in the fall brought them back down the river and wintered them in a cove on the south bank of the river near the mouth. This cove is still on the map as Moore's Cove.

Hazelton rapidly became a busy settlement. In 1871 there were two stores, Farrow & Mitchell and Hankin & Cunningham, besides a number of dwellings and tents. Hankin & Cunningham had sent up over eight tons of trade goods as soon as the ice went out and business was booming. As well as Moore's mule train, the Indians were packing supplies to Babine at ten dollars a hundredweight. Up the river, the freighting was done by the coast Indians in big canoes. These canoes would carry about four thousand pounds and were manned by five men. Their passage was not hindered by the river Indians and for the first year there was no trouble. In the summer of 1872, the Indians at Kitseguecla were attending mass one morning when fire broke out in the village. The cause of the outbreak was unknown as the few left at home that morning were lost in the fire. For some reason the Indians got the idea that the fire was due to the care-lessness of white men travelling through, and they forbade all freighting on the Skeena until such time as they should be recompensed for their loss. Cunningham and Hankin had two freight canoes on the river at the time and they were stopped at Kitseguecla. A Mr. Brown, from Victoria, was a passenger and he returned to Kitwanga, further down the river, and sent a letter to Hankin at Hazelton telling of the incident. Hankin immediately went down and was soon successful in getting his freight through, but Mr. Brown returned to Victoria and reported the matter to the Government. This resulted in the first expedition to the Skeena. The Lieutenant Governor and the Attorney General went up on H.M.S. "Scout" and met a delegation of the Indians at Skeenamouth.[5] After hearing their complaints the Lieutenant Governor explained that their misfortune was the result of an accident and they must not interfere again with the whites. On this occasion the Government would assist them and he distributed six hundred dollars amongst the Chiefs.

It was natural that with miners passing up and down the river intensive prospecting of the Skeena itself should be undertaken. Numerous strikes were made and the most notable occurred on the tributary known as Lorne Creek. Located on the north bank of the Skeena, about two-thirds of the way up to the Forks, it is approximately eight miles in length. The showings were very good and soon a hundred miners were working the area. Several companies were formed, amongst them Booth & Ewing, Larkin Brothers, Cunningham & Co., Young America, Joe Ewen & Co., and French & Moffatt. This activity and the strikes in the Kitselas region added greatly to the traffic on the river.

At first, up-river transport started from Woodcock's Landing. Cunningham & Hankin, who were doing the bulk of the shipping, had some trouble with Woodcock over the land survey and decided to look elsewhere for a location. They chose a site on the south bank of the Skeena just below the mouth of the Ecstall River, and Cunningham took out a pre-emption. This was the customary stopping place for the Tsimpsean Indians returning in the fall from their fishing and trapping up the Ecstall and was called by them "Spokeshute", which means "the fall camp ground". On this ground Cunningham built a trading post and called it Port Essington, the name which had originally been given by Captain Vancouver to the whole Skeena estuary. At this time the chief trading vessel up the coast was the Hudson's Bay Company ship "Otter". The story is told that Cunningham, wishing to convince the captain of the "Otter" of the trading potentialities of his new site, when the vessel hove in sight, had his Indian helper rushing around building a number of fires in the bush. This gave the appearance of a large Indian encampment and Cunningham was able to get what he wanted. The firm had chosen its new position wisely for Port Essington soon became the main entrance point for the Skeena. In the despatches in southern newspapers of that day, it is constantly referred to as the port of call where traffic up and down the river embarked and disembarked.

Cunningham encouraged the Indians to settle permanently at Port Essington and set aside a portion of his pre-emption for their use. The remainder of his property he divided up into lots and sold to settlers. Gradually a small community grew up around the store. Following the example of Duncan he built a sawmill south of the town on a small stream from a nearby lake—the ultimate source of water for the town—and supplied the growing demand for lumber on the north coast.

The Hudson's Bay Company[6] were not far behind Cunningham in seeking to obtain their share of the Skeena trade, and in the summer of 1871, Chief Factor James A. Grahame went up the coast on the steamer "Otter", and after looking over the situation, bought three lots from Cunningham at Port Essington, for the erection of a small store. This was known as "Skeena Post", and was in charge of Matthew Feak, Postmaster. Trading at this point did not prove very profitable and the Company decided to close the store, which they did in September, 1877, transferring the stores on hand to Port Simpson.

The traffic up the Skeena of prospectors proceeding to the Omineca soon petered out as transportation on the Fraser improved, most of them going in by the latter route. However, business on the Skeena did not lag, as the Hudson's Bay Company began to use it for their brigades to and from the northern Forts. In 1876 the first salmon cannery was built at Woodcock's Landing by the North Western Commercial Company.[7] Four years later it became the property of Turner Beeton & Co., and this firm changed the name to Inverness. The name has remained to the present day, although the cannery again changed hands and became the property of J. H. Todd & Sons of Victoria. Other canneries were soon built in the area and by the '90s there were seven scattered around the Skeena estuary. Aberdeen was located on the north bank at the mouth of the Kyex River, Balmoral on the north shore of the Ecstall River, and there were two canneries at Port Essington—Cunningham's and one owned by the A.B.C. Packing Co., known as Boston Cannery. On the south shore of the river, right at the mouth, were Claxton and Standard Canneries. The fishing season made of the Skeena a hive of industry, and workers were recruited from the various Indian settlements up the river as far as Kispiox. The men were employed catching the salmon, while the women worked in the canneries washing fish and filling cans. In the meantime the town of Port Essington had grown apace and there was a permanent population of several hundred. A number of Indians had taken advantage of Cunningham's land grant and built homes, and both the Church Missionary Society and the Methodist Church had established missions there. With the white settlers there came other commercial interests and Cunningham's chief rival was Peter Herman, who built a store, and, eventually, a cannery.

Peter Herman was a native of Saxony, Germany.[8] He came north in 1885 and went to work for Robert Cunningham. After some time he branched out for himself and began the operation of a small cannery and also a general store. He was industrious, and his business thrived and most of the buildings beyond the Anglican Church on the main thoroughfare, called Dufferin Street, were the result of his efforts. In 1901 he took the Post Office over from Cunningham and hired Mr. R. L. McIntosh as postmaster. Thus was introduced to the north a man who figured largely in its development for the next thirty-five years, having business interests in both Terrace and Prince Rupert. Peter Herman was a Liberal, and he was one of the founders of the Liberal Association in the north, being its President for several years. He eventually ran for the Provincial House, but was defeated by C. W. D. Clifford. His political activities probably contributed to his downfall, for his business interests took a turn for the worse after this election. He died a relatively young man at 44, in a drowning accident on the Ecstall River. He and his son Walter and a companion were towing a raft of logs with a rowboat. The logs caught on a snag and the coiled cable in the rowboat began to run out. A loop caught around Herman's leg, and in spite of his companions' efforts, the racing current pulled him over the side, capsizing the boat. Peter Herman was married to a native woman and left six children, some of whom are still living in the district.

Robert Cunningham, however, continued to dominate the scene. With his branch store at Hazelton he did a big business in the fur trade and on the coast he had a multitude of interests. At Port Essington, to care for the travelling public, he built a hotel, and for the local residents, a large town hall. In connection with his cannery he also built a cold storage plant, the first in the north, which began operations in 1892.[9] It was run by a Mr. Bergoff. On Porcher Island, just off the mouth of the river, he was interested in an Oil Reduction plant which produced

Dog Fish and Herring Oil. To connect up these many ventures he owned several steam tugs, notable among which was the "Chieftain", which plied these northern waters for many years.

Like all these early coast settlements, consisting of flimsy frame buildings, and having only a primitive water supply, the village was under the constant threat of fire. At least three disastrous fires occurred in Port Essington, wiping out large portions of the town on each occasion. Always reconstruction was rapid and complete, for the town was essential in the flourishing fishing industry and in the constantly increasing up river trade.

Since the river was closed to freighting in the winter, and the salmon fishing was only a summer activity, life in Port Essington fluctuated with the seasons. Most of the inhabitants drifted south in the fall, like the migratory birds, to return in the spring; but those who were left behind lived a good life. It was then that community social life blossomed, with Saturday night dances, community concerts and Church activities; and for those whose tastes were of a more Rabelaisian type, the friendly atmosphere of the brightly lighted bars of the Essington, Caledonia and Queen's Hotels, with their black jack and poker games in the back rooms, or the sociable gatherings at the houses of Blanche Hart and others of her ilk, were waiting to supply their needs.

The young community was politically minded too, and the rival Tory and Grit Associations held their meetings and passed their resolutions — on the one hand Cunningham and his followers; and on the other Peter Herman and his. Cunningham, himself, did not take much part in politics. Questioned once as to his political opinions, he roared—"Politics? What have I to do with Politics? The Grand Trunk Pacific Railway is my politics!"[10] The town was unorganised, but this did not stop the residents from having their civic elections, and a mock campaign was staged which resulted in the election of G. J. Frizzell as mayor; for aldermen, D. D. McLaws, W. Noel, and A. G. Harris; for Parks, (although there weren't any parks) R. W. Ward; School Trustees, W. J. O'Neill and J. Cauthers; and Licensing, J. Adams. During the long winter months, very little was necessary to start a party, or inspire some wag to promote a practical joke. The Skeena District News of March, 1904, carries the following story, and one can easily visualise the "boys" enthusiastically embracing the opportunity for a fortifying round at the Essington bar before sallying forth; and the riotous session on their return, while each detail of the day's adventure was recounted and relished afresh—

35

"Sam Pearse, a citizen very well known, was loitering about in an aimless fashion in the woods to the rear of the town. Suddenly the dog, that accompanied him, set up a furious barking. Mr. Pearse investigated. The dog was at the mouth of what, without doubt, was a bear's den, and if further proof of that fact was necessary, it was supplied by the constant issuance from the den of stertorous snorts such as only Bruin is capable of making. Mr. Pearse, conscious of his imminent danger, fled, having first turned pale. He did not cease running 'til he had reached town. His idea, hastily formed as he ran, was to ring the fire alarm. He intimated as much to several citizens to whom he had breathlessly explained the situation as to the bear, but the Stipendiary Magistrate and others of those of the better mind did not think the bell should be rung. It was promptly decided, however, to call out for purposes of general defense and attack, such of the able bodied citizens as were possessed of, or could borrow, fire arms. It took only a short time to marshal a phalanx of determined and blood thirsty looking men. Mr. W. R. Lord was chosen general officer commanding with Mr. George Frizzell as chief of staff. Then the cohort was drawn up and briefly and feelingly addressed by the G.O.C. He bade them look about and take a hasty farewell after which the word to march was given. Mr. Pearse was guide, issuing his directions in a loud voice, from the rear. Half an hour later the army was cautiously approaching the enemy. The dog was still at the den, barking to beat the band. The General cried "Halt!" and for a moment pondered as to whether a bold frontal attack should be made, but remembering the fate of Buller at Colenso and Spion Kop, and urged thereto by Mr. Pearse, he decided that a wide flanking movement, so as to turn, if possible, the enemy's left ear and thus enfilade him in his den would be the safest. At this moment the enemy debouched into open view. Whereupon Mr. Pearse took cover and thoughtfully besought the rest to follow his example. Then George Frizzell uttered a piercing shriek and said, "Why, I'm cogswoggled if it isn't my cub Bruno that escaped from me last fall!" The excitement in the army then subsided and those who had begun a precipitate retreat, returned emboldened. Bruno shinnied up a tree and George dauntlessly shinnied up after him. They went up as high as they could get and it was a small tree and the cub got out on a limb. George got opposite him and tried to wheedle him with pet names uttered in dulcet tones, but Bruno resisted these blandishments and would not "come". Then George drew from his pocket, which is usually stored with toothsome articles, a large rosy apple. This proved a fetcher and when Bruno shot his nose forward, he was seized by the scruff of the neck and hauled forward. Then began a battle royal between George and the cub. It lasted quite a while, neither participant apparently having the advantage, when at last the limb broke and bear and man in a firm embrace came crashing down through the branches and landed in the deep snow beneath. Neither was injured and George lifted his prey bodily and started homeward with him. At this moment Dr. Wilson, who had been requisitioned as surgeon to the army, came up with his two sinewy sons, who formed the ambulance corps, but their services were happily not needed and the army wheeling, marched back in triumph to town, Mr. Pearse in the lead."

Speaking of newspapers, there were four which made their appearance in the river town at various times — "The Skeena District News", edited by Wm. Baillie in 1904; "The Sun" by W. J. McKay in 1907; "The Star" by Rev. B. C. Freeman in 1908; and finally "The Port Essington Loyalist" by R. A. Hume, also in 1908. All had a relatively short existence.

To complete the story of Robert Cunningham, a further note on his private life is necessary. His first marriage to a native of Metlakatla ended disastrously. There were five children of this union three of whom died in infancy, and John and George. John, the older of the two who survived, was drowned at 17 years of age in the Queen Charlotte Islands, and in 1888 Mrs. Cunningham met a similar fate while crossing the Skeena River in a canoe with the Rev. Mr. Shelton and his wife. All three were lost!

Five years later, in 1893, Robert Cunningham married again, the bride being Miss Florence Bicknell, a Scottish girl who was living with her uncle, the Anglican clergyman, Rev. Mr. Appleyard. From this union Hazel was born in 1898 and Harold in 1903. Robert Cunningham died in Victoria in April, 1905, and a third child, Edith, was born after his death.

The success which had attended him inspired Robert to share it with his family in the Old Country, and in the early years of Port Essington's development he was joined by John Cunningham, a brother, and George Cunningham, a nephew. His sister Emily also came to British Columbia and married a man by the name of Johnson. There were several children of this marriage, and one son, Bob Johnson, became one of the outstanding figures in the fishing industry on the north coast.

Returning to Port Essington, the town was laid out on two arms of a right angle, centered on a rocky point at the confluence of the Skeena and Ecstall Rivers. Cunningham's establishments occupied the central location around this rocky point and the settlement extending down river was the portion laid aside for the Indian village. The up-river half of town lined both sides of Dufferin Street, the one road-way, which consisted of a twelve-foot board sidewalk built on posts over the tide flats. The buildings on the water side of the road were all on piles and the tide flooding under the buildings every twelve hours adequately cared for garbage and offal disposal. On the other side the buildings clung to the rocky hillside or again were built on piles over the sloughs projecting in from the river.

On Saturday night Dufferin Street was a seething mass of humanity, with representatives of every race, and the vast majority of them in some degree of intoxication. The married women of the town very wisely stayed at home on Saturday night for the two Provincial constables were totally inadequate to maintain order; and brawling frequently halted the stream of people as they eddied around a struggling group. In fact, the constables were often as bad as their charges, and at one time were directly interested in the operation of the numerous gambling dens which were mulcting the careless fishermen, so that, during the days of railroad construction, the district Chief of Police had to come in to clean up the mess.

Stores and restaurants stood open all evening and threw their shafts of light onto the darkened streets. As one walked east on Dufferin, the side wall of Cunningham's store stood flush with the sidewalk on the right, while the homes of the staff were grouped around the rear of the Cannery on the water side. Beyond them stood the "Chinahouse", where the Chinese laborers in the cannery silently shuffled in and out of the darkened door, or sat in groups on the steps stolidly watching the passing crowds and smoking their long tubular pipes.

Across the street was Charlie Katsayama's restaurant. Charlie was a thin wiry Japanese, invariably dressed in work pants and heavy woollen underwear, with a woollen scarf around his waist, while he performed the innumerable tasks of serving meals, and, in between, dishing out ice cream cones to the children clustered about the door. Kind-hearted as he was energetic, he brought up a healthy, happy family.

Next were Louis Hepenstall's poolroom and Lee Wing's restaurant, Mrs. Frizzell's dress shop and Morrow and Frizzell's Meat Market, while on the water side was the No. 2 dock — Frizzell's wharf — the only one not connected with a cannery, and the point of call for most of the upriver sternwheelers. The Anglican Church and the Dominion Fishery offices faced each other at the half-way mark, and then came the old Herman buildings, now occupied by Kameda's store and restaurant — another hard-working Japanese family whose life was shortly to be

—Courtesy of Wrathalls Photo Finishing

Hazelton

—Courtesy of Wrathalls Photo Finishing

Kispiox

—Courtesy of Wrathalls Photo Finishing

Bulkley Gate — part of the Canyon

—Courtesy of Wrathalls Photo Finishing

High Level Bridge at Hagwilget

touched by tragedy, when Essington's bloodiest murder suddenly erupted from their doors. Three drunken fishermen went into the restaurant and for some reason, obscure to all but an alcoholic mind, began to tear the place apart, chasing the Japanese out by hurling crockery at them. The Japanese returned and armed with knives soon got the better of the fray. One man, clutching his throat, slit from ear to ear, rushed out the door and staggered down the road, his blood spraying both sides of the street until he fell in a pool a hundred yards further on. Another spent some time in hospital paralysed from a stab wound in the back of the neck. The community's sympathies were with the Japanese and only jail terms were exacted by a lenient court.

Wadham's Cannery was next on the left — where Peter Herman's original cannery stood — and across the street the Queen's and Caledonia Hotels, with the proprietor, George Kirby, sitting on a chair outside the door; and Kishimoto's store — a wonderful collection of Japanese art and merchandise. A.B.C. Packing Company's Boston Cannery and store marked the end of the road, where a trail led along the shore between shacks occupied by cannery workers and others whose profession is the oldest known to man.

From the south end of town a board walk led along the river bank to Cunningham's Sawmill, a mile and a half down the river. After the destruction of the Mill by fire, the road was maintained to serve the farm at the mill site which was operated by Fuji, the Jap. He kept a few cows and pigs there and daily carried the milk on his four-wheeled cart into town over the old board walk. On Sunday afternoons and in the long summer evenings, the Old Mill trail was the promenade for old and young. Even in later years, when Fuji and the farm had long since gone, the local citizens walked out the slowly disintegrating sidewalk, which led past the cemetery, and crossing two small streams, on precarious bridges, reached the ruins of the mill.

In 1926 this lonely walk was the scene of the brutal murder of the local school teacher. Miss Loretta Chisholm was a tall athletic girl of twenty-one, who had been in Port Essington for the school term of 1925 - 26. On May 23rd, on a Sunday morning, she set out from her boarding house for her usual 'before break-fast' walk, swung along the river road, stopped for a moment at the end of the village to talk to the old German boat builder who had his boat shed there, and started along the Mill trail. She was never seen alive again.

Joe Sankey was an Indian youth of twenty-one whose home was at Port Simpson, but who had been living with his uncle in Port Essington for a couple of months, and working at the Boston

Cannery. He was not particularly robust, being under five feet six and weighing 136 pounds. Like many Indians he lived an improvident existence, and other than his working clothes, he owned only a blue herring-bone suit, which he had been wearing on all occasions, apart from work, for over two years. The suit consisted of three pieces — coat, vest and pants — and the history of these three garments was one of the crucial links in the chain of evidence presented by the Crown in the famous Sankey trial, and in the story for the Defence.

To return to the morning of May 23rd: when the school teacher failed to return for breakfast, her landlady became worried and instituted a search. The Mill Trail was covered with searchers until dark, and the search was resumed at daybreak. Strangely enough the searchers were immediately successful that next morning, for going over the same ground they found the body of Miss Chisholm lying face down in the moss a short distance off the trail. She had been viciously attacked and had put up a strenuous defence, but had finally been killed by suffocation, when her attacker packed her throat and mouth full of moss. There was no evidence that she had been criminally assaulted, although her clothes had been torn off and she was practically nude when found.

Inspector Spiller of the Provincial Police headed the detachment which came over from Prince Rupert to investigate the crime. In a matter of two or three hours the Inspector had solved the crime to his satisfaction and arrested Joseph Sankey as the criminal. How he arrived at the identification is not recorded in the official records of the trial, but suspicion was thrown on the Indian by the German boat builder, Rineholt, who claimed he had seen him following along about five minutes after the girl. He admitted he didn't know the Indian's name, and the method of identification was typical of the ruthless and bullying attitude of the Inspector. The traditional method of identification in a line-up was not used, but Rineholt was confronted with the accused and asked if this was the man. The only other suggestion that Sankey was anywhere near the scene of the crime was the identification of a ten-year-old girl who said she recognized him sitting down in the grass about two hundred yards away as she looked out the window of her house. She saw the teacher pass the seated figure, and when she looked again a few minutes later both persons were gone. The Inspector whose technique reminds one of the sign displayed on the desk of a Hollywood executive —"MY MIND IS MADE UP. Don't confuse me with facts"— was satisfied. When it was pointed out to him that there were other men that day in the vicinity of the crime, he refused to investigate and took Sankey to Prince Rupert, after searching his home and impounding his clothes. There the same ruthless methods were in evidence when the Inspector had the Indian into his office for questioning four times in the one day, and finally, under mental duress, obtained a signed "voluntary" statement.

The trial was held in Prince Rupert in November and was a glaring example of prejudiced atmosphere and confused defence. The Crown introduced the blue suit and proved that it had blood on various parts of both coat and pants. They didn't find the vest which two of their star witnesses saw Sankey wearing, and when the defence produced the vest which had been located by a Dominion Constable in Port Simpson, and it was shown to have been there all the time, their only concern seems to have been indignation that Watkinson, the Dominion Constable, should have presumed to interfere in the case. Even the learned Judge allowed himself to show exasperation with this presumptuous gentleman by referring to him in a disparaging manner in his summing up to the jury.

Sankey himself went on the stand and gave a straightforward account of his doings throughout the day in question—the Crown never did show when the crime was committed—and explained the blood on his clothing as due to two bouts of nose bleed which were attested to by other witnesses. Unfortunately all Sankey's witnesses were natives like himself and it was quite evident from the first that in that particular court an Indian was not to be given any credence. Sankey's story would have carried more weight with the jury had the Crown not been permitted to introduce the "voluntary" statement of the accused which he made when he was badly "rattled" by the Inspector's questioning. There were a few minor discrepancies which didn't help his case. It is remarkable that the presiding Judge allowed this statement to be introduced, but it is even more remarkable that it was done without any protest from the Defence Counsel. This aspect of the trial received scathing comment from some of the Appeal Court Justices.

Sankey was found guilty by the jury and condemned to hang. A new trial was granted and this was held in New Westminster where the accused was defended by Mr. J. Edward Bird of Vancouver. At this second trial Sankey was rapidly acquitted. It is interesting to note that Joseph Sankey is still living quietly amongst his people at Port Simpson, and now, thirty years after the famous trial, he has yet to exhibit any further evidence of that vicious character which he is supposed to have possessed on May 23rd, 1926, in Port Essington.

In the early days administration of the law was frequently unencumbered with legal technicalities.[11] Port Simpson was the center of all Government agencies, and when he was required, the magistrate made a special trip to Port Essington to hold court. The first constable in the river town was James E. Kirby, and he had a small, flimsily constructed shack in which to confine his prisoners. Unworthy of the title of gaol, it was called the Skookum House (a Chinook term). The magistrate holding office in Port Simpson at that time was Mr. Alexander who had been Hudson's Bay Factor at Quesnel, and had come out to Port Simpson in 1888. Kirby would get a list of offenders and Alexander would come down and hold court. On nearly every occasion a half-breed called Joe Blake would appear on the docket. He lived on the reserve and therefore in the eyes of the law was an Indian and could not legally have intoxicants. His Honor invariably dismissed the charge, much to Kirby's disgust, and finally the latter remonstrated with the magistrate. "I can't understand why you always let Joe off. The evidence is conclusive." "Well, Jim," said Alexander, "did you ever hear Joe tell where he gets his whiskey? Don't you admire honor, Jim?" "Yes," said Jim, "I noticed that, but the evidence, your Honor ——" "Oh, to hell with the evidence," said Alexander, "Jim, I admire honor!"

Port Essington finally got its own Justice of the Peace, one Jimmy Adams, an honest little Scotsman, who worked in the local cannery. Jimmy didn't know much law, but he had a sense of justice and fair play. His first court case was one of assault and he was excessively nervous in his new role. He fidgeted throughout the proceedings trying to look dignified and saying nothing, but finally the evidence was all in and the plaintiff and accused awaited his verdict. Solomon in his famous trial showed no more astuteness than Jimmy, who finally managed, "I dinna ken the rights or wrongs o' this case, but I fine ye both fifteen dollars and costs. Aye, and I advise ye both ta keep the peace. Court adjourned!"

Eventually a magistrate was appointed in the person of a man who shall be known by the name of Billy, which, perhaps, was his first name. Billy was well thought of in the community but he had one weakness which caught up with him on occasion. One such occasion was the arrival in town of three travelling men, old friends of Billy's, and their arrival was the signal for a party. A real party this was, extending well past the midnight hour, and finally, as they began to wend their way homeward, the night air was too much for Billy and he collapsed on the sidewalk right in front of Frizzell's Meat Market. The obvious

42

solution was to commandeer one of Frizzell's meat trucks and the boys dumped Billy in and wheeled him down to his domicile at the end of town. The house sat up on a hill with a long flight of steps leading up to it, and it was no small job to get the stuporous magistrate up to the top. Finally they succeeded, propped him against the front door, and proceeded to serenade him with "For he's a jolly good fellow". Suddenly the door flew open and Billy rolled over backwards at the feet of his irate spouse, while the boys beat a hasty retreat down the stairs. They continued their noisy way up the street and eventually ran afoul of the local constable, Johnny Herring, who clapped them in jail. Next morning, somewhat chastened, but nevertheless confident of speedy acquittal, they appeared before Magistrate Billy, who immediately fined them each fifty dollars and costs. The fines were paid and high indignation reigned as they waited outside on the street for the appearance of their erstwhile pal. When he came along, he was greeted with a barrage of all the choice names that came to mind, but Billy was undismayed. As he passed the group he was heard to mutter, "That'll teach you to sing 'For he's a jolly good fellow' to me on my door-step at two in the morning."

With the completion of the railway, Port Essington's importance in the river trade disappeared, and the town's slow death set in. With modern fishing techniques, the supply of fish diminished, and the fishing boundaries were steadily shifted down the river to give the fish a better chance. The up-river Canneries had had their day, and one by one they closed, until the three at Port Essington were nothing but camps, and finally disintegrated from neglect. One of them was destroyed by fire. Today, a handful of Indians and a few families of Finnish fishermen occupy some scattered homes, while Dufferin Street is lined with ruined shells.

CHAPTER EIGHT

Hazelton

While the port at the river mouth was thriving, a corresponding development was taking place at the up-river end of navigation, where the town of Hazelton served as the distributing point for the Omineca gold fields.

In earliest times, there were two Indian villages close to the junction of the Skeena and Watsonquah[1] Rivers. Hagwilget, on the flats below the towering cliffs of the canyon where the Watsonquah cuts its way around the foot of Rocher de Boule, was a Carrier village. Gitenmaks, established by the Gitekshan Indians, was situated on the banks of the Skeena, a mile or two above the Forks.

In 1866[2], William Manson and Thomas Hankin were sent out by the Hudson's Bay Company to explore the Upper Skeena and the territory eastward, and to decide on suitable locations for new trading posts. As a result of that survey, on November 17, 1866, Hankin was sent up the Skeena on the sloop "Petrel" with one man, James Otley, and a temporary assistant, Kiona, to "put up a small house to winter in" for trading purposes. This post was erected at Hagwilget.[3] Trading in this new territory did not prove very profitable. In January 1868 Chief Factor Dr. W. F. Tolmie wrote from Victoria to William Manson that "The furs from Ackwilgate . . . are of inferior quality. . . . We shall probably instruct you to abandon that post in the spring. . . ." It was also found that this post interfered with the fur trade in New Caledonia, and during the summer of 1868 the place was closed and the stores removed to Port Simpson.

Thomas Hankin left the employ of the Hudson's Bay Company shortly after and settled on the hazel flats, across the Watsonquah, on the banks of the Skeena and adjacent to the Indian village of Gitenmaks.

The year 1866 saw the arrival of the work parties for the Collins Overland Telegraph Company, and the first real invasion of the District by the white men. As we know, their effort was short-lived, but some of the men engaged in the project stayed in the area to prospect; and a few of them wintered at the Forks. In

1868 this small settlement on the banks of the Skeena was given the name of Hazelton from the profusion of hazel bushes growing there. And what a spot for a village! The valley of the Skeena at this point is several miles in width, with good agricultural land on the benches above both banks of the river. To the southward, across the Watsonquah, towers the mighty mountain called by the Indians "Stegawdun", which means "brother", referring to the "Seven Sisters" mountains further down the river. From its steep shoulders had come a heavy slide, and the early settlers, probably French Canadian with the Hudson's Bay Company, called it Rocher de Boule — the name it bears to-day, as it stands in majestic solitude above the Forks of the Skeena. Away to the westward are the snow peaks of the beginnings of the Coast Range, while in front of the town, the rushing waters of the Skeena make a picture never to be forgotten.

The Indians of Gitenmaks had a trail running from their village, over the Babine mountains to Babine Lake, and this was the route used by the miners to reach their claims in the Omineca country to the east. As the traffic increased, the Provincial Government, in 1871, let a contract to Cunningham and Hankin to clear and improve the trail. The survey was carried out by a Mr. Dewdney, and the trail cut through by Mr. Woodcock, of Skeenamouth fame. Over it passed the miners in a flood in the rush of '71 and '72. The Indians acted as carriers, charging ten cents a pound for freight, and Captain Billy Moore made regular trips with his mule train from Hazelton to Babine Lake. In that year, 1871, there were six buildings and a tent in Hazelton. Two of these were occupied by the stores of Cunningham and Hankin, and Farrow and Mitchell. Law and order came to the area for the first time in this year also, when Judge O'Reilly [4] held court at Skeena Forks on October 20th. Probably his most popular decision was the granting of three "spirit licenses". These were evidently not granted indiscriminately, for it is recorded that one, Peter Cargotitch, who had started to build a saloon, was refused a license.[5]

The following year a third store was built at Hazelton, operated by Boyd, Reed and Tregonian. By this time it had been demonstrated that the Skeena route was a practical means of reaching the interior of the Province, and in 1880 the Hudson's Bay Company re-entered the picture in Hazelton by purchasing a store of one of the traders already settled there, a man by the name of W. J. Walsh.[6] With this link in the chain completed, the Company started supplying their forts at Fraser Lake, Bear Lake, Babine and Stuart Lake from Port Simpson. The first man in charge of the post at Hazelton was Alfred Sampere, who was transferred from Babine for the purpose. He remained in charge until 1884 when he was succeeded by William Sinclair. Sampere died that winter before he could be appointed to another charge. During 1885 Charles W. D. Clifford was sent to Hazelton and the post was placed in the Port Simpson district under the supervision of R. H. Hall. The buildings were in bad condition and Clifford built a new store that year. He remained in charge until 1891, when he was succeeded by J. H. Lyons.

In October 1890 the post at Hazelton was inspected by Chief Factor J. McDougall. It consisted of a general store and office, constructed in 1886, a warehouse, and a dwelling house intended for the officer in charge, which was still in course of construction. These buildings were "surrounded by a double board stockade 110 ft. by 214 ft. and 12 ft. high with two log bastions 12 ft. square at diagonal corners . . . . . erected in 1888 during the Indian troubles".[7] Outside the stockade the Company owned a dwelling house which had been "occupied as a residence by the trader from whom the Company bought the business, and since then by the clerk in charge". There were also four other dwelling houses which were "usually occupied during the winter by miners who (were) regular customers". McDougall added in his report that " . . . Outside of the land occupied by the buildings 7 acres of excellent land are under cultivation; of this land 4 acres were acquired with the post when purchased and the balance was since obtained from Indian occupants. . . ."

During these early years the history of this pioneer settlement is very meager. The Indians were not very favorably disposed to the white man and altercations were frequent. Open violence was only narrowly averted on many occasions, and appeals were made to the Government at Victoria to intervene. On one occasion Mr. Hankin made the long trip to Victoria to urge the punishment of a brutal murder in Hagwilget, but nothing came of it. The Indians were still in their heathen state as the only attempts at Christianising them were made on the occasional visits of the Roman Catholic priest from Stuart Lake. However, in 1880, Bishop Ridley and his wife arrived in Hazelton to spend the winter. He opened a day school for the children and tended the sick in addition to his religious duties. For the white people he held a social evening every Tuesday in his home, and for their amusement published a small paper called "The Queek"[8] —the first paper of the Interior. Charles Clifford edited it and the printing was done on a gelatin press, the whole being written out in long hand. It was short-lived, coming out in thirteen weekly issues, the first one on December 18th, 1880. Indeed the

Bishop's own stay in Hazelton was equally short for he had to return to his Diocesan headquarters at Metlakatla; and his place was taken by the Rev. Mr. Faulkner.

Besides the mines in the more distant Omineca area, there were other workings closer in, at Kisgegas, Lorne Creek and up the valley of the Bulkley. Some of the miners went down the Skeena to winter outside, but others stayed, and the little community slowly expanded. Ranches were started down the river on both sides, as well as above the town on the way to Kispiox. The Indian problem was largely solved when the Dominion Government appointed R. E. Loring as the first Indian Agent,[9] with a District from Kitselas to Babine; and in 1890 the Provincial Government sent in survey parties to map the country.

While the general flow of traffic was up the Skeena and on to the Omineca and vice versa, the surveys for the Collins Overland Telegraph had pointed out the possibility of using the Skeena as a means of travelling north to the headwaters of the Stikine and Dease Lake. Several attempts were made to develop this route, and during the year 1874 pack trains from Quesnel, following the Telegraph trail, reached Hazelton and pushed on to Telegraph Creek. It was a rugged trip, but might have been practical had not the Indians proved hostile. The last pack train to attempt the trip was owned by a P. Grinder. They made about one hundred and ten miles above Hazelton, when they had to give in to save their animals, casting away 20,000 pounds of freight which fell into the hands of the Indians.[10]

Life in the little community ebbed and flowed with the seasons. Bustling and active from spring to fall, it subsided beneath its blanket of snow and ice in the winter, like the hibernating bear. One must assume that, since there were three liquor licenses, the winter months were occupied with other pursuits besides sleeping, and we do know that all the unattached males were gathered for the Christmas celebrations at the Hudson's Bay Company fort, where the Chinese cook fed the town at noon on Christmas Day. We are indebted to the old Hudson's Bay Company records for a list of those who spent the long winter months in the District.[11] During the winter of 1894-95 we find the following in Hazelton — R. E. Loring, his wife and three children, also Master Arthur Hankin, the Rev. E. C. Stephenson, J. J. May, C. Rolls, Ezra Evans, W. K. Speer, W. B. Forrest, E. O. DeLong, O. M. Dutton, Enos Williams, George Nash, Jas. Wells, Gabriel LeCroix and wife, Joe LeCroix and wife and two children and Master Joe Gardiner, and the Hudson's Bay staff which consisted of J. H. Lyon (in charge), Mr. Moat and R. S. Sargent. There was also a group of eight to ten Chinamen. In the district roundabout were Mr. and Mrs. J. C. Spencer, the Methodist missionary at Kispiox, and R. H. Cole ranching at the mouth of the Bulkley, probably on Mission Point, for we find it referred to as Crosbyville—undoubtedly a reference to Rev. Thomas Crosby, the head of the Methodist Mission which owned land on the point. Four miles below Hazelton, on the bench, were two ranches owned by A. McIntosh and William Keynton, both of whom had their families with them. Then further down the river at Kitseguecla was the Rev. T. Neville and at Kitwanga, Rev. A. E. Price and family. All these made up a scattered group of people, completely isolated from the outside world, with no regular means of communication amongst themselves. Roving parties of Indians would sometimes carry news from one to another, and it is a wonder that there were not more tragedies, with women and children living under such primitive and rugged conditions. However, they were a sturdy race and only occasionally did sickness or accident strike with fatal consequences. Ezra Evans' little girl was drowned at Kitseguecla, falling into the river and slipping under the ice before anyone could reach her; the fifteen-month-old daughter of Joe LeCroix died of some undiagnosed complaint; and on one occasion, it appeared to be the long arm of justice when a horse thief from the Cariboo, escaping to the north, tried to ford the Bulkley, and horse and rider were both drowned.

During these poorly recorded years, the surveys doubtless being responsible, the old Indian names of mountains, rivers and towns were dropped, and their permanent names became affixed. It would be a gradual process, but Stegawdon Mountain became Rocher de Boule, the Watsonquah became the Bulkley River after Colonel Bulkley of Telegraph fame, Gitenmaks disappeared, merging with Hazelton, Moricetown and the Morice River took their names from the famed Father Morice, and so on throughout the District.

In 1891 there arrived at Hazelton R. S. Sargent, whose name was to become as synonymous with Hazelton, as that of Cunningham with Port Essington. He was the son of an Anglican clergyman at Qu'Appelle, and he came across the country in a prairie schooner. He arrived at Hazelton at eighteen years of age and began to work for the Hudson's Bay Company, first as bookkeeper, then as apprentice clerk for five years, and then as chief clerk for another five years. He then left the Company and started out in business for himself, opening a store in opposition to the Bay. At first he was in partnership with a Mr. Stevenson, but later operated alone. Along with his store he also ran the Post Office. In 1911 he married Miss Barbeau, bringing his bride up the river on the sternwheeler "Hazelton". By this time Hazelton had expanded and boasted three hotels, three banks,[12] a Methodist and an Anglican Church, a hospital and a drug store, besides the business houses of Cunningham, Sargent and the Hudson's Bay Company.

But we are getting ahead of our story! Toward the end of the '90s, history repeated itself. Another gold rush was electrifying the country, this time to the Yukon. The route followed was up the Coast by boat to Skagway and then over the famous Trail of '98 to the Yukon. To some of the restless miners of the Cariboo, the long trip to the Coast before starting the journey northward appeared unnecessary, and they headed north over the old Telegraph Trail. So, once more, Hazelton saw pack trains and miners trudging in from the Bulkley and turning north up the Skeena, heading for Telegraph Creek and beyond to Dawson and the Yukon. This was a terrible trail and never became a popular route to the Yukon.[13] Nevertheless it did offer a solution to the problem of communication from this new mining district to the outside. We have already noted the abandonment of Fort Stager and the Telegraph line in 1869. In 1871 the Provincial Government secured a perpetual lease of the whole line and this was taken over by the Dominion Government on the completion of Confederation. However, no attempt was made to maintain or operate the line beyond Quesnel, and soon the only evidence of its existence was the trail extending through the wilderness and here and there, along its extent, a bundle of rusted wire which had been overlooked by the scavenging Indians.

Now with the sudden development of the Yukon, and the demand for telegraphic communication, the Dominion Government set out to connect Atlin and Quesnel. Construction was started in 1899 from both ends simultaneously and it was completed in 1901. It extended for 1100 miles and by 1900 had reached Hazelton from the south and Telegraph Creek from the north. The route followed was the original Collins' trail from Quesnel to Fort Fraser, then along the north shore of Burns Lake and Decker Lake and so into the Bulkley Valley. It paralleled the east bank of the Bulkley until it came to Moricetown where it crossed the river and proceeded to Hagwilget. Again it crossed the Bulkley and reached Hazelton. The work was under the direction of J. B. Charleson, and the pack train was operated by Charles Barrett. These names will appear again as the Bulkley Valley comes into the picture.

From Hazelton the line ran up the Skeena Valley and at the same time was being built south from Telegraph Creek. The surveying must have been done very sketchily, for the two parties eventually found themselves in two valleys separated by a mountain chain and seventy miles of rugged country. Much of the line had to be abandoned and a new trail constructed. Not much wonder then that the estimates in Parliament proved insufficient and subsequent allotments were made in the face of severe criticism from the opposition benches. Relay cabins were built every twenty to thirty miles, and two men stationed at each cabin, one to operate the key and the other to patrol the line for ten miles on either side of the cabin until he met up with his opposite number of the next adjoining station.

While the construction of this portion of the line was proceeding, a branch line was pushed down the Skeena from Hazelton, to terminate on the coast at Port Simpson. It followed the north bank of the river as far as Aberdeen cannery at the mouth of the Kyex River and then, cutting across the narrow peninsula of land at Green River to the head of Wark's Canal, ran west to Port Simpson. This branch line was completed by the middle of June 1901, just a month after the line to Atlin began operation.

Life on the line from Hazelton to Telegraph Creek was a grim business. Supplies were taken in each summer by pack train, and for the remainder of the year the men were completely isolated, except for conversation over the wire. Little wonder that "winter madness" crept into the cabins and more than one operator had to be taken out for psychiatric treatment.

With the turn of the century, interest in the agricultural possibilities of this new area quickened and the Provincial Government continued the land surveys and encouraged settlers. This resulted in the opening up of the Bulkley Valley which we shall consider in detail later on, but the impact on Hazelton was to stimulate a steady growth. Hotels and banks and more stores made their appearance and along the trail to the southward, roadhouses sprang up. Such a one, built at Two Mile, that is, two miles from the town of Hazelton, in 1906, was the scene of a brawl and murder which resulted in the most famous manhunt in the history of the Province.

Simon Gunanoot was a Kispiox Indian who was living at Hagwilget. He was a splendid physical specimen, standing over six feet in height, with a powerful frame, and capable of long hours on the trail. He was a famous hunter, a crack shot with a rifle and generally known as an industrious worker—a "good" Indian. In the spring of '06 Simon returned from his trap line with a rich catch of furs, and after disposing of them went with his brother-in-law, Peter Himadon, to celebrate at the roadhouse at Two Mile. There they met two half-breeds, Alex McIntosh and Max LeClair, who for some reason hated Gunanoot. They immediately began to taunt him, and to cast reflections on the morals of the women of Kispiox, mentioning Gunanoot's wife in particular. In fact, McIntosh said that she was the worst of the lot, and, of course, a fight followed. The men were separated and Gunanoot left to get his rifle, saying he would kill McIntosh. The two half-breeds left soon after and at four in the morning, McIntosh was found lying beside the road on the way to Hazelton with a bullet through his heart, and shortly after LeClair's body was located on the road between Hazelton and Kispiox. Both men had been shot with a rifle, and both through the heart with one shot. They had been riding horseback, so the implication was that the murder was the work of a skilful marksman.

In the meantime Gunanoot had fled up the Skeena Valley, and he was accompanied by Himadon, who had been heard to urge the killing of both the half-breeds at the roadhouse. At the inquest which was held shortly after, Gunanoot was cited as the killer and the R.C.M.P. immediately set out to catch him.

This was more easily said than done. The two Indians knew the country north of Hazelton like a book, and easily evaded the various patrols sent out to find them. It was later found out that one patrol had been so close to the fugitives that Himadon had drawn a bead with his rifle on the constable in charge, but was restrained by Gunanoot; and the constable, unaware of his danger, had decided to turn off the trail at this point and missed his quarry who were crouching in a bush immediately ahead of him. Peter Himadon died on the trail, but year after year, Gunanoot lived his hunted existence. He continued to trap each winter and his relatives disposed of his furs and kept him supplied with food.

Peter Himadon's wife, on her death bed, finally confessed that she shot LeClair when he attacked her while she was on her way to Two Mile to find her husband. She claimed that she met Gunanoot, who said that he would take the blame, and that while they were talking, Gunanoot's father had come along and told them that McIntosh had been killed and that Gunanoot was being blamed and must flee. The authorities were not impressed with this version of the affair and the search went on. Gunanoot's father died finally, making a last request that he be buried at Bowser Lake, forty miles from Hazelton. The fearlessness with which Gunanoot moved about the country is no better exemplified than by his behaviour on this occasion. He put his father on his back and packed him the forty miles to Bowser Lake and there buried him as he had requested.

Eventually the police admitted their inability to outwit Gunanoot and decided to wait him out, for they figured he would finally give himself up. This was, in fact, in the outlaw's mind, but he hesitated to trust the white man's justice. He approached George Byrnes, a rancher up the Kispiox Valley, who was the man operating the pack train each summer for the Telegraph line. Knowing Byrnes well and respecting him, he asked George to get him a lawyer. Byrnes got in touch with the famous criminal lawyer, Stuart Henderson, who agreed to take the case. Even then, Gunanoot hesitated, and it was only after several meetings with Henderson that he finally walked into Hazelton and gave himself up in 1919 — after thirteen years of successful evasion.

He was treated with the respect accorded a brave man and at his trial in New Westminster he was acquitted. No one will ever know who killed the half-breeds — whether Peter Himadon, or Simon Gunanoot, or both—but it is doubtful if anyone cared very much, for the two men had undoubtedly been looking for trouble.

Although we shall deal with the missionary efforts of the various religious denominations as they affected the Skeena in a later chapter, one man stands out so pre-eminently in the history of Hazelton that he must be accorded his place in chronological order in the development of the town.

Dr. H. C. Wrinch was a missionary of the Methodist Church. While undergoing his training in a Toronto Medical School, he intended to volunteer for work in China. However, he heard the story of the heathen Indians of the Skeena told with such graphic power by one of their own race, Rev. W. H. Pierce, when the latter was visiting the Ontario churches on behalf of Home Missions, that he determined to spend his life on the Skeena.

In 1901 he arrived at Hazelton with his wife who was a trained nurse, and since Kispiox was the site of the Methodist Mission in the area, he set up his office in that place. There had been only casual medical service in the past when Robert Tomlinson had spent a few years in the valley and Dr. Spencer had been located at Kispiox for a short time. Neither of these men was qualified to practice medicine in the Province, although both had received medical training.

For a year or two the young doctor and his wife cared for the sick, making the long trek to Hazelton and answering calls from the surrounding district. He soon realized, however, that a more central location was required and he obtained a parcel of land on the bench above Hazelton and about a mile from the town. Here in 1904 he opened the first hospital and built his home. There was nothing haphazard in the undertaking, for Dr. Wrinch knew farming and loved the soil. The land was carefully cleared and landscaped, and a prosperous farm was developed to supply the needs of the mission hospital in garden produce and cattle. A small lake was located on the property and, in the winter, ice was cut and stored to supply the hospital through the hot summer months.

In the town of Hazelton he opened an office and dispensary, the forerunner of the first drug store, and from this central point he travelled on horseback and afoot to minister to the sick up and down the river.

He was a large, powerful man physically and his character and mental development were in keeping. While at times brusque in manner, he loved the people, both native and white, and he loved the country. His efforts were evident in every phase of the community life. Although primarily concerned with administering to the sick, he was also an ordained minister of the Church, and found time when opportunity offered to conduct religious services. He was a leader in all community activities, particularly in things horticultural, and eventually in 1924 he was elected to the Provincial Legislature as a Liberal member. He held this seat from 1924 to 1933, contesting two elections.

Dr. and Mrs. Wrinch raised a family of four sons and a daughter—Leonard, Cooper, Arthur, Ralphena and Harold. The oldest son, Leonard, followed in his father's footsteps and for a time was in charge of the hospital after his father's retirement. All the children have since left the District, scattering across Canada from coast to coast. Mrs. Wrinch died in 1923 and for a few years the doctor carried on alone with the able assistance of his daughter Ralphena as his official hostess. In 1927 he married again. The bride was the daughter of the pioneer coast missionary, Rev. William Hogan, affectionately known as Father Hogan. The doctor's health began to fail in 1936 and he retired to Vancouver where he died in 1939. His name will long be remembered in Hazelton where it is perpetuated in the new H. C. Wrinch Memorial Hospital, which he built just before his retirement.

With all its importance as a distributing center, Hazelton never took on the habiliments of a town. It was never organized and remained to the end a place of temporary abode for the traveller rushing east and west. Even the essentials of sanitation were neglected, for the visitor in the village in the 1920s could still see the Chinaman delivering water from door to door in oil cans filled from the river. The building of the railroad down the west side of the Bulkley and on down the Skeena was a hard blow to Old Hazelton, and for a time threatened its very existence. The promoters of the new townsites of South Hazelton and New Hazelton, along the rail line, confidently expected the town to move bodily across the Bulkley and join in the march of progress. But the old-timers of Hazelton were stubborn and refused to be stampeded, and the town continued to be the distributing centre for the District, in spite of the efforts of the rival townsites to displace it.

Of course, much of its glory faded and the population dwindled. Fire and the ravages of time destroyed many of the old landmarks, and only an optimistic old timer could see any hope for the future. R. S. Sargent passed away in 1945, but the family remained, and a second generation continued to operate the store which was now the largest in the area. A hotel was added and when these were destroyed by fire, the Sargents built again—bigger and better. In 1956 they opened their new up-to-date general store and fully modern hotel. Its beautiful site on the bank of the river is somewhat marred by the proximity of a number of old shacks, relics of an earlier day; but, once within its portals, the attractive decor and comfortable surroundings leave nothing to be desired.

The town has now been incorporated and, in co-operation with the Hospital and the Department of Indian Affairs, they have piped in water from Hospital Lake.

Once more there is hope on the horizon for Hazelton. The Dominion and Provincial Governments have announced their intention of completing the road from Stewart to Cassiar, and this road will undoubtedly be joined to Highway 16 by a link from Stewart. It will probably come down the old Telegraph route to Hazelton, and when this is completed, Hazelton will again be the Gateway of Empire.

—Courtesy of Wrathalls Photo Finishing

Skeena River with Railway and Highway

—Courtesy of Wrathalls Photo Finishing

Bulkley Valley

Port Simpson — 1884

—Courtesy of B.C. Archives

—Courtesy of Wrathalls Photo Finishing

The Slough — one of the mouths of the Skeena River

CHAPTER NINE

Bulkley Valley

With the turn of the century, reports of a railway to be built across the country and down the Skeena stimulated a Province-wide interest in the Central Interior of British Columbia. Actually, little was known of the country east and south of Hazelton, except that there was a great valley extending southward, through which flowed the Bulkley River.

The Telegraph trail from the Cariboo followed this valley, and intermittently it had been used for pack trains heading north, but beyond the trail it had been little explored.

Leaving the Forks, for the first twenty-five miles the Bulkley River cut its way through deep canyons with forbidding banks and a minimum of bench land above, as the mountains encroached almost to the river's edge. At the upper end of this stretch was the Indian village of Moricetown, located by the side of a waterfall, where the river boiled and raged as it entered the first of the series of canyons. Moricetown was not the original home of this band of Indians. At one time they lived around the mouth of the Bear or Susqua River. According to Indian legend, there was a rock slide which blocked the Watsonquah River near its mouth, raised the river level, and flooded their village. The Indians fled up the river and finally settled around the canyon at the site now known as Moricetown. The legend explains the origin of the name of the mountain—Rocher de Boule or Fallen Rock.

From this point on the valley began to widen, although there were occasional protrusions of the mountain chain to the west. The country was fairly open, expanses of grass lands alternating with clumps of pine, spruce and poplar. This open country was rich with wild pea-vine and red top grasses and eminently suited to grazing. The soil of the bottom land near the river was black and rich and well adapted for agriculture. Throughout the valley were numerous lakes, richly stocked with fish which the Indians caught and cured for food.

About sixty miles from Hazelton the Telkwa River entered from the westward and from here on the valley steadily spread out until it reached its maximum width at the junction with the Morice River flowing in from the southwest. Preliminary surveys of the Bulkley Valley were undertaken by Poudrier[1] for the Provincial Government in 1890 to 1892, when he surveyed nine townships and laid out a wagon road from Hazelton to Moricetown. This was not followed by settlers, however, and the first attempt to farm in the District was made by the Hudson's Bay Company, when they established a ranch in the neighbourhood of Driftwood Creek, which entered the east bank of the Bulkley about fifteen miles south of Moricetown. It was started in 1898, was managed by George Hill, and was used chiefly to winter their pack horses.

When the Dominion Telegraph line was completed in 1902, Edward Charleson, the son of the man in charge of construction, and Charles Barrett, who had been running the pack train which carried supplies to the construction crews, formed a partnership and purchased the pack train. They established a ranch near the junction of the Morice River, calling it the Diamond D, and from this headquarters supplied the various cabins of the Telegraph line, and also provided transport for other ventures in the area. Their cattle were herded up from the Chilcotin and fattened on the rich grass lands of the valley. J. C. K. Sealy joined the partnership for a short time, but he and Charleson eventually withdrew, and Sealy went into the hotel business at Hazelton.

Several attempts were made by the Government and by land speculators to promote settlement of the Bulkley Valley, but the warning issued by the Government in a bulletin published in 1902[2] was not conducive to an ill-considered land rush.

"It is not desirable, either in the interests of the Province or of the (then proposed Bulkley) Colony itself, that the development of the enterprise should be hampered by men and women who are unused by experience to the trials of pioneer life, unfitted by training to take up the work of actual farm labor, and unable by physical endurance to withstand the hard labor involved. It must be understood that settlers who go in there will, for some time, be wholly isolated, and that, for three years at least, their property will be unproductive. The prospects for success in five years' time, or as soon as railway communication is afforded, are very good, and all accounts are favorable to the belief that the Bulkley Valley is one of the most fertile in British Columbia, and particularly well adapted for stock raising; but the way to success is long and hard, and without pluck, untiring industry, intelligent effort, self-reliance, physical endurance, and some capital to back up these qualities, disappointment and failures are sure to result.

Those who are not prepared to accept the situation as stated and stick with it, had better remain where they are. Discontented, discouraged, heart-sick settlers will be the greatest possible drawback to the country, and every person, especially with a family, should weigh well the step before taking it. Those who are prepared and qualified to enter the valley with the same spirit that actuated the early settlers of Eastern Canada will, in all probability, never regret it.

"Similar remarks apply to the whole northern interior, as without communication and without market, except that afforded by local mining development—still in its infancy—it requires some capital and a good deal more pluck to await patiently the day when railways will afford both."

Undoubtedly sage advice, but I'm afraid the north country would have waited long for settlers with those qualifications; and who ever saw a country developed by patient waiting? As pioneers well know, it is only the impatiently clamoring settlers that get Government action finally on roads, public utilities, etc. Consequently a few settlers did make the venture. Gabriel LeCroix, noted in the list of settlers in Hazelton in 1894, was one of these. He took up land at Round Lake. George Duhaml, who had been a linesman on the Telegraph, settled south of Moricetown and built a roadhouse known as Glacier House. He soon went broke but remained in the district for many years, eventually working in the mines. The first real settlement began along the shores of Aldermere Lake, known as Tyee Lake and now as McLure Lake, on a ridge between it and the Bulkley River. Fred G. Heal was one of the first to settle here but the town was staked by John Dorsey in 1904. Dorsey had entered the valley in 1901 and built a roadhouse known as Bulkley House, a log hotel on the same ridge just above the river. Besides putting up travellers, he kept a few supplies for sale—the first store in the Bulkley Valley. From this point the trail swung down to the river, emerging opposite the entrance of the Telkwa River.

By May 1906, there were seventy-four permanent settlers in the valley and the following year a village was surveyed adjoining Aldermere, on the banks of the Bulkley, called Telkwa — the same name as the stream entering on the opposite bank. During 1907, the first sawmill was brought into operation by William Croteau, in partnership with Joe Bourgeon and Tom Thorpe, and finished lumber became available, all buildings previous to that time being of log construction. The first store at Aldermere was built by Len Broughton and Jack McNeill, who also had a warehouse and a hotel.

While this preliminary settlement was proceeding, other visitors to the valley were interested in the mineral possibilities of the surrounding mountains. One of the early prospectors was Mr. Frank Dockrill, who is still an active citizen of the District, operating the Telkwa Collieries. Let him tell in his own words of his arrival in the Bulkley Valley:[3]

"In company with William McCullough I left Vancouver the first week in January, 1905, on the steamer Cutch and landed at Port Simpson, the seat of Government of the District of Omineca. John Flewin was the Government Agent and Stipendiary Magistrate in charge of the District. . . . About the tenth of April we boarded the river steamer Hazelton for the trip up river. At Little Canyon we encountered Mr. George Little, whom we had met earlier at Port Simpson. He had not waited for the first boat, but had come up river by canoe with the Indians and filed a preemption at that point which he later sub-divided and named Terrace.

"Owing to low water, we were ten days reaching Hazelton, which is the head of navigation on the Skeena. On the day after arrival, we rented a cabin from an Indian and settled down as it was early yet to travel owing to shortage of horse food. On the days following, we called and paid our respects to the following gentlemen: First, the Government Agent, then Mr. Loring, Indian Agent, and then Mr. Boyd, factor of the Hudson's Bay post. All three were men of consequence of the period, not the least of whom was Mr. Boyd, the Hudson's Bay Factor, through whom all banking business with the outside world was carried on; and last, but not least, the Hudson's Bay Company were the importers of all alcoholic liquor brought into the country and carried a large stock in what was known as the 'stone cellar'. This was quite a commodious building built of stone at the time of the establishment of the Fort to safeguard the storage of commodities, especially ammunition and liquor, in case the Indians became troublesome. At the time of the advent of the writer, it was used solely as a liquor warehouse, and it was quite a sight, as all spirits came in oak casks, and the casks were lined up around the walls on racks, lying on their sides with the wooden spigots in the end to facilitate the drawing of either large or small quantities.

"The itch to move was upon us as the weather had turned warm, so we proceeded to buy a pack horse and assembled our outfit including camp utensils, tents and food. My partner, McCullough, thought he knew how to throw a diamond hitch, but alas, we had not gone far before the ground was covered with our various 'iktus',[4] and then a man who knew how to throw the diamond hitch came to our assistance. I realised right there that it was up to me to learn to pack a horse, and we never had any trouble afterwards.

"Our destination was a point in the Bulkley Valley about fifty-eight miles from Hazelton opposite the mouth of the Telkwa River. The weather was beautiful, we walked, leading the pack horses in turns, and enjoyed every minute and made our destination the third night. The country appealed to me, what with the budding light greens of the aspens in the foreground with patches of new grass and the dark greens of the pines and spruce rolling into the background, made a beautiful picture. Prospectors and land seekers were arriving daily and we learned that a general store was to be opened on the bench by two men named Len Broughton and Jack McNeill, which assured us of a place to renew our supplies when we would return from the hills.

"With the aid of our Indian canoe, we swam our horses across the Bulkley River and started west for the mountains known as Hunter Basin, named after an old prospector who had staked claims there the year before. After spending some time looking over the mountains in the Hunter Basin area, we continued west crossing Glacier Creek on to Sunset Creek. Here we spent some time and staked some claims showing copper ore, continued on west across Gold Creek and Dominion Basin and down the south fork of the north fork of the Maurice River. Evidences of copper ore were found on almost every range, but nothing outstanding. Owing to the abundance of game and fish, our supplies had lasted longer than expected, but we got nearer our source of supply which would be the new store at Aldermere opposite the junction of the Telkwa River with the Bulkley River. On our way up the north fork of the Maurice we found coal float and traced it for miles, finally entering Gold Stream, and followed the float into what we later called Coal Creek and near the head of this small creek we found a nice seam of high grade bituminous coal which later proved to be seven feet thick. After staking six sections of coal lands, we procured generous samples, for by this time our pack horse was travelling light and headed for the Bulkley Valley. It was September by this time, and on our way out to the valley we shot quite a number of young blue grouse, and upon our arrival in the valley we procured some new potatoes from one of the early pre-emptors, a Mr. John Grey, and while these potatoes were just a little bigger than marbles, they were delicious fried with young blue grouse. We entertained some of the prospectors who had come out of the hills ahead of us, among others a Tom Jefferson, who we thought would founder himself before the fry pans became empty. After laying in the valley for a while we headed for Hazelton, as at that time the steamer did not run late into the fall owing to low water and lack of business. At Hazelton we made arrangements for the wintering of our pack horse and in the meantime, having a generous supply of coal samples, we optioned our coal claims to some Butte interests. We later took the last trip of the river steamer to Port Essington and the coast steamer for Vancouver."

A rough survey of the valley during those early years, before the railway construction began, would show Billy Clark, an ex-lineman, at Bulkley Lake, Harry Davis at Pleasant Valley—just up the Bulkley from the Morice River — the Diamond D ranch just below the Morice, LeCroix at Round Lake, the Wakefield family at Deep Creek, who, incidentally, brought the first wagon into the country when they emigrated to the Bulkley Valley from the United States, and a considerable settlement around Aldermere and Telkwa, and the Hudson's Bay Company ranch at Driftwood. This latter ranch gave its name to the prominent mountain across the river on the west bank, which dominated the area and was crowned with an impressive glacier. Hudson Bay Mountain and Hudson Bay Glacier are still the outstanding landmarks of the District.

The first Protestant missionary to serve the Bulkley Valley has much to tell of the conditions in those early days and should be mentioned here. Rev. F. L. Stephenson was an Anglican clergyman who had served in various places in the Diocese of Caledonia and in 1906 was stationed at Atlin. He volunteered for service in the Bulkley and essayed to travel there by foot. This he did by following the route of the Telegraph line, visiting all the cabins on the way. He made his headquarters at Aldermere. This is what he says:—[5]

"My nearest clerical confrere was at Hazelton, seventy-odd miles by trail. No roads, no automobiles, no planes, no radio. Ah, if we could have had some of those things! But you never heard a grouch or a kick. Generous, active, helpful, their motto was 'The latch string hangs on the outside of the door. Pull it and come in'. If none was home and you wanted a meal or stay the night you were as welcome as though mine host was there. All that was expected was, leave the place clean and tidy with wood and kindling ready for his return. Locks, there wasn't one in the whole country. To use one would be an insult, or at least a sign you were a che-chako (new-comer). No robberies, petty thieving or hold-ups.

"What did the people do if taken ill? Well, they took a chance on me, and if they needed a doctor after that, well, they had seventy or more miles to go or bring him. Almost invariably they took a chance on me, and Dr. Wrinch, one of the most splendid men I have ever known or worked with, was my help and stay. He is outstanding in both his profession and the work he has achieved. He was the originator of the first hospital in Hazelton and by his untiring efforts this has been replaced by a modern and up-to-date one. No call for his help was ever turned down. Weather, distance, inconvenience, even his own physical condition, were secondary matters when called to a sick or injured man or woman. Transportation was done by cayuse (pack horse) or you packed your own load, unless you hired an Indian. Many a time I have thought that the only difference between me and a mule was in the length of my ears. The load, the stubbornness, the muddy trail were all mine, but I lacked the ears and the melodious voice.

"Provisions were packed in by pack trains in the summer. In wet weather the trails were shockingly cut up by these trains. Each horse stepped into the same hole the one in front had made in the soft ground and when too sloppy and deep, tried a fresh place to one side or the other. In time a right-of-way eight or ten feet wide was hammered down, resembling a railroad track without rails, the ties or sleepers being the ridges between the steps of the horses, and the intervening spaces mud sometimes three feet deep. Provisions consequently were expensive. In addition to the original cost, you paid three freight bills on every pound: The coastwise freight, the river steamer to Hazelton, and the pack-train from that point of distribution to where you were located."

Telling of one of his patients who required the attention of Dr. Wrinch, he recounts a tale of getting the doctor and the two of them riding on horseback to see the sick woman. "After a bite to eat, the doctor and I were in the saddle and 'silently stole away' reaching the patient shortly after noon. An operation was necessary, but how to get her into hospital over that long rough trail was the problem. Riding was altogether out of the question, and we could not get a vehicle over the trail. So a stretcher was improvised. I got five other men to volunteer and we packed her in in two days. Dr. Wrinch operated two days later. It was successful and I went to Synod the next day. That was practical as well as muscular Christianity, which will, I believe, be counted to those men (who profess little but are emulators of the Good Samaritan) as Righteousness."

The trails mentioned by Mr. Stephenson were slowly improved to wagon roads by the Provincial Government. In 1908 the trail to Aldermere from Hazelton received attention and was built into a road with the necessary bridge at Moricetown. The work continued the following year and at the same time a road was built up the Kispiox Valley to supply the farmers who had already entered that part of the country.

Settlers were increasing in the Bulkley Valley and many of the farms were assuming major proportions. The Barrett Ranch was the most outstanding and in 1908 Charlie Barrett brought in a threshing machine. The produce from this particular ranch for that year sold for $28,000,[6] so it was quite evident that initiative and energy could make a success of farming in the valley. In fact, the growth was, in many cases, phenomenal, and in one of the stores in Hazelton there was exhibited a twenty-six and a half pound turnip. Only a market was needed and the imminent arrival of the Grand Trunk Pacific Railway promised that.

CHAPTER TEN

Terrace and Kitamat

Once upon a time, far to the south, there lived a band of Indians on the banks of a river at the head of Rivers Inlet. They were known as Owikenos and formed part of the great Kwakiutl nation, which covered the Coast from midway on Vancouver Island to Millbank Sound. As the result of a tribal quarrel a group of these people fled from Owikeno and travelled north until eventually they settled at the mouth of a river at the head of Douglas Channel. Here they lived in peace and plenty for many years, for their new river had a good supply of salmon, and also a run of oolichan in the spring.

One day they noticed a piece of carved cedar floating down the river — a sure sign that others were living in the vicinity — and going up the valley they met a band of strangers: Indians of different appearance and talking a strange tongue. They made friends with the newcomers and invited them to join them at the river mouth. There the two groups lived together, and thus, according to Indian legend, came into existence the Kitamats. Ethnologically the story is probably substantially correct, for the Kitamat people are a distinct group, resembling, yet different from, their neighbours to the north and south.

The up-river group were Gitekshan who had come across the divide from the Skeena River, and as the years went by there were doubtless others who made the journey of forty miles from the Skeena to salt water on Douglas Channel. The Kitamats certainly would visit their relatives on the Skeena from time to time, and so a well-worn trail extended up the Kitamat Valley and over the low divide to Kitselas. The traveller on the trail passed through a broad fertile valley, heavily timbered with cedar, spruce and pine, and skirting a lake about halfway across, entered another valley which extended far to the north. This valley crossed the Skeena at right angles and reached almost to the Naas. It was a place of singular beauty, ringed 'round with the rugged peaks of the Coast Range, while level terraces of sandy gravel formed the floor of the basin. It must have seemed a peaceful paradise to the Indians, for its mild climate produced a plentiful crop of wild fruits, its rivers and lakes were full of fish, and wild animals, including the cariboo, abounded. Even the mighty Skeena forgot its boisterousness as it burst through the canyon on the eastern rim to wander peacefully across the valley.

To the prospectors and settlers, this happy combination of valleys deep in the heart of the Coast Range offered a welcome short cut to the upper Skeena; and in the winter months when travel on the lower Skeena was practically impossible, the hardy traveller could reach the river with a two or three day march from Kitamat. This was the route used to bring in the mail during the winter on the occasions when it was possible to find men willing to take the contract for its delivery to the settlement at Hazelton.

The fabulous Barney Mulvany [1] renowned throughout the north country, now living in retirement at Burns Lake, began his experiences on the Skeena when he carried Her Majesty's mail by dog team and on his back from Kitamat to Hazelton. His was a roving character and in his own words "my first ambition was to start at the mouth of every river in B.C. and go to the head of it to see what was on the other side of the summit". This he claims to have accomplished, but the Skeena was his first love and his wanderings always brought him back to its banks. Like so many of 'nature's noblemen', he had a poetic soul and his later years have been occupied with recording his experiences in prose and verse. His ballad of "Kitselas" recounts a legend of the Skeena doubtless gleaned as he camped with his Indian friends along the trail from Kitselas to Hazelton.

KITSELAS
(A legend of the Skeena River)

The aged chief of the Tsim-sians had summoned his son to his
    side;
"What ails ye? For years I have waited and still ye have taken
    no bride,
Too long ye have tarried along the coast, 'mid the salt-chuck's
    easy life;
Go forth and come not back again less ye bring to me your wife.

Go furnish ye the great canoe and choose of our braves the best;
Pick five young men for company, men that can stand the test
Of rocky rapids, the canyon's roar, and the strain of the towing
    line,
And go ye up the Skeena seeking a bride where I found mine."

We-oak-us, the son, replied: "I have listened to what you have
      said,
And the maidens here do please me not, or surely I would wed.
Tomorrow we leave with the great canoe, loaded with stores that
      are rare,
To our brothers from the far inside, with the foods for which they
      care."

Kaien, his father, answered: "I am pleased that ye obey;
Go choose your men at once, and I will load the canoe today
With grease of the oolachan, sea foods all, and remember ere
      ye go
That your mother was strong and brave and true, and came from
      Old Kuldo."

The morning wind was light and fair when the merry crew set
      out,
Sailing the salt-chuck easily, o'er an oft familiar route.
Till they entered the mighty Skeena and a favourable tide
Carried them up the river, till the weight of the salt-chuck died.

And then to pole and paddle, and hours on a straining line,
But their labour was lightened with laughter, for the weather
      was benign;
Steadily up the river, for the water was low and slow,
And calm and quiet and peaceful—as such mountain rivers go.

Past village after village, at none of which they stayed,
But just to say "Kla-how-ya", although many a pretty maid
Eyed them with coquettish glances, and sighed as they would
      pass;
And yet they would not linger till they came to Kitselas.

Here the river valley narrowed to two frowning canyon walls,
With but sixty feet between them full of rocks and reefs and falls.
We-oak-us went ahead and looked, then came back laughing, said:
" 'Tis only easy water, let us keep on going ahead."

The mile of the canyon mastered, ever on and on they went,
Past Means-kin-isht to Kitwanga, and all the time intent
On getting up the river while the spring was low —
Lining rapids, poling riffles, with a progress far from slow.

At the mouth of the Hagwilget River, where Hazelton now stands,
They found a large encampment of many Indian bands;
And Kaien's cousin, Tsinlet, was chief of the Kit-ex-shen;
He bade We-oak-us welcome, and made tent-room for his men.

But on the morrow camp was struck and all the different flocks
Headed in one direction—to the village of Kispiox,
Where many tribes were gathered—Sikanee and Kish-ga-gas,
Stikine, Babine and Kuldo, and even from the Naas.

With dance and feast and frolic, We-oak-us and his crew,
Generous with their store of food, made a potlatch, too.
And Tsinlet was their sponsor, always at We-oak-us' side,
For to him he had confided he was seeking for a bride.

The rains came on, the river rose, but still the dancing feet
In the potlatch house responded to the tom-tom's steady beat.
And We-oak-us, always careful, went to look at his canoe,
To see that everything was safe as he was wont to do.

Then on his way returning past a little single tent
He stopped and gazed a moment, and then to Tsinlet went.
"Come quick and tell me who this is; there's a girl I want to
        know."
And Tsinlet looked and answered: "Janet the Sitkum from
        Kuldo.

"But you need not try to win her, for she's shortly to be wed
To Unguz the Wolf of Kish-ga-gash, tho' she were better dead."
Said We-oak-us, "I'll talk to her, and see if her heart is won;
If not, she'll be mine tomorrow ere the setting of the sun."

Quickly he wooed and won her, as she told him of her fear
Of the long, long winter travel and the snow-shoe trails so drear.
"Take, please take me far away, ere some ill shall come to pass,
For the mother of Unguz is Dow-it-zie, the witch of
        Kish-ga-gash."

And Unguz looked black and angry, but his mother only said:
"Be still, it will never happen that they shall ever wed,
Tomorrow we leave for the salt-chuck to meet the salmon run,
And the river is high and wild and wicked, and many things may
        be done."

In the morning the last good-byes were said and Stikine and
        Sik-a-nee
Took trail for the Omineca or the Tahltan illahie.
But the Kit-ex-shan must answer the lure of the salmon call,
And many canoes were leaving, with Tsinlet leading them all.

Janet travelled in Tsinlet's canoe, with We-oak-us astern that day;
And the rising flow of the river flood hurried them on their way,
Till nightfall found them camping at the eddy near the pass
Where the half-mile-wide wild river converged to Kitselas.

Then the council drums were sounded and the chiefs expressed
        their view
That none should run the canyon; they would portage the canoes.
But Unguz sneered and muttered, "Let We-oak-us lead the way
In his great canoe and we'll follow; 'twill save us one whole day."

And We-oak-us then answered, "We are not afraid to try;
We have listened to the council, and we know that dangers lie
In hidden rock and whirlpool, while the waters are so wild."
And he looked at his companions, who nodded "Yes" and smiled.

"We will make the trail at day-break, ere the floods begin to rise."
Then turning met the "Sitkum" with the tear drops in her eyes.
"Oh, We-oak-us, I am fearful: please make the portage too."
But he answered, "I have said it and I have to see it through."

That night, at darkest of the moon, the camp all wrapped in sleep,
Dow-it-zie, the witch of Kish-ga-gash, so stealthily did creep,
With axe in hand most carefully, with cunning stroke and true,
Notched the great stern sweep which steered the Tsim-si-an
        canoe.

Then early in the morning the tribes the canyon lined;
Dow-it-zie spoke to Janet in a voice that sounded kind;
"Come with me to the whirlpool where the greatest danger lies,
If they pass the point in safety there is no need for your sighs."

At the landing all was ready, but just before the start,
Tsinlet, the cousin of Kaien, came with the speed of a dart;
"I will go in the bow with you that it may not be said by men
That the Tsim-si-ans had shown a lead to the Chief of the
        Kit-ex-shan.

"Watch out for the crooked channel, and swing on the top of the
        swell;
When we make the canyon entrance we enter the Gate of Hell."
And the crew just raised their voices in a song of joy and pride,
But the answering notes of the death-song came from the canyon
        side.

The canyon safely entered when a sudden splintering crack,
And the craft now sideways drifting, caused the bow-man to
        look back.
The broken sweep now useless, the canoe was uncontrolled,
Met the next swell broadside, smashed against the wall and
        rolled.

Down below the whirlpool Janet stood with bated breath,
Till the cries from up the canyon warned her of the threatened
  death.
Then from the whirlpool vortex a head and arm appeared,
And We-oak-us grasped a juniper the rocky wall had reared.

And white-faced Janet the Sitkum was making a rope of her
  clothes,
When behind her the witch Dow-it-zie silently arose
With a great uplifted boulder which she crashed on his drooping
  head,
And back in the swirling water he went to join his dead.

Then Janet said, "You wanted that I be strong and brave;
What matters it when you are gone and there are none to save?
But above all things you told me was to be always true.
I will, Oh Kitselas," she cried, "And now, please take me too."

There lies a midstream island at the head of Kitselas,
And there may be seen a totem-pole lying in the tall rank grass;
Though mouldy and rotten, the Bear of the Tsim-si-ans will show
With the salmon of the Kit-ex-shen and the Raven of Kuldo.

The advantage of this route to the Interior appealed to other
than prospectors and in 1900 the Provincial Legislature granted
a charter to Charles Clifford and associates for a railway from
Kitamat to Omineca. With the charter went a guarantee of a
cash subsidy of five thousand dollars per mile provided the sum
of one hundred thousand dollars was spent in construction before
1907. The promotion never got as far as actual construction and
the charter was eventually purchased by the Grand Trunk Pacific
in 1905.

There had always been considerable mining activity in the
Kitselas area and some of the properties found the Kitamat route
advantageous for supplies during the winter. In fact, the first
cleared trail was put through in 1898 by a New York syndicate
who were developing a mining property on O.K. Mountain.[2] The
guide for the party was Harry Franks, later one of the early
settlers of Terrace.

Another of the pioneer settlers in this area came in over the
Kitamat trail in 1905. George Little[3] came out of the Yukon that
year, as did Mr. Dockrill, because of the new railroad which was
to come down the Skeena. After a short stay in Port Simpson,
he headed for the Kitsumgalum Valley where the Provincial
Government was shortly to open the reserve of land for public

sale. He, along with others, staked extensively and thus began the settlement ultimately known as Terrace. At first it was called "Eby", in recognition of the man and his wife who built a store and hotel at the landing on the river bank. As on the Bulkley, settlement was not rapid, and after two years, in 1907, there were about fifteen pre-emptors on the ground. Charles Weeks, Fred Bohler and Harry Franks were among those early pioneers.

The valley proved to be eminently suited to agriculture. Two types of soil were present. The low-lying land on either side of the Skeena was rich alluvial deposit, while northwards was a level plateau about three hundred feet high, consisting of clay sub-soil with a gravel and sand topping. The vegetation on this plateau was mainly birch, alder and willow and, being easy to clear, made way for excellent orchard land. Small fruits and vegetables did amazingly well on the lower levels and, given adequate population, this valley showed promise of becoming the bread basket for the north coast settlements. Its productivity was in reality due to the benevolent climate. Midway between the bitter colds of the Interior and the heavy rainfall of the coast, it shared the best characteristics of each. Winters were mild and the summers moderate with long hours of sunshine. Water supply was adequate with only about half of the rainfall of the neighbouring coast.

With the coming of the railroad a townsite was surveyed in 1910. The settlement had been known for some time as Kitsumgalum, and the new townsite, which was laid out on property largely owned by George Little, was first called Littleton. However, there was already a "Littleton" in Canada and the name of Terrace was finally settled on for the new community. It was planned with wide streets and, with an eye to its future beauty, George Little planted shade trees of maple and birch down the main street. For the days of construction Terrace boomed, since it was a principal point of call for the steamboats on the river and a hive of industry for the railroad construction crews. With agriculture, mines and forests it seemed inevitable that the district would develop rapidly, but progress in all three was spasmodic and the stagnation which settled on the whole north line of the railroad with the coming of the First World War smothered the hopes of Terrace too. With a population of approximately three hundred, it drifted along through the Twenties, rousing momentarily for incorporation as a village in 1927, and dropping back into somnolence, until destiny called it with the bugles of the Second World War.

CHAPTER ELEVEN

Missions

The first clash of native and white man was disastrous for the poor Indian. The introduction of firewater by the early traders with its accompanying inevitable degradation and the contact with new and decimating diseases worked havoc amongst the Coast and Interior tribes, which the trader made no attempt to alleviate. Not until the middle of the 19th century was there any effort made by the forces of organized religion to penetrate the district and rescue the inhabitants.

Three denominations played a major role in the movement —the Roman Catholics in the Interior, and the Anglican and Methodist churches on the coast and up the river as far as Hazelton. It is unfortunately true that rivalry between the three was bitter, and the efforts of a second denomination in any area were considered as a form of proselytizing which was deeply resented. The methods used by the three Churches did not vary greatly, although the men and money available in some cases delayed the attainment of the goal. Discipline and authority in dealing with these primitive and often savage people were essential and, in the case of Duncan of Metlakatla and the Roman Catholics under Bishop Durieu, the discipline was carried to the extreme of corporal punishment, which gave rise to severe criticism from the white population.

The arrival of a fourth Church organization on the scene— the Salvation Army—further complicated matters, for they went on reservations where Churches were already established, and in most cases left their infant congregations in charge of native leaders. The ease with which a recalcitrant communicant could cross the road to the rival Church completely demoralised church discipline, and was the reason for the resentment against the "Army" which was voiced by the missionaries of that day.

ROMAN CATHOLIC

The Roman Catholic Church had established a mission in the vicinity of Fort Vancouver on the Columbia,[1] and, in 1842,

Father Demers made a journey up the Okanagan and Cariboo to Fort George, finally reaching Fort St. James, before he returned to the coast. Three years later he was followed by Father Nobili, who again visited Fort St. James, but did not get any further west. He returned the following year—1846—and this time visited the Indians around Fort Babine, where he spent a couple of weeks. Father Nobili was therefore the first Catholic priest to visit the Indians of the Skeena, but his visit was not the first word these people had heard of Christianity.[2] William McBean who was in charge of Fort Babine in the 1830s was a half-breed from across the Rockies who had been educated and was deeply religious. He undertook to impart Christian teaching to the natives around his post, although his methods were novel to say the least. He mixed his doctrines with some of their own heathen practices and the resulting religion was a remarkable combination of singing and dancing.

Following Father Nobili's visit there was a long period when no priest was available for work in this remote region, but a number of pseudo priests or prophets made their appearance amongst the natives themselves. Amongst the Babines appeared a man called Uzakla, who had a wide following even among the Tsimpseans. It is not surprising that such success generated opposition and jealousy, and amongst the Hagwilgets a man named Kwes decided to start his own brand of religion. By means of a series of cataleptic fits he impressed his fellow tribesmen and, changing his name to Peni, soon became famous at home and abroad. To quote Father Morice: "Gradually he formulated a set of religious tenets, consisting of a mixture of Christianity with many beliefs and practices congenial to the native mind. He taught his followers to make the sign of the cross, composed songs with a strong religious bias, destined to accompany heathenish dances, preached repentance and atonement of sin, introduced an organisation whose object was to watch over order and morality, bestowed names on his adepts in imitation, no doubt, of the christenings by the white priest he must have heard about, united native couples, and in every way played the part of a minister of religion. He went even further. As the number of his followers increased, he set upon prophesying, and declared that the future had no secrets from him. Strange to say, all the living witnesses, white as much as Dene and Tsimpsean, are unanimous in asserting that all his predictions have since been fulfilled to the letter."

Twenty years elapsed before the first Bishop of the new Vicariate of British Columbia, the Rev. L.- J. D'Herbomez, accompanied by Rev. Father McGuekin, managed to cover the

71

district as far as Babine, where they stayed several days exhorting and instructing the Indians who had gathered for a potlatch.

The following year—1869—Father Lejacq came to the north and was the first priest to visit the natives at Hagwilget. For the following eleven years he ministered to the inhabitants of a parish extending from the Forks of the Skeena to Fort McLeod, and north to Fort Connolly. He operated from Fort St. James as his headquarters, where the Mission of Our Lady of Good Hope was established. In this work he was assisted by Father Blanchet. A Protestant clergyman, Rev. D. M. Gordon, in his book "Mountain and Prairie", has this to say of the work of Father Lejacq:[3] "On our way we met Pere Lejaques, the missionary of this district, whose charge embraces the whole territory between the forks of the Skeena and Fort McLeod, east and west, and between Fort Connolly and Fort St. George north and south. After leaving the valley of the Skeena and of the Naas, all the Christian Indians of the Interior throughout this northern district are Roman Catholics. The mission is under the direction of the Oblate Fathers, and the missionaries, if all like the devoted Pere Lejacques, are 'in journeyings often and in labors abundant.' "

His name is perpetuated in the naming of the Indian Residential School at Fraser Lake. This school was begun at Fort St. James in 1916 and was originally housed in a day school which had been erected there in 1908, and was enlarged to accommodate the new students. Father Joseph Allard was the first principal. It proved inadequate for the needs of the district and, in 1921, a new school was built and opened on the south shore of Fraser Lake. This school was named Lejac, an abbreviated form of the name of the pioneer Catholic missionary.

The origin of the school is interesting, and has to do with the salmon fishing on Babine Lake. When the first Dominion Fisheries Inspector visited Babine, he found the Indian traps completely across the mouth of the river as it left the lake. He destroyed them and forbad the Indians to place them there in future. This, of course, gave rise to great indignation on the part of the Indian chiefs, who declared that, had they been there when the destruction took place, they would have killed the Inspector.

A conference was then held with the Indians, when the Government placated them by allowing them sole fishing rights in the area and agreed to supply them, in perpetuity, with nets to be used in place of traps. They also agreed to give them a residential school. To implement the last clause in the agreement, the Government negotiated with the Roman Catholic

Church and the establishment of the Lejac School was the result.

With the departure of Father Lejacq to his new appointment at Kamloops, there came to Fort St. James Father A. G. Morice, without doubt the most outstanding man in British Columbia missions in any denomination.[4] He was born in France, and, after completing his training, arrived in British Columbia in 1880. The first years of his mission were spent in southern British Columbia and the Cariboo and he was transferred to his northern post in 1885. Then began a period of remarkable achievement. He was a man of tremendous energy, both physical and mental, and in his vast new mission there was unlimited challenge.

His first concern was to master the language of the inhabitants and in this he was aided by the knowledge he had already acquired of the Chilcotin tongue. Within a year he was able to converse passably and on his departure knew more about their language than the natives did themselves. Following the example of a Protestant missionary among the Crees, who had elaborated a syllabary, Father Morice developed a written language for the Carrier people, and by means of a primitive printing press, published religious documents in their own language. The beauty of the new system was its simplicity, which enabled the natives to quickly master it; and the written word thus made available to them promoted the spread of Christianity amongst them in a way that nothing else could have accomplished.

By the time Father Morice arrived there were fourteen mission centres scattered over the vast territory already outlined, and to these missions the Father travelled at regular intervals. His knowledge of the language and his sympathetic insight into the native mind, made a powerful appeal to these primitive people, and over the years he came to have a tremendous influence with them. As one Hudson's Bay Company official once put it, he was "the king of the country". Before he completed his mission, he had the satisfaction of seeing all the villages under his care, at least outwardly Christian, the last to embrace the new faith being the Hagwilgets, who signalled their final surrender by publicly burning all their heathen paraphernalia before the visiting Bishop.

Father Morice's efforts were not confined to his missionary duties although these were not neglected. He had a deep interest in the shape and characteristics of this new, largely unknown, country and on his continual journeying from village to village, he made voluminous notes and observations which he later drew up in a map of the country. Indeed he made many trips which were solely for geographical purposes, and was the first white man to explore and describe the country south and east of the Skeena and the headwaters of the Bulkley. It was his contention that the river which now bears his name was the true Bulkley River, and in his original map, he so labelled it, assigning his own name to the river now called Bulkley, above the entrance of the Morice. The lake now called Morice, he christened Loring Lake, and gave his own name to the Great Eutsuk Lake in Tweedsmuir Park which he discovered. The Provincial Government, for reasons best known to themselves, changed the nomenclature on subsequent maps.

Such prodigious exertions as he constantly made might have been tolerated had his living conditions been better. However, he lived alone, with no servants, and made the least possible concessions to the demands of the flesh. His food was poor and his meals poorly prepared. He literally lived out of a frying pan. It seemed he begrudged the time for such trivia and he labored long into the night on his printing, writing and scientific studies. In truth, he burned himself out, and in 1904 his superiors transferred him from his beloved Denes to work in the south. We are not concerned with the rights or wrongs of the matter, save to note that it was a terrible disappointment to Father Morice, who felt that no one could carry on his work as well as he. He was later transferred to Manitoba and relieved from ecclesiastical duties so that he might bend all his energies to his scientific work. His writings are numerous and brilliant as historian, ethnologist, anthropologist and journalist, and he died knowing the satisfaction of world-wide recognition and acclaim.

Before following up the story of his successors, a short description of the methods used in the Indian Missions by the Roman Catholic Church is in order here. The missions on the mainland of British Columbia were under the charge of the Oblates of Mary Immaculate with headquarters at New Westminster. In 1875, Father Durieu was consecrated as Bishop of New Westminster and he instituted the "system" which was to characterise the work of the Church in the following years. Father Morice summarises it:[5] "Being a grown-up child, the native must be constantly watched, often reproved, and his persevering powers at times tested. Hence the establishment of the watchmen, who are the eyes of the village chief. But a correction cannot be administered without the proper means of enforcing orders; this accounts for the presence among Durieu's neophytes of the so-called 'soldiers', or policemen, who are the arms of the chief, whose role in the native social economy is that of the head in a well organised body.

"With the spiritual progress of the people still another, and more important, office has come into existence. This is that of the 'Eucharist watchman', who to-day renders communicants or the candidates for the first communion the same services as the Chiefs did formerly to common people. The duties of these Chiefs are now regarded as partaking more of a civil or temporal character. That watchman virtually replaces the priest when he is absent; he comforts the weak and afflicted, stirs up the lukewarm, and raises up the fallen by kind words and a salutary penance.

"This penance may be of a moral or of a corporal nature, and the love of the same is sedulously inculcated into the faithful. As a consequence, that discipline recalls many points of that in vogue during the first centuries of the Church. Especially during retreats or missions, which are periodically given at relatively short intervals, it is not rare to see Indians, tied up or free, kneeling down or standing up in front of the whole congregation as a means of atoning for public delinquencies."

On the coast, the efforts of the Roman Catholic Church were confined to the area south of Queen Charlotte Sound. Only one excursion to the north is recorded and that in 1864.[6] Fathers Fouquet and Lejacq, the latter at that time being stationed at Fort Rupert on Vancouver Island, left for the north on the Hudson's Bay Company's steamer. They visited Kitamat for two days, baptising a number of Indian children, and then proceeded to Port Simpson. Here they spent two days, and, hiring a canoe, travelled up the Naas River and across to the Queen Charlotte Islands. This trip was made with only two Indian companions, one from the Fraser River and the other an Iroquois. Without any local knowledge, their journey across Hecate Straits and back to Fort Rupert was an amazing feat, accomplished as it was in the early part of the year when storms are frequent. This trip was in the nature of an exploration, and lack of men made it impossible for the Church to follow up the information gathered with the establishment of missions.

In 1908[7] a Prefecture Apostolic was established to include the Yukon and that portion of British Columbia lying north of the 54th parallel, and Father Bunoz was named as the Prefect Apostolic. Father Bunoz at that time was laboring in the Yukon and after his appointment he journeyed down the coast to Vancouver, stopping en route at the infant port of Prince Rupert, where he spent some little time. The land was not yet on the market, but Father Bunoz erected a small chapel near the wharf before continuing his journey. He returned when the land was released for sale in May and June, and purchased several lots, on some of which he began the construction of a church. On an adjoining lot he built living quarters and a small chapel. The church was completed in 1909, but shortly after, in a severe November storm, the building listed about fifteen feet. Fortunately it was capable of restoration and the repaired foundations have maintained the building four-square to the winter storms ever since.

Father Bunoz was joined in his work the following year — 1910 — by Father Godfrey and the latter was assigned to mission work on the Skeena River.[8] Father Godfrey was christened Gottfried Anthony Eichelsbacher, and he was born in Hansen, Germany. He came to Canada in 1901 and was sent to the Yukon, where he served until his transfer to the Skeena. Late in October 1910, Father Godfrey made his first journey up the Skeena, going by steamer as far as Kitselas, and from there he travelled on foot to Hagwilget.

Hagwilget was the western boundary of the Babine District and had had a church and mission for some years. The original building had been erected by Father Marchal, but had been replaced in 1908 by Father Coccola. A small house had been built for the priest and this Father Godfrey enlarged and it became his home that winter. The following year he journeyed up the Bulkley Valley visiting the settlers en route and finally deciding on Telkwa as the site of a church for the white population. The funds for this building were raised by the ladies of the district.

He continued to work in the area and in 1912 began construction of a new church for the Indians at Moricetown. An interesting item in regard to this structure is the history of its bell. Father Bunoz had intended to install a bell in the church at Prince Rupert and for that purpose had procured a one thousand pound bell from Grenoble, France. Through delay in constructing the necessary tower, the bell had been stored for some time and Father Godfrey finally prevailed upon his superior to let him have the bell for Moricetown. It was duly installed even though it bears an inscription for the church at Prince Rupert.

In 1913 the townsite of Smithers was put on the market and Father Bunoz selected and purchased four lots for a church site. Father Godfrey proceeded to raise the money for the erection of a church, which was finally completed in 1915 when it was opened and blessed at Easter by Father Bunoz.

With the outbreak of the First World War, feeling against Germans in this country ran high, and Father Godfrey did not escape. Following some indiscreet remarks attributed to him, which got him into trouble with the civil authorities, the Church removed him for a time from the district. He was transferred temporarily to Fort St. James, and his place taken by Father Joseph Allard. However, he returned in the fall of the year 1916, and opened a school in Hagwilget with a lay teacher.

Father Coccola succeeded Father Morice in the mission at Fort St. James and we find him making frequent visits to the villages of the upper Skeena, assisting Father Godfrey. Eventually he was appointed principal of Lejac School, in succession to Father Allard, and in 1934 became Chaplain to the new Catholic Hospital in Smithers, which position he held until his death on March 1st, 1943 at the age of 89. He gave a lifetime of devoted service to the district and was very highly thought of by Catholic and Protestant alike.

In 1936, Father Godfrey removed to Babine where a new church had been built by Father Coccola in 1915. At the Old Fort Babine a church had been erected by Father Allard in 1925 and Father Godfrey remained in charge of these missions until 1941, when he was appointed pro-vicar of missions and transferred to Smithers. During his absence at Babine, Father Murie had been in charge of the Smithers work; he now returned to the care of Moricetown, Telkwa and Houston. Father Godfrey held his appointment until 1944 when he assumed the position of Chaplain to the Smithers Hospital, which he holds to the present time. His place in the parish was taken by Father LeRay.

In 1916 the Prefecture of Yukon and Northern British Columbia was raised to the rank of Vicariate, and Father Bunoz was made the first Vicar Apostolic of the Vicariate of Prince Rupert and the Yukon. His district extended east to include the town of Prince George and the southern boundary was set at the 53rd parallel.

Bishop Bunoz continued to preside over this vast district, gradually opening up the work as the population increased and new communities came into existence. In 1936 he was given a co-adjutor in the person of Bishop J. L. Coudert, and in 1944 the Vicariate of the Yukon and Prince Rupert was divided, Bishop Bunoz presiding over Prince Rupert to which was added the Peace River area of Dawson Creek and Fort St. John.

The Bishop was a real ecclesiastical pioneer in northern B.C. and the Yukon. For nearly half a century, he carried the message of the Church along trails and streams, travelling for the most part by primitive means — the canoe, horseback, dog sled and snowshoes. The life was hazardous and trying and on more than one occasion his life was in danger. On one trip his travelling companion, Father E. Allard, was drowned when the two of them were spilled out of their canoe on the treacherous Dease River. The work of the diocese steadily increased during his administration, and when he died on June 3rd, 1945, there were missions at Telkwa, Houston, Babine, Smithers, Hagwilget and Terrace, in the Skeena District.

In lay activities also, the Church had been active. In August 1916, the Sisters of St. Joseph arrived in Prince Rupert and began a day school in the Parish Hall. In the meantime, a convent was being erected for them on property in the center of the city, and this building was opened in October 1917. Classes are today being conducted in these two buildings from kindergarten through to Grade Ten. In Smithers, a small hospital had been built, but it was inadequate for the needs of the area, and in 1934 the Sisters of St. Ann opened a new hospital, known as the Sacred Heart Hospital. In deference to the wishes of the local residents, the hospital is known officially as the Bulkley Valley District Hospital. Modern in construction and well equipped, it is a credit to its founders and the people of the district.

Bishop Anthony Jordan, O.M.I., the present incumbent,[9] who succeeded following the death of Bishop Bunoz, still has a tremendous Diocese to supervise. Travel over some of it is still very primitive and difficult, being accomplished on horseback, along old trails. On one such trip the Bishop was making his first visit from Fort Babine to the village of Takla and, as companions and guides, had two Babine Indians. Their knowledge of English was very slight. The trail, which was the old route used by the miners in going in to the Omineca, was overgrown, and it was necessary for the Bishop to loop the reins of the horse over the pommel of the saddle and use both hands to fend off the bushes on either side, as he rode along. His horse was a noble animal, in sharp contrast to the nags used by his guides, and the Bishop was curious as to where the Indians had got him. With difficulty he asked about the horse. One of them replied, "Get him white man. Him savvy English damn good!"

On another occasion the good Bishop was preaching a mission at a small native village when he found his supply of tobacco had run out. He went to the shack of Chief Charlie, and, pointing to the pipe in his hand, asked him if he had any tobacco. The Indian and his wife dug around in their possessions and finally came up with a small package of "Ogden's" which had been opened and was pretty dry. However, it was tobacco, and the Bishop was enjoying his first smoke in several days, when a knock came on the door, and there was Chief Charlie with a tin cup in his hand. From it he poured out a collection of silver amounting to two dollars and thirty-five cents, which he said he had collected around the village. He had gone to each door and held out the cup, saying, "Bishop too poor to buy tobacco."

Bishop Jordan's sojourn in the Vicariate was destined to be short, for early in 1955 he was appointed coadjutor-Archbishop of Edmonton.

ANGLICAN CHURCH

As already recounted, the work of the Church Missionary Society on the northern coast of British Columbia began with the arrival of William Duncan at Port Simpson in 1857, and the establishment, a few years later, of Metlakatla. In the years that followed several ordained clergymen were sent out to assist Duncan on the new field. The Rev. L. S. Tugwell was the first of these men and he arrived on the coast in 1860, joining Duncan at Port Simpson. His stay there was short as, after a year, Mrs. Tugwell's health necessitated a return to England. The Rev. R. A. Doolan followed, whose labors were centered on the Naas River, and therefore beyond the scope of this narrative. The Rev. F. Gribbel arrived soon after, but he found it impossible to work with Duncan and only remained approximately two months. His departure was overlapped by the arrival of another man of far different caliber, the Rev. Robert Tomlinson, who spent his life amongst the Indians of this district and whose name is still revered up and down the Skeena.

Robert Tomlinson was educated in Ireland where he took his B.A. degree and a course in medicine.[10] While completing the course, he did not take all his final examinations, and the explanation given for this is certainly novel. It was his intention to work in the foreign field under the Church Missionary Society, and lest he should be tempted to leave the work and practise medicine, he neglected to take his qualifying examinations.

He arrived in Victoria in 1867 and while waiting for transportation north stayed with Archdeacon Charles Woods. The Archdeacon had a brother Richard who lived on a farm situated along the Gorge, which he calley "Garbally". Robert met the family and formed an attachment for Richard Woods' daughter Alice.

He journeyed up the coast with William Duncan on the latter's boat, the schooner "Kate", when part of the load of freight carried was a sawmill for the village of Metlakatla. They arrived safely at their northern destination, although they managed to strike a rock entering the port. Tomlinson was given the choice of remaining with Duncan at Metlakatla or joining the Rev. Doolan in the work on the Naas, and he chose the latter. Duncan claimed that Tomlinson was prejudiced against him by conversations he had in Victoria with the Rev. Gribbel, but his subsequent behaviour towards Duncan would indicate that the prejudice, if any, was of a very transitory nature.

In Mr. Tomlinson's work on the Naas we have no particular concern, except to note that he remained there for twelve years, and was responsible for moving the mission station from Greenville to a new site near the mouth of the river and establishing the village of Kincolith. As on other fields, the missionary passed through many trying times and undoubtedly his life on occasion was in jeopardy. An amusing incident which occurred shortly after his arrival was credited with contributing in no small measure to his survival. In preparation for his departure from England, Robert had purchased a supply of linen, and to secure it from loss had carefully marked it with his initials in India ink. Being of an artistic nature he had, as well, drawn in ink a dove, as being a suitable symbol of his mission. When he first moved to the Kincolith site, he took with him two natives who looked after his household needs while he was engaged in building his new home. One day they rushed up to him in great excitement and exhibited some of his handkerchiefs they were washing, and asked if the black bird was his crest. Tomlinson said, "Yes, I suppose it is!" The only black bird the Indians knew was the raven, and from that day Tomlinson was considered a member of the Raven Clan and the local Chief of that clan made it his personal business to see that no harm befell him.

During the days and nights on the Naas, Tomlinson's mind often turned to Victoria and the young woman, Alice Woods, he had met there. After a year on the field, he procured a canoe and with a crew of eight Indian men and one Indian woman, as company for his intended bride, made the long trip to Victoria. There he married Alice at an impressive ceremony with five bridesmaids, which was attended by all of Victoria society. One can easily imagine the impatience of the young missionary with all these frills, for it is recorded that the wedding was delayed for two weeks so that the bride's father could have a road cut through the forest from Douglas Street in Victoria, so that the guests might reach the farm on the Gorge."

The journey back to the Naas took twenty-four days, but was accomplished in safety and Alice went about the task of making a home for Robert Tomlinson. At the end of the twelve years at this mission, it was decided that Tomlinson should open up work on the upper Skeena. In preparation for the move, he went to Victoria and purchased two horses with foals, and several head of cattle. He brought them to Kincolith and, when all was ready, loaded the animals on a scow and sent them up the river on the rising tide, with a crew of Indians. His wife and children went in one canoe and Tomlinson followed later in a second. They were to rendezvous at a point previously arranged some distance up the river. Tomlinson arrived there after dark to find his wife and family, but no sign of the scow. They set out to search the river, and, in the dark, finally located a light which turned out to be the missing scow. It had swung off to the opposite side of the river in the changing tide, and then grounded on a sand bar. The frightened animals stampeded, some entering the water, and a horse and foal were lost and some of the cattle drowned. The rest were gathered up and order restored and the party continued up the river to the head of navigation.

There the long trek was begun over the grease trail to the Kispiox River. This trail, at one point, crosses the Cranberry River, and here trouble was again experienced with the cattle. The prize bull was lost when he panicked, got his head under water, and was drowned. Misfortune continued to dog their footsteps, for Mrs. Tomlinson came down with Typhoid Fever, and being too ill to travel, it was necessary to camp for some weeks while the doctor nursed her through the crisis. The long delay depleted their food supply, and it was a hungry and travel-weary party that finally reached Kispiox. News of their approach had preceded them, and the missionary considered it intervention by the Almighty when they were met on the trail by an Indian woman from Kispiox, sent by the Chief of that village, with a sack of potatoes.

The Tomlinsons settled on a flat, called Ankitlas, about seven miles up river from Kispiox village. Here they built a home, but winter came upon them before it was completed, and that first winter in the harsh interior climate was a bitter experience still recounted by the family. Under these unfavorable conditions another child arrived, a third daughter, Annie.

The dissension in the field which had developed with the arrival of Bishop Ridley was evident even in this remote spot. Tomlinson was under the impression that he had been sent to Kispiox, but the Bishop wanted him to go to Hazelton. To get things straightened out Mr. Tomlinson made the long trip back to England and was confirmed in his appointment to Kispiox. From funds he raised in the Old Land, he constructed a brick yard for the natives on his return.

The Bishop was determined to secure the work at Hazelton for his Church, and had the Rev. Mr. Falconer in view for the appointment. In the meantime, word came that the Methodist Church were sending the Rev. C. M. Tate to Hazelton. The Bishop immediately sent the Rev. Mr. Collison up to establish the mission and hold it, pending Mr. Falconer's arrival. Mr.

Collison visited Tomlinson at Kispiox and the latter asked what he was doing at Hazelton. Collison replied, in the words of the famous hymn, "Hold the fort, for Tate is coming!"

His work at Kispiox continued to be in disfavor with the Bishop who appointed the Rev. Falconer to Hazelton and, Tomlinson claimed, instructed him to oppose him. It was an impossible situation, and in 1883 Robert Tomlinson left Kispiox and joined William Duncan at Metlakatla. At the same time he sent his wife and family down to Victoria where his last daughter, Nellie, was born. The children were sent to school in Victoria, Robert, the oldest, attending a school held by the Rev. Percival Jenns. It is hard to realise at this distance the intense feeling engendered amongst the Anglicans on the coast by the rivalry between William Duncan and Bishop Ridley, but when it was learned in Victoria that Tomlinson was working and siding with Duncan, his son Robert was dropped from Jenns' school.

For the next four years, Mr. Tomlinson worked at Metlakatla, and when Duncan left, he returned to his work on the Skeena. It is related that, at his departure, Duncan dismantled and took with him those things which he considered belonged to the people and not to the Church, and the old sawmill was one of these. He gave it, all dismantled, to Mr. Tomlinson to use in his new field up the Skeena; but after Duncan's departure, Bishop Ridley had his men seize the machinery during the night and lock it up in a shed where Tomlinson could not get it without breaking and entering.

In November 1887, the Rev. Tomlinson went up the river and spent the winter at Kitwanga. There he gathered a nucleus of converts around him and the next year looked about for a site on which to build a new Christian village. In this he was following Duncan's example and his own experience on the Naas with Kincolith. They settled on a place down from Kitwanga, and on the opposite side of the river, and called their new village Minskinish, which means "under the pitch pines". To-day it is known as Cedarvale, which seems singularly appropriate, for a large grove of cedars adorns the bank at the landing. The missionary called his new home Garbally after the original in Victoria.

This mission was strictly non-sectarian, as Tomlinson had resigned from the Church Missionary Society. The missionary used his personal funds to purchase a sawmill which was erected on the opposite side of the river. The business this small industry was able to bring helped to carry the expenses of the mission and Tomlinson and his band of converts were able to keep ahead of starvation and slowly build up their village. To hold the land for the natives, Mr. Tomlinson pre-empted the village site and then leased it to the Indians for one hundred and ninety-nine years. His son, Robert, pre-empted across the river for land for the sawmill, and built his own house thereon. In later years the railroad ran right through the center of Robert's property, and his house became the Cedarvale postoffice.

The experience of the brickyard at Ankitlas was put to good account and Mr. Tomlinson taught the Indians to make bricks for the chimneys in their new homes — an important development, for fires were a constant threat in the early villages from the tin stove-pipes commonly used. The little sawmill was kept running constantly and proved a great boon to the whole upper Skeena. The Anglican Church at Hazelton and the Hazelton Hospital were both built from lumber cut at Minskinish. As all along the upper Skeena, the soil here was excellent for farming, and once the land was cleared, gardens flourished. Mr. Tomlinson brought in sheep which thrived well and provided a welcome change in diet.

The first building erected was used as a church hall for several years, but eventually, by dint of careful saving and all voluntary labor on the part of the Indians, they built themselves a beautiful little church, complete with bell and stained glass windows. Since they were an independent mission, this was done without any outside help beyond some small donations received from interested friends round about.

Tomlinson patterned his new village after the model of Metlakatla and ruled the people strictly. Particularly in the observation of the Sabbath was this noted, and up and down the river the new village was nicknamed the "Holy City". None dared land or leave on Sunday, nor was any work performed on that day. When the river steamer happened to arrive on that day of the week, the mail was left on the river bank and not touched until the following morning.

Mrs. Tomlinson had rejoined her husband, and for over twenty years they labored amongst the native people at Minskinish, bringing up their own children, six in number—Robert, Alice, Lily, Richard, Annie and Nellie—in a dedicated Christian home.

During the summer of 1908 Mr. Tomlinson visited Duncan at New Metlakatla. Duncan was getting on in years and needed help. He also needed medical care for his people and he persuaded Mr. Tomlinson to join him once more. Accordingly, that fall Mr. and Mrs. Tomlinson and Robert moved to Alaska, leaving Richard in charge of the mission at Minskinish. The autocratic Duncan was probably even more set in his ways and young Robert Tomlinson did not agree with him in many things. In

1912 Robert resigned and determined to return to Canada, and his parents decided to come with him. Duncan was so bitter about it that he would not come down to see his old friend off on the boat.

When Mr. Tomlinson returned to Minskinish he found the mission badly run down, and this disappointment, together with his sadness over the break with Duncan, undoubtedly hastened his death which occurred in 1913. With the death of Mr. Tomlinson, Robert, the oldest son, felt responsible for the mission and he asked the Indians to decide which Church they would like to have oversee them. They decided on the Methodist Church, and the mission property was deeded to that denomination. Actually, the Methodist Church gave little attention to the village. Richard went over to the Salvation Army and held services in the old Church Hall, and so another Christian village was divided in its allegiance.

Robert Tomlinson Jr. is another of the outstanding pioneers of the Skeena. His early years were spent amongst the Indians where he learned to speak the Nishga tongue before he mastered English. His formal education was very slight and was mostly supplied by home instruction. Nevertheless, his own native ability lifted him above the mediocrity which might easily have been his. He operated the sawmill at the village for years and later worked on the Government Telegraph Line. Then, as we have seen, he worked for Duncan at New Metlakatla for several years.

When he returned to Canada in 1912, the Rev. Walter Rushbrook was just starting the northern coast mission and Robert joined him as engineer of the "Northern Cross". Here, his knowledge of the native language and his Christian devotion were of inestimable help in making the new venture a success. He and Mr. Rushbrook were a congenial pair and the arrangement might have lasted indefinitely had not fate stepped in, in the person of one of the lady teachers at the Crosby Girls' Home in Port Simpson. Robert married Miss Ethel Collins and, entering the service of the Methodist Church, took charge of the mission at Kispiox. His labors here were saddened by the death of his wife who left him with three small children. In 1921 he married a Salvation Army nurse at Glen Vowell, and in 1924 he moved his family to Hazelton to get school facilities, taking a position with the Hazelton Hospital as steward, in charge of all outside activities.

Following the death of Mr. William Duncan in 1918, Robert Tomlinson was invited to take charge of the Church at New Metlakatla. At first he demurred, but finally, after several invitations, he moved to Alaska in 1932 and took over the mission. He labored there for six years until 1938, when he built a home for himself in nearby Ketchikan, where he still lives in retirement.

We have already mentioned the Rev. W. H. Collison as relieving at Hazelton. He came out as a lay worker to assist Duncan in 1873, accompanied by his wife. Mrs. Collison was a remarkable woman. She had trained as a nurse and deaconess, and had nursed the sick in the Franco-Prussian war. The devoted couple were sent across to the Queen Charlotte Islands to open a mission at Massett, where they lived for six years, until Duncan called them back to work at Metlakatla. Mr. Collison was ordained by the famous Bishop Bompas[12] who made a visit to Metlakatla to conduct confirmation services. Mr. Collison was subsequently sent to the Naas where he spent the remainder of his life amongst the Nishga Indians. His book, "In the Wake of the War Canoe", is a classic of missionary enterprise. As the first Archdeacon of the Diocese of Caledonia he was a well known and highly respected figure of the north coast.

With the formation of the northern half of the Province into the Diocese of Caledonia in 1879, the Church Missionary Society sent out Bishop William Ridley to superintend this vast area. It would be doing a great disservice to the Bishop's memory if we allowed what has already been said regarding his dealings with William Duncan to loom very large in the picture of his life. Indeed it played a very small part in the history of this great man's service. He was sent to organise and advance the work of the Diocese, and the twenty-five years he gave to his Church in this area were years of great accomplishment.

For the first few years the Bishop had few helpers and since he was far from welcome at Metlakatla, he spent much of his time travelling around his territory and personally ministering to the needs of the natives. In this work he was assisted by the gift, in 1881, of a small steamship, the "Evangeline", which was the first of the Anglican Mission boats which became so well known along the coast. By these personal visitations, which in the case of Hazelton lasted all one winter, the Bishop became familiar with the needs of his field, and as he received additional helpers was able to place them more advantageously.

In 1884 he opened a mission at Port Essington, sending there the Rev. A. H. Sheldon. The latter labored there for four years and then was drowned in a canoe accident off Point Lambert on the Skeena — the same accident which took the life of his wife and of Mrs. Robert Cunningham. After Mr. Sheldon's death, there was no regular missionary at Port Essington under the Anglican Church until 1895 when the Rev. B. Appleyard was appointed. He was responsible for the building of the first Anglican church there.

When Duncan removed to Alaska, the Bishop made his head-quarters at Metlakatla and began to restore the mission. He divided the mission house into three parts, utilising one end for a residence, the other end as a home for some boys he was training, and the central portion was made into a home for children of mixed parentage. The latter was placed in the charge of Miss Margaret West, a lady who had come out from England and worked without salary. This was the beginning of the Ridley Home, so called in memory of the Bishop's wife who died at Metlakatla. The name really applied to the new building which was put up following the disastrous fire in 1901 which wiped out all the mission buildings. Miss West continued in charge of the new building and was assisted by Miss R. M. Davies. These two ladies operated the home for the following twenty years until it was finally moved to its present locality in the City of Prince Rupert.

In 1866 [13] two more men joined the Diocese, Rev. R. W. Gurd and Rev. J. Field. The former worked at Kitkatla and later at Metlakatla, while the latter was sent to Hazelton. Mr. Field had been working in Africa and Ceylon, but had to seek a different climate for the sake of his wife's health. They lived in Hazelton for thirty years. During that time they were more than once in grave danger, owing to the disturbed conditions amongst the natives, and once were advised by the authorities to leave. Mr. Field built a church which ministered to white people and Indians alike, and both he and his wife were held in deep affection by the inhabitants. Mrs. Field was known as "the good angel of Hazelton", and Mr. Field was called "the St. John of Hazelton".

Three years later another pioneer missionary of the Skeena appeared on the scene. He came out as a layman and was ordained by Bishop Ridley and sent to open up the work at Kitwanga. His name was Mr. A. E. Price. He spent many years with the Indians of this village, learned their language and translated the prayer book and some of the gospels into their tongue and printed them on his own press. In the translation he was assisted by Mr. Robert Tomlinson. The first church in Kitwanga was built by Mr. Price. Two of this man's many experiences emphasise the hazards of life on the river in those days.[14] The river steamer had called at Kitwanga, and the Rev. Mr. Price took his sack of mail aboard and picked up the bags for the village. In doing so, he inadvertently picked up the bag he had brought on to the ship. When he discovered his error the boat had already pulled out into the stream. With an Indian, he jumped into a canoe and paddled out to the ship and threw his bag on board. In trying to get clear, the canoe was carried by

River Boats during Railroad Construction

Railroad Bridge across the Skeena at Kitseguecla

Terrace

—*Courtesy of Wrathalls Photo Finishing*

Old Kitselas

—*Courtesy of Wrathalls Photo Finishing*

the current under the paddle wheel which was, at the moment, going rapidly astern. The Indian jumped to the guard of the steamer but the missionary was carried under the sternwheeler, the paddles smashing the canoe to pieces. Price held on to the broken canoe and eventually came to the surface where he was rescued by the crew of the ship. One month later, the same river steamer was on her way upriver and Price decided to go with her, up to Hazelton. As he was ascending the plank to board the ship, the steamer swung out into the current, the plank pulled away from the shore and Price was dumped into the icy river, loaded down with a sack of books he was carrying. Fortunately he was a strong swimmer and managed to regain the bank in safety.

The following year a young Canadian clergyman was engaged by the Bishop, the Rev. F. L. Stephenson, and after three years at Kitkatla he was sent to open work amongst the white population at Port Simpson. He spent five years in Port Simpson and then went to the far north. However, in 1908 we find him as the first Anglican missionary in the Bulkley Valley.*

The need for medical service amongst the natives was still great. Mr. Tomlinson had been trained as a doctor, and for two or three years a Dr. Bluett-Duncan, a wealthy Englishman who was a cousin of Mr. Tomlinson's, had lived with William Duncan at Metlakatla, giving his services freely. In 1889 Dr. Vernon Ardagh, a graduate of Edinburgh University, was sent out by the Society, and he set up practice in Metlakatla. In 1900 he spent the winter up the Skeena River at Kisgegas, and in the spring of 1901 returned to Metlakatla where a small hospital was improvised from two empty native houses. This hospital was staffed by Miss Davies, a trained nurse from England, and two helpers, and Dr. Ardagh had as assistant a Dr. Webb, sent over from Australia by the Church Missionary Society there. The work was short-lived, however, doubtless due to the fire of 1901, and Dr. Ardagh returned to England where he was in practice for ten years. In 1911 he returned to British Columbia and was ordained to the priesthood and sent to take charge of the mission at Kitwanga, where he lived until his retirement to Port Coquitlam. There he spent the remainder of his life engaged in translating the Gospels into the Gitekshan dialect.

Two other men who became prominent in the work on the Skeena remain to be mentioned. William Hogan appeared on the scene in 1893 and for a while assisted the Bishop at Metlakatla. In 1899 he was sent to take the place of the Rev. Mr. Stephenson

---

* For further information on Mr. Stephenson, see "Bulkley Valley".

at Port Simpson and he remained there for ten years. Affectionately known as "Father Hogan", he built up a strong Anglican community amongst the white residents at that point and erected a church and a rectory. He was an immense man of tremendous strength, with a broad Irish brogue and a handclasp that could crush the unwary. The story is told that at Port Essington, there was a Mr. Stapleton, a cannery man of similar girth to Mr. Hogan, who likewise had a tremendous grip and delighted in using it on all and sundry. The meeting of these two men was anticipated with great delight by their friends, and Father Hogan was duly warned. To the satisfaction of Stapleton's victims, the canneryman was brought to his knees by the doughty Irishman — as Hogan recounted it later, "Mon, he gave a mighty oath!" Mr. Hogan was later transferred to Massett where he served until his death.

Rev. W. F. Rushbrook joined the Diocese in 1903 and was sent to Port Essington to relieve Mr. Appleyard who had built up a healthy congregation with church and rectory. Mr. Rushbrook, in addition to his clerical qualifications, was a master mariner and the maritime nature of his parish appealed to him. In 1909 the Bishop supplied him with a small gasoline launch and he was thus enabled to cross the Skeena and visit the settlements up and down the river, from his headquarters at Port Essington. The same year Port Essington experienced one of its numerous fires and the Anglican church was completely destroyed. Mr. Rushbrook set about rebuilding and by fall had the new structure ready for use. Just one year later another fire swept away the new church. This time there was insurance on the building, and that, with the help of a generous donation from the local Japanese Association, was sufficient to again rebuild. The Japanese had been one of Mr. Rushbrook's particular cares, and they showed their appreciation in a tangible way.

The marine work which Mr. Rushbrook had begun on the Skeena was extended to include the whole northern coast in 1911 and he was appointed Superintendent of the Prince Rupert Coast Mission. A new boat, the "Northern Cross", was obtained and Mr. Rushbrook began regular monthly visits to all the settlements along the northern coast. He had as his engineer Mr. Robert Tomlinson and these two men became well known and welcome visitors at all the homes in the area. He continued in this work for many years until his health was no longer equal to the labor, when he was transferred to St. Peter's Church in Prince Rupert. His place was taken by the Rev. Bruce Jennings, and a succession of men to the present incumbent, Rev. F. W. Mitchell.

Bishop Ridley retired in 1904 and was succeeded by Bishop DuVernet who held the position for twenty years. He was another outstanding man and was elected Archbishop for British Columbia in 1915, a signal honor! Bishop DuVernet had charge of the Diocese through stirring, as well as troublous times. He saw the building of the Grand Trunk Pacific Railroad with the opening up of the country, and the building of the City of Prince Rupert. This meant a tremendous increase in the work of the Diocese and the necessity of procuring many new men to supply all the new settlements. He also had to direct the Diocese through the difficult times of the First World War when all activity in the district was virtually brought to a standstill, while the men went overseas. In spite of these handicaps the work of the Church prospered, in no small measure due to the wisdom and ability of the Bishop.

During Bishop DuVernet's term of office three men of note were brought into Caledonia. Rev. G. A. Rix took charge of the church in Prince Rupert in 1913, Rev. J. B. Gibson was appointed to Anyox and later Smithers, and Canon Marsh opened up the church work in Terrace, building the first church there in 1912. These men came from elsewhere in Canada, Rix from Ontario and the others from work on the prairie. In Prince Rupert, a series of men had charge of the church for varying lengths of time—Laycock, Des Barres, James, Petter and Burch —until the Rev. Rix took the permanent appointment. Following Bishop DuVernet's death in 1924 there was a vacancy in the Bishopric for several years, while the Diocesan funds were built up to a sufficient level to support a new Bishop. In 1928 Rev. G. A. Rix was elevated to be the third Bishop of Caledonia, and the following year he made the church at Prince Rupert his Cathedral and appointed Rev. J. B. Gibson the first Dean.

During Bishop Rix's tenure the present Bishop's Lodge was built next to the church. In 1913 a mission had been opened at Seal Cove in the east end of the city under the charge of Rev. W. E. Collison, a son of the Archdeacon on the Naas, and, in 1928, when Mr. Rushbrook, who was now Canon, retired from the captaincy of the "Northern Cross", he took over this church. Up the Skeena the church finally penetrated the Kitwancool valley through the efforts of the Rev. Mr. Proctor, the minister at Hazelton, and a church was built there in the village of Kitwancool in 1930. Another change of note was the moving, in 1923, of the Ridley Home from Metlakatla to Prince Rupert, where it occupied three cottages still under the care of Miss West and Miss Davies. Miss West died in 1931 but Miss Davies continued in charge for many years, and, in recognition of her long years of service to the children of the area, she was awarded the O.B.E. in 1934.

Bishop Rix died in 1945 and was succeeded by Bishop Gibson who had been Dean of the Cathedral throughout the Bishop's incumbency. His term of office was short as he died in a tragic car accident in 1952, and he was followed by the present Bishop, Dr. H. G. Watts. With the elevation of Bishop Gibson, the Rev. Basil Prockter became the Dean of the Cathedral.

Before concluding the history of the work of the Anglican Church, one branch of their endeavours must be mentioned. In the latter part of the nineteenth century, the Salvation Army made its appearance in Victoria, and the Indians on their visits there were immediately attracted by the musical instruments and the uniforms of this religious organisation. They brought back their enthusiasms to their reserves and, finally, in self defence, the Anglican missionaries had to organise something of a similar nature in their missions. This resulted in the formation of the Church Army, which in many ways followed Salvation Army methods. It was an immediate success with the Indians and, over the years, proved a real value to the Church, resulting in the development of many strong Christian leaders amongst the Indian people. Nevertheless, the emotional character of this type of religion, while appealing to the primitive mind, is not always productive of stability in Christian character, and the present policy of the Church is to emphasise the desirability of membership in the established Church, with the result that Church Army activity is not nearly so prominent to-day.

METHODIST CHURCH

While the first Protestant mission began in Port Simpson, the work did not continue there. After Duncan removed to Metlakatla, the Simpson Indians were left largely to their own devices, although native workers from Metlakatla undoubtedly visited the village from time to time. Nevertheless, a change of heart did occur amongst these proud people and on their frequent visits to Victoria they came in contact with the missionary efforts of the Methodist Church in that area, and some of them were converted. Among these, but a generation apart, were two high-ranking princesses of the Tsimpsean tribe. Deax was a native princess in the very early days of Port Simpson. She belonged to the Gitandou branch of the Kispalotz tribe, one of the sub groups at Port Simpson. She had great power, but was equally bound by tribal laws; and, like the other women of her tribe, had no voice in the disposal of her hand in marriage. Thus she learned to her dismay that she was to be given to an old man; and on the eve of his arrival, she ran away from her home and sought protection in the Hudson's Bay Company fort. We do not know whether she had any right to expect a particular welcome there, but in any event, she was taken in; and there she married a young Frenchman by the name of Dudoier. He was a tailor by trade and was in charge of a group of men who looked after the clothing and equipment needs of the fort. There was only one child of this marriage, a boy, Alfred. He and his mother went to Victoria where he received some education in the schools of the day and, for the moment, there we will leave them.

Mary Holmes was born of a Tsimpsean mother, the sister of the famous Chief Shakes. She belonged to the Gitna-khan-geak tribe, another sub group at Port Simpson. Her father was a certain Captain Holmes of Victoria. Mary was educated in a convent in Victoria and later taken into the home of a naval officer in the same city. Although educated in a convent, she was confirmed in the Anglican Church. While in Victoria, she met Alfred Dudoier and eventually married him, and the young couple went back to Port Simpson, where they reverted to the heathen life of their people.

Deax remained in Victoria, where she was well known around the reservation, and one day in 1872 she wandered into a Sunday School meeting. This led to other meetings, until finally she was converted. Dr. Crosby, in his book[15], says: "She was a woman of commanding appearance and of great force of character, and exerted a powerful influence over her people. . . . She was the means of leading into the Light quite a number of her own people who were wandering in sin on the streets of Victoria."

Shortly after this, Alfred Dudoier and his wife and child, with a number of their people, visited Victoria in one of their big canoes. Deax immediately set out to tell her son the gospel story, and eventually persuaded him to attend some meetings where he was converted to Christianity. This was not the first that Alfred had heard of religious teachings, for he had been brought up a Catholic. At any rate, this was a red letter day in the history of Port Simpson, for Alfred Dudoward and his wife Kate returned to their village changed people, and became the founders of Christian civilisation in that northern town. The change in name is attributed to Mr. Crosby who was in contact with them in Victoria and later in Port Simpson. It was a common practice for a new name to be taken when the people were converted by the early missionaries.

Together they taught the day school and the Sunday School

as assistants to the various missionaries who, in turn, labored at Port Simpson. Alfred Dudoward was the official interpreter in those early years, while his wife was busy with her rapidly growing family—William, Alice, Flora, Ernest, Fred, Rufus and Charlie. Of these, more anon! In later years, Kate took on the task of interpreter, and what an interpreter she was! The writer has seen her sit on the platform, quietly listening to a full length sermon, and then, when the minister finished, get up, and without a note, repeat the sermon verbatim. That there was no improvisation has been vouched for by those who could speak both languages.

They were a striking couple as they walked about their village, attended service in their church, or entertained in their home. Alfred predeceased his wife by some years, while Kate lived on in the Eagle House, with her grown-up family around her, in quiet dignity leading her people in the Christian way of life. With the death of Alfred Dudoward, the succession of chieftainship normally would pass to a nephew. As there was no nephew, Alfred Dudoward, before he died, adopted his son Rufus into his crest, and the chieftainship passed to him. As might be expected from the union of two such remarkable families, the children kept the name of Dudoward high in the esteem of their people. They were gifted musicians. Flora, who married Captain Magar of river-boat fame, had a beautiful soprano voice and for years was the first soloist in the local choir. Alice, while not as gifted as her sister, loved music and also sang for many years in the choir. She also married a river-boat captain, Watson by name. Charlie, the youngest boy, was probably the most artistic of the family. He had a truly remarkable voice in a very low register, and in his youth did a lot of singing. Later in life he took up painting and then carving. To-day, he is the outstanding carver amongst the Simpson people. Ernest, as a boy, received lessons on the organ from the wife of one of the early missionaries and became very proficient. Throughout his life he was the leader in things musical in the village, playing the church organ, conducting the church choir and also the village concert band. He and his wife, who was also musical with a beautiful contralto voice, were an outstanding couple, staunch supporters of the local church and of high intelligence. Ernest for many years was the chief councillor of the village. Much more could be written of this remarkable family, but perhaps enough has been said to indicate the contribution made by two princesses of the Tsimpsean nation, Deax and Mary Holmes.

As the result of urging from Alfred Dudoward and his wife to the Rev. Mr. Pollard, the head of the Methodist Church in the Province, it was finally decided to enter the mission field in the north, and Mr. C. M. Tate was sent to Port Simpson to open a school and teach the people until a missionary should arrive. Mr. Tate reached Port Simpson in 1873 and was warmly welcomed by Mr. Charles Morrison, the clerk in charge of the Hudson's Bay Company fort, who took him into his home.

In a few months the Rev. Thomas Crosby and his bride arrived to take on the work and begin a mission which lasted for over twenty years. Again the missionary received every assistance from the Morrisons and in a short time a church and a mission house were erected. Mrs. Crosby taught the day school, and she was assisted by Alfred Dudoward and his wife, an old Indian house being used for the purpose. At this stage Port Simpson was still a collection of old-style Indian houses grouped around the fort, and the mission house and the church were the first modern buildings to be erected. In 1875 a sawmill was built at Georgetown, about seven miles down the coast, and the lumber cut at this point soon effected a transformation in the Indian village.

Crosby persuaded the Indians to organise themselves into a municipal council and to build new homes, lay out streets and erect bridges. This was, of course, a gradual process, and from time to time met with setbacks and difficulties. The church, which was a particularly large and imposing edifice, was designed to accommodate about one thousand people. Just after it was completed, the entire roof was blown off, in a November gale, with debris being scattered far and wide; only prompt work by the Indians with ropes and braces saved the main body of the building. The defect in the architecture of the roof was corrected and the church restored, and it stood for many years as the most prominent landmark in the village.

One of the particularly deplorable results of the impact of civilisation on the savages of the coast was the debasement of the young women. Many of them were sold into slavery and others debauched with whiskey and prostitution. First one and then another of these young girls approached Mrs. Crosby for help and she responded by taking them into her home. It was not long before their numbers increased to the point where some additional accommodation was required and an appeal was made to the Ontario Churches. As a result of funds donated a new mission house was built and the original building was devoted entirely to the care of these unfortunate girls. Thus came into being the Crosby Girls' Home.[16] In 1882 the Women's Missionary Society of the Methodist Church sent out a matron to take charge of this Home in the person of Miss Hendrie of Brantford,

Ont. She was followed by Miss Knight and then Miss Hart. During the latter teacher's incumbency the Society purchased land and erected a large school which was capable of housing over forty girls with class rooms for education. Over the years a number of the teachers staffing the institution married missionaries in the area and remained to devote their lives to the work of Christianising and educating the Indians of the north coast.

The Rev. Thomas Crosby was not content to confine his efforts to Port Simpson. He was a firm believer in the command "to preach the gospel to every creature". As soon as he had things organised at Port Simpson, he began the journeys by canoe to surrounding tribes which were to make him famous and which soon established him as a maritime missionary.

In 1878 Crosby headed for the upper Skeena, travelling up the Naas river and crossing over the "grease trail" to Kitwancool and Kitwanga. He made the trip about the end of April when the Indians were returning from the oolichan fishing on the Naas, and his description of the sights on that trail of the throngs of Indians is worth repeating:[17]

"This work (the making of oolichan grease) ended about the last of April when, with borrowed canoes, they would make their way up the Naas River to the end of the trail, which was one hundred and forty miles in length. Sometimes, when they had a big catch, it would take them weeks to 'pack' their stuff away. Some of the women were the greatest 'packers' among them and carried these great grease boxes, some of them weighing from one hundred and fifty to two hundred pounds each. They started from camp in the morning, mother and father, and even little boys and girls, each one with a pack on his back, attached by a rope to a strap around the forehead. Even the dogs, if there were any, had their packs also. They went a distance from their camp, putting down their loads where they thought they could bring up all their belongings during that day by making a sufficient number of trips over the same ground. With hundreds of people scattered for miles along this wonderful trail, there was a lively scene during the month of the exodus or that of the homeward trip."

He travelled on up to the Forks and pushed as far as Kispiox holding services at all the Indian encampments. This was not the first visit of a Methodist missionary as the Rev. A. E. Green, who was stationed on the Naas, had been over the ground the year before; but as a result of this journey the Church did send in as a teacher a Mr. Mathiesen, who opened a school at Hazelton. Unfortunately his stay was short, and, as we have seen, the

Church Missionary Society sent a missionary to open the Anglican work at Hazelton about this time.

For several years the only Methodist work on the upper Skeena was carried on by occasional visits from the Rev. Mr. Green from the Naas and the Rev. Mr. Jennings who had opened a mission under Crosby at Port Essington. However, in 1885 a native preacher, W. H. Pierce, was sent to Kitseguecla.

William Henry Pierce [18], one of the most colorful personalities in the history of the Methodist Church on the north coast, deserves special mention. He was the son of a Scotsman, an employee of the Hudson's Bay Company, and a Tsimpscan woman who died three weeks after his birth at Fort Rupert in 1856. His Indian grandfather claimed the child and William was raised at Port Simpson in a heathen home and schooled in all the heathen practices of that day. However, he did attend Mr. Duncan's school when it was established in Port Simpson, and as a youth of twelve obtained employment as a cabin boy on the Hudson's Bay Company steamer "Otter". This took him to Victoria, where a few years later he came under the influence of Crosby and was converted. He was taken in hand by the missionaries in Victoria and given some rudimentary education; and when Thomas Crosby went to Port Simpson, William Pierce joined him and began his life of Christian ministry. He saw service with the Church on the Naas, in Alaska and at Bella Bella and then was entrusted with opening the mission at Kitseguecla. This mission was intimately associated with the famous "Skeena River Affair", which is graphically recounted by Pierce in his book "From Potlatch to Pulpit". As it resulted in a military expedition to the Skeena it is worthy of detailed recording.

A young chief of the Kitwancools who, in all the accounts, is only referred to as Jim, was married to a Kitseguecla woman. During a measles epidemic, two of their children died and the mother, who was heathen, claimed they had been killed by the machinations of a witch doctor of her village, Kitseguecla. She taunted her husband with his indifference and finally Kitwancool Jim went out, met the witch doctor on the trail and shot him dead. The Kitsegueclas, who were visiting in Kitwancool at the time, immediately returned home and prepared for war. Pierce remonstrated with them and better judgment finally prevailed, and the Christian Indians contented themselves with protesting to the Government.

Pierce left for Port Simpson shortly after and travelled by way of the Kitwancool grease trail to the Naas. On the way he met and talked with Jim, who defiantly sent a message by

Pierce to the Government Agent at Port Simpson, that he would kill anyone sent to apprehend him, and no doubt in this he would be supported by the members of his tribe.

A warrant was sworn out for Jim's arrest and in the execution of it, one of the special constables, a white man by the name of Green, shot and killed the murderer. There is considerable confusion regarding the true state of affairs, some claiming Jim was resisting arrest, and others that he was shot in the back. In any event there was great excitement amongst the Indians who apparently threatened the white people, and it was deemed necessary by the authorities at Victoria to make a show of force.

Accordingly, "C" Battery, consisting of eighty-five men, was despatched on the H.M.S. "Caroline" to the mouth of the Skeena, where they disembarked and camped just above Port Essington at the mouth of the Ecstall River—since known as Soldier's Point. Superintendent Roycroft and a detachment of police went up the river and were successful in quelling the natives, but not without leaving a feeling of deep resentment which persisted in the Kitwancool valley for another generation. In fact, as late as the 1920s it was still difficult for a white man to pass through that area. Amongst the Indians themselves the trouble was not settled until two more violent deaths occurred.

In 1887 W. H. Pierce was ordained at the first Methodist Conference to be held in British Columbia, and three years later he was married to a teacher of the mission school at Port Essington, Miss Hargreaves. The Methodist Church had opened up a mission at Kispiox and in 1895 Mr. Pierce was transferred to that point. Here he labored for fifteen years and saw the village pass from heathenism to Christianity; and assisted in organising the Indians into a model village with elected Council and modern homes, in the construction of which their own sawmill played no small part.

In 1910 he was transferred to Port Essington to succeed the Rev. B. C. Freeman who had followed the Rev. D. Jennings, the original minister at that point. This was his last appointment and he held it for twenty-two years, finally retiring in 1933, to spend the closing years of his life in Prince Rupert. Even then he remained active in the work of his beloved Church, befriending the members of his race who were experiencing all the degrading influences of a sea-port city. His knowledge of the Indian people and their Art made him a person much in demand as a speaker on native lore, and he was a familiar figure for years in the Museum at Prince Rupert, lecturing to the tourists until his death in 1948.

W. H. Pierce was an outstanding example of what can be

accomplished amongst these native people with Christian teaching and direction. His education was limited but his devotion to his early training was complete. He had all of the native gift for apt expression, and to hear him preach was an experience never to be forgotten. On several occasions he visited eastern Canada to rouse interest in Home Missions and his journey through the Ontario Churches was in the nature of a triumphal procession. Amongst his own people, he was a powerful influence, counselling and directing them in the many problems of advancing civilisation.

The development of the early missions on the Skeena, as elsewhere, is in reality the biography of individuals. At Kispiox we meet another of these devoted men whose names are still held in respect on the north coast, the Rev. J. C. Spencer.

John Clark Spencer [19] was born in Ontario in 1859, the son of a farmer and shoemaker, John Spencer. At twenty years of age he began to teach school and two years later volunteered to the Methodist Church for Home Missions. There were no openings, or more correctly, perhaps, there was no money. However, J. C. Spencer had his face turned westward and he took employment with the Canadian Pacific Railway, then under construction, and arrived in British Columbia. Eventually he reached the coast and in 1888 was sent by the Methodist Conference to assist Thomas Crosby at Port Simpson.

Mr. Crosby was anxious to get work started on the upper Skeena and W. H. Pierce had been sent to Kitseguecla. Another native worker, George Edgar, had been stationed in Hagwilget to open a school, and now Mr. Spencer was despatched to Kispiox, where he arrived in late November. There were about four hundred Indians living in the village, and one of them, Edward Sexsmith, had gained some education on the Naas— sufficient for him to act as Spencer's interpreter.

The following year, Mr. Spencer was accepted for the ministry and he was ordained in 1893, the intervening years being spent at Kispiox in the winter and with his people during the summer months on their travels to the Naas for oolichan, and to the mouth of the Skeena for fishing.

The early missionaries had little or no medical training and the prevalence of serious disease amongst the natives, due to their debauchery and unhygienic living conditions, was a depressing factor with which they had to contend. Convinced of the need for physical as well as spiritual help, Rev. J. C. Spencer obtained leave of absence following his ordination and entered medical school in California, where he completed his first year, the limit to which his financial resources extended at that time.

He then returned north and, marrying Miss Hart, the matron of the Crosby Girls' Home, resumed his charge at Kispiox. This time he went directly up the Skeena and Mrs. Spencer describes her sensations on her first journey on the Skeena River:[20]

"We left Port Simpson on August 26th and came to Essington on the Skeena River, hoping to get up to our own mission without delay; but travelling on the river was impossible, as the water was running so high that it was not until after three weeks that we commenced our river trip. Even then the water was very high; but we had a good strong canoe and a reliable crew of Indians, five in all. I had rather dreaded this part of the journey, having heard so much about the Skeena River. It has a fall of eight hundred and sixty-five feet in the two hundred miles; from that you may judge it does not flow very quietly or slowly.

"We made our start at two o'clock one morning, having got everything ready the evening before, but too late to leave on that tide, and waiting until daylight meant losing the most of another day. The night was cloudy and showery. I hoped to be able to sleep; but, though I had the best place in the canoe, I found it very uncomfortable and sleep out of the question. Daylight found us at the head of tide water. At seven, we stopped for breakfast. A heavy shower of rain did not add to the comfort of that meal and my sympathy for missionaries who have to do much travelling on the river began greatly to enlarge. I thought I was realising what some of their discomforts were, but the rest of the party did not seem in the least affected by the rain.

"Breakfast and prayers over, a little warmed by the camp fire, but not drier, we embarked again on our way. But travelling was slow. The canoes have to keep near the shore to avoid the strong current. It is not often deep enough for paddles, so long poles are used; thus our canoe is pushed along. When the water is deeper, paddles are used. More force can be applied with the poles, but poles and paddles are put down whenever there is a beach or even a foothold along the water's edge. Then three of our crew would take a towline and pull the canoe, the other two remaining in to keep the canoe off the rocks; this was the fastest mode of travelling. If we let our eyes rest on the water we would imagine that we were speeding along at a most rapid rate, but one look at the shore told us we were travelling at a snail's pace. I soon learned to be thankful when we got along even at that rate, for so often there would be places to mount where we could scarcely hold our own for moments at a time although every nerve was strained to the utmost to force our way up against the water, which would almost seem to be pouring down on us and often would come into the canoe. Then again we turned rocky points that jutted out into the rapid current. Those were exciting times indeed; paddles and poles were kept in readiness. It astonished me to see the intense alertness of our men, one second pushing with all their force against the rock with a pole, the next paddling with every power till the next point was reached; then down went the paddle, and the pole was put into use again.

"But what I dreaded the most was crossing the river. Sometimes they would cross in a comparatively quiet place, but usually the water rushed with all its force. In the power of those waters it seemed to me as if we must be swept away with some of the swirling eddies long before we reached the opposite shore, or crash with such force on the shore that nothing would be left to pick up. However, neither of these things happened. On the whole, we made a good trip for the time of year; and I realised what made it so expensive travelling on the river or getting goods up. It cost us almost the price of our supplies to get them up the river; indeed, some things cost more than their price, so that nothing that can be done without is brought up.

"Our crew was very kind in pointing out all the interesting things along the river. One place they indicated was a bold, rugged rock, rising perpendicularly from the water. Here the people in olden times believed the river god resided, and in their coming and going offered sacrifice that they might have his protection. But what impressed me most on the river was the great amount of driftwood, heaps upon heaps. It seemed as if forest after forest must have washed down to supply such islands of debris. I learned that every year the water changes more or less. Often whole islands are swept away and in other places new islands formed. Sand bars are carried away and deposited in other places so that the course of the river is ever changing."

After a further year at Kispiox this pioneer missionary was transferred to other fields and did not again return to the Skeena. He completed his medical course and after years of service at Bella Coola and on the Queen Charlotte Islands was posted to Port Simpson where he had charge of the field for the ten years from 1914 to 1924. He was then moved to Bella Bella where he served until his death. He will long be remembered by natives and whites alike, for his saintly character, his great kindness and happy disposition, and his quiet humor.

It has been intimated repeatedly that disease was rampant amongst the Indians. While the white population was mostly composed of young and sturdy adults, there was frequently serious illness amongst the children, in many cases contracted from the natives with whom they were in close contact. Epidemic diseases swept through the native populations with ease, as a knowledge of the laws of hygiene was completely lacking, and the death rate in these epidemics was abnormally heavy. For example, W. H. Pierce, coming out of Kitseguecla one spring, reports two hundred deaths from fever during the winter.[21] The missionaries' families were not immune and Rev. Mr. Crosby lost four of his children during the early years of his stay in Port Simpson.

Dr. Ardagh had started practice in Metlakatla, but he was the only doctor in the whole of the north country. Mr. Crosby, on one of his trips to Ontario, spoke frequently of the need for medical men and his words fell on sympathetic ears. Dr. A. E. Bolton completed his medical training at Queen's University in 1888 and took post-graduate training in New York. He was deeply interested in Church work and wrote the General Secretary of the Missionary Society of the Methodist Church, offering his services for medical missionary work in Canada. His offer was rejected with the excuse of lack of funds. He then returned to Canada and began practice in Portland, Ontario. Here he heard the appeal of the Rev. Mr. Crosby for a medical missionary and again offered his services to the Church. Again he was refused as the Church had never undertaken medical work and appeared reluctant to make the move.

Dr. Bolton was not to be deterred. Some of the missionaries in the field offered financial assistance and the Indians also pledged support, so the good doctor and his wife set out for British Columbia at their own expense. They arrived in Port Simpson on November 17th, 1889, and went to work. There was no lack of patients for the Indians soon heard of his coming and journeyed to Port Simpson from far and near. It rapidly became obvious to the doctor that he must have a hospital in which to care for his patients. Conditions in Indian homes were impossible when it came to surgery. At first he and his wife lived in the mission house and then in the Boys' Home—a residence for native boys which had been built by Mr. Crosby—and some of his patients from outside points were cared for in tents on the beach or in the guest house of the Hudson's Bay Company.

Still the Church had no funds to promote the medical work and Dr. Bolton turned to industry and Government for assistance. With donations from Indians and white residents he succeeded in raising sufficient funds to build the Port Simpson General Hospital, and a house close by for himself and family. It was completed in 1891 and was operated as a general public hospital, owned and directed by a Hospital Association made up of the white residents of the district, and incorporated under a special Act of the Legislature.

An excerpt from a letter written by Dr. Bolton in 1890 gives some idea of the extent of his labors.[22] This was written at the end of his first year's work:

"To instruct in hygiene, to check the progress and alleviate the suffering of seated disease, to soothe the dying agonies, and at the same time to point to Jesus, the Saviour, as the healer of the soul, have been my work, together with preaching occasionally and helping with class-meetings, Sabbath School, Day School and Boys' Home. Under Providence I hope I have done some good. I have treated over fifty-four hundred patients."

During the summer the Indians journeyed to the Skeena River for the fishing season, and the medical needs of the thousands of people employed in the canneries inspired the opening of a branch hospital at Port Essington in 1895. A similar situation prevailed at Rivers Inlet during the summer months and Dr. Bolton opened a second branch hospital there in 1897, and attempted to operate all three hospitals—an impossible task. The Rivers Inlet hospital was turned over to other hands and forms no part of our story, but the hospitals at Port Essington and Port Simpson were operated continuously, the former during the summer months and the latter the year round. The Women's Missionary Society sent out a nurse for the new hospital and Miss Spence was the first matron, remaining for thirteen years.

In 1901, Dr. Bolton left the mission field and retired to practice in Victoria and later Vancouver. Undoubtedly the hardships he experienced and the unremitting labor he expended in the care of the sick over the whole north coast contributed in no small degree to his early death. His name must ever stand high in the annals of his Church as the man who pioneered the establishment of medical Home Missions, a branch of Christian service which later blossomed out into one of the principal efforts of the Methodist Church.

He was succeeded by Dr. W. T. Kergin, a young man recently graduated from University of Toronto Medical School. Shortly after his arrival at Port Simpson he married Miss Fanny Stevenson, a teacher at the Crosby Girls' Home. Dr. Kergin operated the two hospitals at Port Simpson and Port Essington until the end of 1910. A man of outstanding ability in his chosen profession, he also was an active member of the community. During this period at Port Simpson he served one term as Liberal member in the Provincial Legislature, and at various times he was associated with the development of the natural resources of the country in mining, lumbering and fishing. Upon his departure from Port Simpson in 1910, he settled with his family in Prince Rupert where he became the leading surgeon until his retirement in 1940.

For the next ten years the medical work at Port Simpson was under the care of the Rev. R. W. Large, M.D. Dr. Large came out to British Columbia under the Methodist Church in 1898 and had been in charge of the Hospital and Mission at Bella Bella for ten years. His appointment to Port Simpson was under the Provincial and Dominion Governments but he kept his connection with the Church and took an active part, as his predecessors had done, in the Mission work. He also was a victim of the hardships and overwork of pioneer days and passed away in 1920, at the comparatively early age of forty-seven. His exceedingly good baritone voice, his engaging personality and his dedicated life served to make his another of the honored names in the history of the Church on the north coast.

With the growth of Prince Rupert, the town of Port Simpson steadily diminished in importance, and the church work there gradually moved to other points. The two boarding schools eventually closed and the hospital, after being taken over and operated by the United Church of Canada in 1932, was finally closed and dismantled completely in 1947. The church built by Dr. Crosby was destroyed by fire in 1931 and a new and smaller building was erected to replace it. To-day a resident minister is all that remains of what was once the largest mission on the coast.

One other village in the Skeena District should be mentioned, namely Kitamat. While the village was visited by two Roman Catholic priests in 1864, the work thus begun was not followed up. As happened so often among the natives, the first contact with the Protestant Church came through visits to Victoria to procure whiskey. They wandered into prayer meetings and thus heard the Bible story. In some cases conversion took place and the convert returned to his home to spread the glad tidings. Such a man was Charlie Amos of Kitamat who was converted in 1867 by the Rev. Mr. Pollard in Victoria, and returned to his village to preach the new gospel. He and a few others with him built a small log church early in the following year, and then went to Port Simpson to ask Mr. Crosby for a teacher. They stayed in Port Simpson until the next spring attending school; and on their return were accompanied by George Edgar, the native teacher who was at one time stationed at Hagwilget. Opposition from the heathen element was strong and some of

Totem Poles at Kitwanga

"Seven Sisters" Mountain at Cedarvale

Main Street in New Hazelton

New Hazelton Bank Robbery

the early Christians were undoubtedly murdered under the guise of witchcraft.

In 1883 the first white teacher was sent to Kitamat, Miss Susan Lawrence, and with her coming there was a religious revival. Led by Charlie Amos the natives built a combined school and church. This devoted woman spent a number of years laboring among the Kitamats before her health broke down.

In 1893 the first ordained minister came to Kitamat in the person of the Rev. G. H. Raley. With his arrival the work was greatly expanded. A residential school was built, similar to the Crosby Girls' Home at Port Simpson and a Mr. and Mrs. Anderson were sent in to take charge. A new church was erected, as well as a new mission house and, with the strengthening of the mission, the forces of heathenism were quickly routed. Mr. Raley spent thirteen years in Kitamat and was then transferred to Port Simpson where he had charge of the mission and the Boys' School for a further eight years, during which time he was also Chairman of the District. While in Kitamat, Mr. Raley edited and printed a small magazine called "Nanakwa", in the pages of which are recorded much interesting information of the early days on the coast.

In 1914 Mr. Raley left the north to take charge of the Coqualeetza Institute at Sardis, B.C.—a residential school for native children, both boys and girls—where he remained for twenty years. Although now retired and in the tenth decade of life, Dr. Raley is still pursuing an active existence in Vancouver, a recognised authority on native lore and social customs, and taking a constant personal interest in native organisations, as well as in the private lives of the Indians living in and around Vancouver.

SALVATION ARMY

Owing to the unfortunate loss of all written records of the Salvation Army in Northern British Columbia during the Second World War, it is a difficult matter to record the history of this organisation's activities. The advent of the Army in Victoria aroused an enthusiastic interest amongst the natives visiting there from the northern villages. They wanted drums, flags and uniforms too! The two Protestant Churches responded with the formation of the Church Army and the Epworth League, respectively, both of which organisations operated on much the same basis as the Army, but under the direct supervision of their respective Churches.

In 1896 Ensign Edgecombe surveyed the Coast with a view

to establishing detachments of the Salvation Army in strategic villages. He had settled tentatively on Port Simpson and Port Essington, two villages which were already served by the Methodist Church. In an attempt to persuade him to choose villages which were still without missionaries, Rev. Thomas Crosby took the Ensign on the mission boat "Glad Tidings" for a tour of the coast.[23] All went well until they reached Queen Charlotte Sound, when the boat grounded on a rock and was holed, necessitating several days' delay while they beached her and made repairs. Apparently the rigours of this trip did not impress Ensign Edgecombe favorably, for he shied away from the heathen villages and started work in the two Christian villages already mentioned. There was, of course, a reason for this, as the Army did not have the personnel to carry out missionary work on a large scale, and relied in most cases on dissenting native leaders of the established Churches and their disgruntled followers.

The situation which developed at Kispiox is an example of how such a fission can result from a relatively insignificant incident. A young Indian had tried to rape one of the girls in his village and, contrary to usual custom, the matter was brought before the Indian Agent, Mr. Loring, for settlement. The young Indian was found guilty and sentenced. On his return to the village, he and his friends, who resented his disgrace, broke away from the rest of the tribe, and since there was only one church, they set up their own organisation. Feeling ran very high and eventually it came to blows between the Epworth League and the new group who called themselves Salvationists. Finally the head chief of the village ruled that there could be only one church in Kispiox and the dissidents appealed to Mr. Loring. At that time there was a second reserve belonging to the tribe a few miles down the river from Kispiox, where the village sawmill was located. Mr. Loring divided this area in two, giving half to the Salvationist group, and he sent up a Mr. Vowell to survey the ground and lay out the lots. The resulting village was called Glen Vowell after the surveyor.

The new village of Glen Vowell came into existence in 1898, and when the Salvation Army headquarters heard about it, they sent up as a missionary Ensign Thorkalson. The village prospered and has been the principal stronghold of the Army on the Skeena. A white worker has been kept there continuously and we note such names as Sharp, Hanna, Parkinson, Watson, Brierly and Cooper. They built a school and staffed it, and one of the teachers, Captain Drysdale, married Mr. Robert Tomlinson when he moved from Kispiox to the Hazelton Hospital. She was a graduate nurse and is still active in her profession in the City of Ketchikan.

A similar situation developed in the village of Kitseguecla and Mr. Loring followed the same procedure to establish the village of Andemaul on the opposite side and a short distance down the river from Kitseguecla. This too remained a Salvation Army post, although it is now deserted.

The first detachments of the Army established at Port Simpson and Port Essington were under native leaders. They were followed by a mission at Metlakatla also native-led. The supervision of the work was in the hands of the Salvation Army in Alaska, and each year a Congress was held at Port Essington at the end of the fishing season, before the Indians dispersed to their villages. It lasted for several days and engendered great enthusiasm, but did little towards the guidance of the people throughout the rest of the year.

With the completion of the railroad and the incorporation of the City of Prince Rupert, the Army entered the form of work for which it had been originally intended. They purchased property in the City and erected a residence and a Barracks in 1910, the buildings being officially opened just before Christmas.[24] Ensign Johnson was in charge and was succeeded by Captain Kerr. Over the years the Salvation Army has filled an important place in the religious life of the community, and during the days of the depression their organisation handled a lot of the relief work, and did a great deal to alleviate the hardships and sufferings of those difficult times.

In 1946 the Salvation Army opened a hostel in Prince Rupert for native girls who were attending High School in the City. This has been a real success in giving the girls from the reservations round about an opportunity to further their education in the City High School, meanwhile protecting them from the moral pitfalls of that portion of the City which is normally frequented by visiting Indians.

CHAPTER TWELVE

Transportation

The development of a country is vitally dependent on its transportation; and other things being equal, it will keep pace with the improvement of its transportation facilities.

In the earliest days of the Skeena and the north coast, the sailing ship and canoe provided these facilities, and we noted the change in the site of Fort Naas to Port Simpson because of its inaccessibility to sailing ships. A few years after the founding of that Fort the Hudson's Bay Company introduced the first steam ship to the coast, the "Beaver", although this ship still carried sails. This heralded a new era of coastal trade, but it was a long time before the sails were completely superseded by mechanical power. On the Skeena, and in the adjacent waters, the canoe was the only method of transport.

The ocean-going canoe was made of cedar, hollowed out from one large tree trunk. Until the coming of the white man the only attempt to strengthen the hollow trunk was made by steaming the shell and inserting spreaders, and these were designed to improve the riding qualities of the hull rather than to make the structure any stronger. Under the stresses of heavy seas, the use of sail, or the pounding of fast running water, it was not uncommon for the cedar canoe to split, with disastrous results for the passengers. Possibly for this reason and because cedar was not as prevalent up the river, the river canoes were generally made of cottonwood. The trees being smaller, the resultant canoes were narrower, with less freeboard.

In spite of these limitations, the ocean-going canoes of the Haidas reached a high level of perfection. The cedars on the Queen Charlotte Islands attained an immense size and allowed for the construction of canoes up to seventy feet in length with the rest of the canoe in proportion. The style varied with different tribes, but generally the bow and stern were built up to avoid broaching seas. As with the early sailing ships, native artists oftentimes decorated these raised bows and sterns with weird figure-heads.

When the missionaries started using canoes for their trips

around the coast, they taught the Indians to bend ribs and strakes into the canoes, thus strengthening them and making them far safer for ocean travel.

In travelling the Skeena, the coast Indians used their cedar canoes of smaller size for the river navigation, while the cottonwood canoes were employed by the upriver Indians. An average canoe would carry a crew of five, a helmsman in the stern and four paddlers, and would be capable of transporting several tons of freight as well as passengers. In negotiating the faster stretches sometimes it was necessary to "line" the canoe along the shore.

This form of travel was far from being comfortable. The trip was slow and often hazardous, and for long stretches of the river the banks did not lend themselves to suitable camp sites. Lying exposed throughout a wet night on the bare rocks was poor preparation for the rigours of another day of struggle against the current. The experiences of such a trip have already been well described in a letter by Mrs. Spencer.*

With the establishment of Hazelton and the opening up of the mines to the east, freight traffic up the Skeena developed rapidly and the Hudson's Bay Company used this route to supply their inland forts from Port Simpson. The same traffic accounted in large part for the development of Port Essington which became the main point for up-river trade, and for the transfer from steamboat to canoe. It is rather remarkable that the Hudson's Bay Company were content to use this expensive method of transportation for so long when steamboat traffic had been in use on the Fraser for years; and in 1866 the Skeena had been shown to be navigable for river boats at least as far as the canyon. As a matter of fact, their clerk at Port Simpson, Mr. C. F. Morrison, recommended the building of a river steamer in the 1860s, but nothing came of it, and it was not until 1888 that Mr. John Flewin, the Government Agent at Port Simpson, is credited with persuading Mr. R. H. Hall, the factor at that point, that the idea had merit.

From the time of the establishment of the Company's post at Hazelton in 1880 the goods for Babine had been regularly forwarded by the Skeena River route.[1] Some goods for the other New Caledonia posts were also usually forwarded by this route, but an attempt in the summer of 1882 to bring in the greater portion of the New Caledonia outfit by way of Hazelton was not very successful, owing to the breakdown of arrangements which had been made for a pack-train to transport goods across the Babine portage. During the summers of 1883, 1884 and 1885,

* See Methodist Missions

therefore, the Babine goods only were forwarded by way of Skeena River. Although the New Caledonia goods were brought in by this route in the summers of 1886, 1887 and 1888, the lack of satisfactory transport up the river made the task a difficult one and on October 17, 1888, Junior Chief Trader R. H. Hall, who was then in charge of the Port Simpson district, wrote to Assistant Commissioner Thomas R. Smith as follows:

". . . For the current year's work a pack-train was engaged to operate on the Skeena portage, but the attempt to bring horses 400 miles to do our packing and then take them back the same distance has proved to be a mistake, and I think we should have foreseen that it would be . . . Had the trail and bridges been put in order prior to the arrival of the pack-train at Hazelton, considerably more work might have been done, but the animals should be on hand to commence work early in the season; and to have freight at Hazelton in May we must have a Steamer.

"It seems therefore obvious that the pack-animals should be the property of this District and wintered at Hazelton; and that without a Steamer the Skeena Route cannot be largely utilized for New Caledonia . . . I very much regret the necessity of again reverting largely to the Fraser River route for the work of New Caledonia Outfit 1889, but without proper equipment we cannot undertake it by way of Skeena . . ."

Captain George Oden of New Westminster was commissioned by the Hudson's Bay Company to survey the Skeena, and in particular the Kitselas Canyon; and as a result of his recommendations a stern-wheel river steamer was built in 1890. It was called the "Caledonia", and under Captain Oden's command made the first successful trip to Hazelton in 1891. She was one hundred feet long, but proved difficult to handle, and the following year was cut in two and lengthened by thirty feet. This improved her handling qualities, and under her new skipper, Captain Bonser, she travelled successfully up and down the Skeena each summer for the next five years. In the spring of 1898 she was towed back to Victoria and her engines were transferred to a new "Caledonia", a larger ship.

Robert Cunningham was the other heavy shipper of freight on the river, and he was content to use canoes for many years. However, in 1900 he put the "Monte Cristo" in commission, and the same year the Hudson's Bay Company added the "Strathcona". With two firms operating great rivalry developed over the river trade, and more commodious and faster ships were the order of the day. The following year, Cunningham replaced the "Monte Cristo" with a new ship, the "Hazelton", which eventually turned out to be the fastest on the river. The Hudson's Bay Company replied with the "Mount Royal", a much larger vessel which supplanted the "Caledonia" and "Strathcona", and the race was on.

Captain Bonser was in charge of the "Hazelton" and Captain Johnson of the "Mount Royal". In July 1902, the river water was at a particularly favorable level and the "Hazelton" made the round trip from Port Essington to Hazelton in 2 days, 7 hours, and 55 minutes. Two days later the "Mount Royal" completed the same trip in 2 days, 6 hours, and 15 minutes, and four days later the "Hazelton" chalked up the record of 47 hours. These times included all the regular stops and the lay-over at Hazelton while unloading freight.

Competition between the two Captains was intense and all sorts of tricks were used to get the advantage over the rival ship. Cordwood was loaded for fuel at regular stops and sometimes extra wood would be taken by one or the other to deprive the ship following of an adequate supply. The climax was reached one day when the two ships were racing neck and neck up the river. Captain Johnson endeavoured to crowd the "Hazelton" into shallow water, so Bonser turned his ship, and striking the "Mount Royal" amidships pushed her right up on the beach. The story goes that Captain Johnson was so infuriated that he grabbed a rifle and started to shoot at Bonser. This disgraceful exhibition put an end to the racing.

The fast times we have reported were not the usual story in river traffic. With the rapid rise and fall of water, conditions often prevented the ships from completing their runs, and freight would have to be unloaded part way up and held for the next trip. Seven to ten days for the trip was a much more common length of time and passage at certain points was a difficult and tedious procedure. Kitselas Canyon was the principal obstruction, and here the ships were aided by the crews' hauling with their capstan on a cable fastened to the shore. Captain Bonser devised an ingenious method of slipping this cable at the upper end of the canyon so that the ship could proceed without delaying to put a man ashore. A looped cable was fastened to the deadhead on shore. The looped end of the ship's cable was passed through this first loop and a block of wood inserted to keep it in place. When the ship had reached the upper end of the canyon, the block of wood was retrieved by a line attached to it, thus releasing the cable.

With the coming of these commodious river steamers, the trip up the Skeena became, for the passenger, a pleasant and rewarding experience. From the recorded accounts of some of these early travellers it is easy to visualize the delights and interests of such a trip.[2]

"Our steamer, the Hazelton, is moored to Frizzell's wharf at Port Essington, loading the last of her freight; and with her passengers already aboard. These are mostly on the upper deck, but there is a group of Indians with their bundles camped on the forward deck, quick to learn the advantages of the white man's mode of travel. A blast on the whistle, the lines are cast off and we nose out into the current of a favorable rising tide.

"We quickly cross the mouth of the Ecstall River and Port Essington fades in the distance. About six miles up on the right bank we notice a cluster of small buildings, from one of which steam is rising. This is the famous Hot Springs frequented by fishermen and others to cure almost every ailment. The volume of water is small but it is very hot as it issues from two or three separate clefts in the rock.

"On the other bank, we are soon abreast of the Kyex river and the site picked by certain optimistic gentlemen as the terminus for the proposed railway. Kyex City has been staked by McIntosh, Lorenz and partners, but so far it is nothing but bush and doesn't hold our interest long. Rounding Telegraph Point, the location of one of the cabins on the Dominion Government Telegraph line to Port Simpson, we are soon at the limit of tide-water and the river narrows down. Numerous islands covered with cotton-wood, and bars piled high with old snags choke the river and Captain Bonser has to know what he's doing to find his way along the tortuous channel.

"Snow-clad mountains tower above us on either side, broken occasionally by the entrance of mountain tributaries—the Kasiks and Exchamsiks on the left and then the Gitnadoix on the right. Gitnadoix valley, with its lofty snow-capped mountains on both sides, spreads itself out to the south of the Skeena towards the head of Kitamat Arm and the headwaters of the Big Falls on the Ecstall River. Although a very swift stream for a distance of five miles up from its mouth, the Gitnadoix River runs comparatively sluggishly from there on for a distance of eight miles to a lake some three miles long. A large stream joins it a few miles below the lake where many years ago an Indian village used to be, but a spot now ornamented only by the picturesque hunting lodge of Charlie Jones. This stream runs east to the divide between it and the Wedeene River, which empties a broad body of water into the Kitamat River. Several quartz claims have been recorded on the Wedeene, and considerable work has been done upon them, showing excellent prospects in copper-gold ore.

"Gitnadoix Lake is hemmed in on the north and west by high and steep mountains. There must be extensive deposits of iron in the mountains at the foot of the lake, as all the streams are stained red with iron oxide. At one place there are barrels of pure oxide which has been deposited by a little rivulet oozing out from a crevice in the rock, and the Indians in years gone by used to get their supplies of red paint from that particular spot. The area is a hunter's paradise with bear and mountain goat plentiful and good fishing in the lake and streams.

"Speaking of mountain goat, as we pace the deck of our steamer we can see them from time to time, high up on the rocky cliffs, standing still in remote isolation or picking their way along the precipitous mountainside. As the evening approaches we arrive at Graveyard Point[3] and there tie up for the night, having travelled fifty miles from Port Essington. This is the site of another Telegraph station and we find it under the care of Slim Dobbie and J. D. Wells. We are called to a satisfying dinner in the dining saloon, and after watching the crew for a time as they take on a fresh supply of cord-wood, we retire to our cabin and a comfortable night's sleep on a spring bed. What a far cry from the canoe and the rocky shore!

"Captain Bonser has us under way again early the next morning and as we come abreast of the Lakelse River, regales us with stories of his fishing experiences on that wonderful trout stream. Indeed it was often called Trout River and the Captain claims to have caught twenty-five to fifty trout there on many an occasion in an hour's fishing. The remains of an old Indian village can be seen near the mouth, and the land is still an Indian reservation. It was used originally by some of the Port Simpson Indians. The Captain also tells us of the wonderful Hot Springs close to the lake at the head of the river. Steam can be seen rising for a hundred feet into the air, and the spring forms a pool of unknown depth with water close to the boiling point. It has a very considerable flow and some day will undoubtedly be of commercial value.

"Just above the Lakelse River we pass another river on the opposite bank, flowing in from the north, and this is the Kitsumgalum. At its mouth is another Indian village, still occupied, but by only a few Indians. Most of the tribe have moved down to Port Essington to live on the special reserve given them by Robert Cunningham. This river too drains a lake, and there are reports of gold up the valley. Two prospectors, Harvey Snow[4] and Captain Madden, have been working some claims up there on a creek near the headwaters of Lorne Creek. Our interest in the Kitsumgalum is speedily diverted, however, by the ugly-looking riffles our boat is now navigating; but the Captain knows what he is doing and we pass over them successfully and approach the Little Canyon, where we tie up at Thornhill's Landing.

"Thomas Thornhill is one of the early pioneers and he has a patch of one hundred and sixty acres, with about four acres already in cultivation. He is proud of his flower garden, and when we go in for lunch some of his flowers bedeck the dining table.

"The Skeena at the Little Canyon is only about one hundred yards wide, with mountains on the north side and a low point of rock on the south shore. During the freshets it is a nasty piece of water, but navigation has improved since the Dominion Government blasted out a large rock in the center of the channel. About a mile further on, we pass Bill Bostet's ranch, only recently pre-empted, and then on the north bank we see Dave Stuart's place, where we tie up to his landing. Dave is another old-timer and his ground is producing wonderfully with cherry, apple and plum trees and a good assortment of vegetables. A look over this small farm, and an inspection of its products, convinces us that great agricultural possibilities lie dormant in the valley of the Skeena, awaiting only the advent of the railroad to render them available.

"Right across the river from us we can see the outlet of the Zymoetz, or Copper River. It is one of the Skeena's largest tributaries, a wild mountain stream that is impossible of navigation. It takes its rise far in the interior to the south, and at times of freshet its muddy waters can be traced right to the mouth of the Skeena. It is called Copper River because of the large amount of copper-stained float that has been found in its channel. M. C. Kendall was the first quartz prospector on this stream and in 1896, in company with Henry Frank, he located a promising quartz lead. It did not pan out and he extended his prospecting a little further up the Skeena where he located the I.X.L. and Emma groups of claims near the Kitselas Canyon. As we approach the Canyon, we are right in the heart of the most promising mineral area so far discovered on the Skeena. There are numerous other prospects besides those mentioned and the coming of the railroad and cheap transportation is all that holds up their development.

"Just before we reach the Canyon we pass the Kitselas Indian village, where there is a Methodist Mission, and at the foot of the canyon we tie up at the Telegraph Station where Mr. Daoust is in charge. There is also a Hudson's Bay Company warehouse here and a road has been built to the upper end of the canyon. The Canyon, eighty miles from the coast, is about half a mile long and one hundred and fifty feet wide, with high cliffs on both sides, between which the Skeena, at high water, forces itself with a roaring noise and great velocity. Today it is comparatively peaceful and we pass through with little trouble, though to the novice it appears awe-inspiring and a little frightening.

"We are now encountering some very sharp riffles, but the river seems to be remarkably clear of rocks. The mountains on both sides gradually draw away from the river, and one begins to feel that he is getting away from the coast and the coast climate. We have passed the divide of the Cascades and are getting into the Interior country. High benches take the place of low land. Some, but by no means all, of this is agricultural land. Birch, maple, pine and aspen groves are now becoming common, and as we approach Lorne Creek, thirty-five miles above the Canyon, we know that we are beyond the moist atmosphere of the other side of the mountain range behind us.

"Lorne Creek empties into the Skeena on the north side and is not a large stream. It is the only creek flowing into the Skeena on which very rich placer claims have been located. During the later 80's, about two million dollars in gold was taken from about a mile of ground on the creek by hundreds of men who flocked in after the first discovery was reported.[5] The Creek is now considered worked out, but several hydraulic properties are being got into shape to be worked on a large scale. The Dryhill property is attracting the chief attention at present. The Dryhill is a very large deposit of auriferous gravel about a mile long and hundreds of feet high, situated about a mile from the mouth of the creek. It has been worked on a small scale for many years by Messrs. Raynard, McArthur and others, and with good success. It is now proposed to construct a flume from higher up on Lorne Creek and run the water over the Dryhill. Twenty men are presently at work there and an up-to-date dredging plant is also to be installed on Lorne Creek this summer.

"For the next twenty-five miles the scenery continues unchanged and we finally come up to the Indian village of Minskinish, a mission established by the Rev. Robert Tomlinson. Across the river is a sawmill and telegraph station. This is a clean-looking, up-to-date Indian village, with about two hundred people. After dropping the mail and a little freight, we push on to Kitwanga, a larger Indian village on the north side of the river, close to the mouth of the Kitwancool River. This village

113

is strung along the river bank for some distance and the houses are fronted with a number of fine totem poles. This is an Anglican Mission and also a Hudson's Bay Company post. There is supposed to be placer gold on the Kitwancool but the Indians will not allow anyone to mine it.

"Andemaul, a little further up, calls for a short stop, and then we cross the river to Kitseguecla on the south bank. This is one of the old Indian villages and the site of another Methodist Mission. It is located at the mouth of the Kitseguecla river which also is reported to have gold in small quantity, and further up the valley there are reports of coal deposits.

"We have had some exciting moments on the passage thus far, particularly at points with such picturesque names as Hardscrabble Rapids, Devil's Elbow, Sheep's Rapids, Whirly-gig and Klootchman's Canyon, but the captain assures us that the hardest part of the river is yet to come. After leaving Kitseguecla we find the river very rocky and a string of boulders right across the river is called the Beaver Dam. It requires careful navigating to squeeze between two of these submerged rocks, apparently the only opening which would permit the passage of a boat this size. No sooner is that behind us than the whole river seems to be full of boulders and the Hornet's Nest is a very descriptive name. However, all things come to an end and eventually we push our way up stream until the mouth of the Bulkley River appears, and, crossing it, we tie up to the landing in front of the village of Hazelton."

The necessity for rivalry between the "Hazelton" and "Mount Royal" disappeared when the "Hazelton" was purchased by the Hudson's Bay Company in 1903, and the two ships were operated by the Company. The "Pheasant" appeared on the river in 1905, but her stay was short as she came to grief at the Beaver Dam in November 1906. When the boat struck and heeled over the galley stove spilled out its burning coals; and the purser, grabbing a bucket, doused the fire with river water. Just as he finished, the Captain came down and with great indignation said, "What in hell did you do that for? Don't you know we've got fire insurance, but nothing for wrecks?"

Considering the hazards of the trip up the Skeena, there were very few serious accidents. The first one was the loss of the "Mount Royal" in 1907.[6] She was descending the river with a load of passengers and thirty thousand dollars in gold dust. At Kitselas Canyon she hit "Ring-bolt" island and got crossway of the current. The Captain was able to hold her temporarily and get all his passengers off safely on to the island. However, in the subsequent efforts to get her free, she finally capsized and six members of the crew were lost, including the purser. A graphic description of the wreck is given by Mr. George Little of Terrace, who was present when it occurred. He was working on the roof of the hotel at Kitselas with a companion when he looked up and saw the "Mount Royal" coming through the canyon bottom up. As he watched, the wreck hung up on a bar below the canyon mouth, so the two men rushed down to the river bank and launching a dugout canoe paddled across. They climbed on top of the flat bottom of the boat, and were walking around discussing the accident, when they noticed a human hand waving through a hole in the hull. They rushed over and pulled out the engineer, Mr. Maddigan. He had been trapped when the boat capsized and had been washed into the bilge between the bottom deck and the hull. Here he had floundered around until he saw some light, and reaching the hole, thrust his hand through. Little said to the engineer, "I guess there must have been some air down there!" To which Maddigan replied, "I don't know about air, but there was a hell of a lot of water!"

With the loss of the "Mount Royal", the "Caledonia" was brought back into service for a short time until the "Port Simpson" was built in 1908. She was a larger boat than the "Hazelton", and to avoid the hazard of the Canyon passage, the "Hazelton" was sometimes left above the Canyon and the "Port Simpson" operated below. These two ships continued in the service of the Hudson's Bay Company until the Grand Trunk Pacific Railway was completed, when they were laid up permanently. The "Port Simpson" operated on the Stikine for a year or two, but eventually disintegrated on the beach in Prince Rupert Harbour. The "Hazelton" was sold to the Prince Rupert Yacht Club, and for years served as a club house and dock. She too left her ribs and keel on the beach.

With the beginning of construction of the railroad, the G.T.P. management put the "Distributor" on the run, and the contractors, Foley, Welch and Stewart, had a number of stern-wheelers—"Contractor", "Operator", "Conveyor" and "Omineca". Pat Burns who supplied meat to the construction camps put on the "Skeena". All these ships were strictly construction equipment and were disposed of as soon as their usefulness was passed. Another stern-wheeler which made a momentary appearance on the Skeena was the little "Craigflower". She was owned by Mr. Troup of Victoria and was designed for trips up the Gorge near that City. Enthused by the reports of great profits to be made in trade up the Skeena, Mr. Troup brought his boat north and essayed one trip up the river. She was much too small and underpowered for river navigation, and only got up as far as Minskinish. She was jokingly referred to as the "Cauliflower".

The last commercial ship on the Skeena was the "Inlander", built in 1909. Placed in service the following year, she was owned by a group of local business men, amongst whom was Wiggs O'Neill, who sailed on her as purser. Two of his brothers were in the engine room. The boat was of very shallow draft, and it was said she could sail on anything a trifle moist. The veteran Captain Bonser was in command and the "Inlander" continued in operation until September 1912 when she was put up on the beach below Port Essington, where she slowly rotted away.

The riverboat days on the Skeena have left a notable list of Captains—Johnson, Bucey, Jackman, Gardner, Magar, Watson and Bonser. Their success was due, not only to their own skill, but often to the ingenuity of the men in their crews. Emergency repairs frequently averted disaster. The "Hazelton", on one occasion, was coming down river below Lorne Creek. She had taken on a load of wet wood and the fireman couldn't keep a head of steam on the boilers. The ship lost steerage way and crashed head on into a rock, staving in her bow. They managed to get her on a bar and the ship's carpenter and Robert Tomlinson, who was a passenger, built a bulkhead across the bow and filled it with dirt. With this temporary patch they got down the river to a point where some suitable trees grew on the bank, and there the two men chopped out a crook and fashioned a new bow stem. It was all part of the day's work.

There are numerous stories told of those trips. Wiggs O'Neill, now a resident of Smithers, has recorded many of them, and we take the liberty of quoting him:—[7]

"The water was very low in the river and still big cakes of ice could be seen on the river bars, so our progress was very slow, feeling our way up the channels. When we got to Thornhill Landing at the Little Canyon, which was at the end of the present Terrace bridge, the Captain decided to lay up and wait for the water to rise. Time was dragging on our hands, so the passengers organized a mock trial. Mr. Hall (general manager for the Hudson's Bay Company) was named judge, three fellows named prosecuting attorneys and three named for the defence, among them Mr. McGregor who was a real lawyer. Billy Steele was the prisoner and was charged with stealing the hanging wall of

J.M.L. Alexander — prominent Port Simpson resident and his daughters (left to right) Mattie O'Neill, Minnie Alexander and Madge Alexander

G.O. Rudge — stonemason. He carved the rock for the Parliament Buildings in Victoria.

Captain Bonser's mineral claim. I was called as a witness for the prosecution. Some smart Joe had placed some rocks in Billy Steele's bed, and as his bed was on my side of the ship, I had to make his bed, and of course, found the evidence. In summing up, the Judge said the only thing he could find against the prisoner was his name (Steele)."

Mr. Wiggs O'Neill, who has been associated with transportation in one form or another for most of his life, is worthy of special mention as one of the colorful characters of early Skeena days. His father was C. P. O'Neill of Barkerville who died five years after Wiggs was born, in 1887. Mrs. O'Neill later married Mr. J. M. L. Alexander, the Hudson's Bay Company factor at Quesnel, who was a widower with nine children. With the three O'Neill children, this made a family of twelve whom Mr. Alexander brought with him to the coast and up to Port Simpson in 1888. His decision to go to Port Simpson was probably determined by the fact that his first wife's brother, R. H. Hall, was the factor there.

Mr. Alexander's first venture in this north country was to attempt cattle ranching on the Queen Charlotte Islands and he took a load of cattle over to Massett. His previous experience as a factor with the Company led to his being appointed in charge of the post at Massett when the current incumbent, Mr. Dodd, passed away. However, Massett proved too isolated for successful cattle ranching and a couple of years later he chartered a tugboat, the "Nell", and brought his family and a boatload of cattle to Port Simpson. The cattle he took down to Elizabeth Island, off the mouth of the Skeena. Of these, he only salvaged two as the animals drowned trying to swim across to nearby Porcher Island. The bulk of his herd, three hundred and fifty strong, left at Massett, broke out of their pasture and went wild; so the cattle business was a distinct failure.

For many years Mr. Alexander was a prominent citizen of Port Simpson, which at that time was the government center for the north. He was Collector of Customs and Civil Magistrate until his death in 1901. From his second marriage there were three children, James, known as Tiny, Homer and Hannah. The children, of course, have scattered over the world, but several of them are still well known in the Province. Four of the girls trained as nurses. Mattie, the oldest O'Neill, was a telegraphist, the first at Port Simpson, and later married Mr. Boss of the Dominion Telegraph. She is still living and has written extensively of her experiences in the north. Homer studied dentistry and after practising for a time in Prince Rupert is now one of the prominent dentists of Vancouver. Another daughter married George Rudge, a stone mason. Mr. Rudge quarried the rock for the Parliament Buildings at Victoria and afterwards opened a business in Port Simpson. He was a gifted artist in stone and for years carried on a profitable trade with the Indians in tombstones. With the destruction of the totem poles in Christian villages, the natives enthusiastically embraced the white man's totem pole, the tombstone, and sometimes carried the idea to extremes. George Rudge, who had a great sense of humor, used to delight to tell a story on himself involving one of his stones.

A prominent Indian from the Queen Charlotte Islands was drowned in the turbulent waters off Rose Spit, and his relatives came to George to have him make a stone in keeping with the exalted rank of the deceased. They chose red marble and Mr. Rudge put in long hours of painstaking work carving the three-tier stone. At last it was finished, a real work of art, with lettering in gold leaf. The Indians paid him seven hundred dollars and loaded it into their canoe, for the trip to the Islands. One can imagine Mr. Rudge's chagrin when he learned that the party had taken the stone to the approximate site of the drowning and there committed the stone to the deep. As he remarked, "If I had only known, I could have saved my gold leaf and used gilt paint!"

To return to Wiggs, the second member of the O'Neill family. He went to school in Port Simpson and attended high school in Portland, Oregon, and then started work in a bakery. He came north again in 1901 and started a bake shop in Port Essington. He soon tired of that and for some years was connected with the Dominion Telegraph line, being stationed at Telegraph Point and Aberdeen. In 1907 he decided to branch out for himself and built a gasoline launch called the "Strongheart", and thus began a passenger and freight service up the Skeena from Port Essington to Mile 54 on the railroad which was then being built. He was servicing the construction camps and he connected each day with the "Chieftain", a steam tug belonging to Robert Cunningham, which ran from Prince Rupert to Port Essington. After operating this service for three years, he was instrumental in organizing the company which built the "Inlander", already mentioned. The following year he sold the "Strongheart" and built a tunnel boat called the "Gitekshan", which he took up river where he continued to service the construction camps, first between Sealy and Hazelton, and then on the Bulkley River from Telkwa to Barrett's Ranch. When the "Gitekshan's" usefulness on the Bulkley was finished, the boat was transported overland to Francis Lake and there she functioned as the first ferry. In 1912

Wiggs bought a Packard truck and a Russell Knight passenger car and operated a taxi service between Hazelton and Telkwa. Continuing his interest in transportation, he eventually opened a garage in Smithers, and, obtaining the General Motors agency, has been selling and servicing cars ever since.

With the completion of the railroad, the era of canoe and steamboat came to an end and a new day dawned on the Skeena, which we must now consider in detail.

CHAPTER THIRTEEN

The Railroad

When it was decided to construct a transcontinental railroad, the Canadian Pacific Railway did extensive surveying throughout the Province of British Columbia to settle on the route and the Pacific terminus. In the course of this investigation, Mr. Charles Horetzky travelled through the mountains and down the Skeena and Naas valleys arriving at Port Simpson early in 1873.[1] While the Canadian Pacific Railway was eventually located in the southern part of the Province, Mr. Horetzky reported that there was a very favorable route for a railway along the line he had travelled, and this knowledge gave rise to a general confidence amongst the settlers in the Skeena district that some day such a railroad would be constructed.

It was naturally assumed that Port Simpson, as the only port on the north coast with an adequate harbour, would be the ultimate terminal and early in the twentieth century an American Company announced its intention of building a railroad from Port Simpson to Hudson's Bay. A townsite was laid out and the gullible public filched by the sale of lots. Their representative in the north was a Colonel May who, to give credence to the reports and, incidentally, promote the disposal of the lots, actually brought a small crew of men up to Wark's Canal and began construction of a wharf or float and what was supposed to be a hotel. In fact, it was nothing more than a shack and the whole thing folded up over night.

Kitamat was the other port which attracted the railroad builders. In 1900 an Act of the Legislature granted a charter to a group of Victoria and Vancouver business men, headed by C. W. D. Clifford, to build a railroad from Kitamat to, or adjacent to, Hazelton. The company was known as the Pacific, Northern and Omineca Railway; and, provided the sum of one hundred thousand dollars was spent in actual construction work by some date in 1908, the company was to receive a cash subsidy of five thousand dollars per mile. This project also came to naught, but in 1905 the charter was purchased by the Grand Trunk Railway.

The Grand Trunk Railroad[2] operated in the Province of Ontario, chiefly in the southern half of the Province. Its northern terminus was North Bay. In 1902 Charles M. Hays had returned from a short stay in the United States to resume his position with this railroad as General Manager. He found the Company in difficulties trying to compete with the Canadian Pacific Railway, and he turned his eyes enviously to the western half of the country where the Canadian Pacific had a monopoly of the grain from the prairie and the trans-Pacific trade. He conceived the bold plan of constructing a second transcontinental railroad, and in Sir Wilfred Laurier, the prime minister, and his government found receptive ears. At first with diffidence, but then wholeheartedly, they embraced the idea of sponsoring a new railroad. The C.P.R. had been the child of the Conservatives under Sir John A. Macdonald; this line would be a monument to the farsightedness of the Liberal party!

At first the Government tried to get the Grand Trunk to join with the Canadian Northern, a road then operating as far as Port Arthur and building westward, but was unsuccessful. In fact, ultimately, the two roads were built parallel to each other and in many cases only a few feet apart. In 1903 an Act was passed incorporating the Grand Trunk Pacific Railway Co., and granting extensive concessions. The new railroad was to be divided into two sections; the first, extending from Moncton to Winnipeg to be built by the Government; the second, from Winnipeg to Port Simpson, or some other port on the Pacific coast, to be constructed by the Grand Trunk Pacific Railway. When completed, the first division was to be leased to the Grand Trunk for fifty years with option of renewal. The bonds issued by the new Company were to be guaranteed by the Government up to 75% of their value.

The building of the road across the prairies proceeded rapidly and by 1910 had passed Edmonton and reached Wolf Creek. The western portion was then constructed from both ends simultaneously. To do this it was first necessary to decide where the railroad was to go. When it came to choosing the western terminus for the road, a remarkable series of events took place, and to properly understand what happened we must review a bit of the history of the north coast.

It had been the understanding for years that eventually another railroad would be built, and conjecture as to its probable route was a popular sport. In the press, and amongst the citizens generally, the two most favoured sites for the terminus were Port Simpson and Kitamat. For long there had been speculation in land in these two areas, particularly around Port Simpson where all the land in the immediate vicinity owned by the Provincial Government had been sold. This is a point which should be remembered as bearing very considerably on later events.

To stop the continuing speculation, the Provincial Government in 1891 put a reserve on the land of the Tsimpsean peninsula, north of a line running due west from the head of Wark's Canal. It must be realized that, when this reserve was put on, the land in the area had only been partially surveyed, and the only maps were Admiralty Charts. For this reason, no one in the Government knew, in stipulating the reserve as on the Tsimpsean peninsula, just what the nature of that land was; but the intent was certainly to cover all Crown lands north of the aforementioned line. Of course, subsequent surveys showed that some of that land was in the form of islands and not really peninsula; and to a literally minded individual this fact suggested the possibility of evading the land reserve.

Such a person was George Kane, a Vancouver millwright, who came into possession of some "South African War Land Grant" scrip, which entitled the holder to locate and receive title to one hundred and sixty acres of any unoccupied Crown lands. Mr. Kane, as a result of shrewdness, or possibly private knowledge, decided that Kaien Island in Tuck Inlet was the probable site of the Grand Trunk Pacific terminal, and he filed for six hundred and forty acres on the island. The date of his application was March 1904.

This Kaien Island was part of the land put under reserve in 1891, and the Commissioner of Lands, Mr. Green, refused the application on the grounds that the land was reserved; and, in order to make sure there was no future doubt, a further reserve was put on. George Kane continued to fight for the right to stake the land in question, but without success. In 1909, he applied to the Supreme Court for redress of the wrong which he considered had been done him, as the lands he originally staked became eventually the business section of the City of Prince Rupert.

This continual importuning by George Kane, and various rumors which became rife in the press, resulted in the final release of the information that the Government had indeed sold certain lands on Kaien Island to the Grand Trunk Pacific. The controversy boiled over into the House and was made much of by the Opposition. Finally a special commission was set up to investigate the whole matter and its findings were eventually made public.[3] Substantially they revealed the following story:—

Peter Larsen was a millionaire railroad contractor of Helena, Montana. He had done work for the Canadian Pacific Railway and was conversant with affairs in Canada, and friendly with certain people in railroad circles. Whether he was approached by the Grand Trunk Pacific or not was not revealed, but he conceived the idea of trying to anticipate the location of the terminal, or even influencing the choice by procuring desirable lands in advance. In 1903 he visited Victoria and formed a working agreement with a Mr. James Anderson, who had been connected with the Victoria and Sidney Railway. Mr. Anderson was to go north and look over the country and collect information.

Mr. Anderson made two trips and became convinced that Kaien Island offered the best opportunity. Accordingly, he and Larsen decided to go ahead with their plans to acquire the land, and instructed their solicitor, Mr. E. V. Bodwell, to approach the Government. Mr. Bodwell studied the problem of the reserve and decided it could be solved under a clause of the Land Act which empowered the Government to dispose of land by Order in Council for the "encouragement of immigration or other purposes of public advantage". Bodwell therefore wrote the Government in January 1904, suggesting that ten thousand acres be sold to a company to be formed by his clients, with the understanding that the land would be used for the Grand Trunk Pacific terminal; and if the company were not successful, the land was to be returned to the Government and the purchase price would be refunded.

The Government immediately advised Bodwell that they were prepared to sell the land on his terms, but would only do so directly to the Grand Trunk Pacific, and they would have to be assured that he was representing the railroad. This certainly changed the picture as far as Larsen and Anderson were concerned, but they continued to interest themselves in the deal. Anderson made further trips north and conducted a detailed survey of the lands, employing a Mr. Twigg and later Mr. Ritchie. While it was, no doubt, a disappointment to them to have to drop their idea of a company, they had not exhausted the possibilities of profit from the transaction.

Bodwell got a wire from Mr. Hays, authorising him to proceed on behalf of the Railway, but without binding the Railway Company; and the Government, on the strength of that wire, passed the order in council selling ten thousand acres to the Grand Trunk Pacific Railway for one dollar per acre. They, at the same time, reserved one quarter of the proposed townsite for themselves, including one quarter of the waterfront. This latter part of the agreement was the justification given by the Government for their action, as they maintained, and correctly, that the choice of Kaien Island was for the public good—that is, the Provincial good—since, if the railroad went to either Port Simpson or Kitamat, the Government did not own any adjacent land with which they could make a deal.

There is no doubt that, from the first, the Grand Trunk were cognizant of what was going on, and approved. One might reasonably suppose that they had some private arrangement with Larsen, although this was never shown. Larsen maintained, according to Bodwell, that he was not interested in making any money out of the land, but only wished to ingratiate himself with the Grand Trunk Pacific company, so that he might later obtain contracts for the construction. We will see later to what extent he succeeded. Not so, Anderson, however; and this gentleman finally went to Montreal and dickered with the Company for a separate deal. As a result, an agreement was drawn up between the Company and Larsen & Anderson, which Anderson signed on behalf of the two of them, since he had Larsen's power of attorney. This agreement was to pay the two men forty thousand dollars if the railroad decided to use the Kaien Island site. It appears that when Larsen found out what Anderson had done, he refused to have any part of it, and destroyed the contract. He subsequently paid Anderson ten thousand dollars in cash for his trouble, as well as defraying all expenses incurred by Anderson in his work over the site. Further, the Grand Trunk paid Anderson twenty-five hundred dollars to complete the preliminary survey work for them.

The special committee reported that there was no evidence that anyone in the Provincial Government had profited in the transaction and that the Government had consummated an advantageous deal for the Province. Since the committee had no power to subpoena witnesses outside the Province, they never did succeed in getting testimony from Mr. Larsen or any Grand Trunk official, so no one knows to this day what Larsen got out of the railroad. It was generally admitted that he got most of, if not all, his expenses paid.

The principals in the matter did profit, however, in another way. All the negotiations with the Government were strictly secret, and even after the order in council was passed no information was released. Accordingly, it was the Larsen group alone who knew where the railroad was going, and they had time to acquire strategic land. This they proceeded to do, and Anderson again went north, this time with Mr. Ritchie, a B.C.

land surveyor, and staked all the land surrounding Kaien Island, now the Port Edward townsite. To handle this, and other townsite land which might offer, Anderson formed the Pacific Coast Realty Company.

Charles M. Hays then visited the coast and looked over the Kaien Island site. He was favorably impressed, but worried about the harbor. The existing charts showed a rock right in the entrance,- so Hays ordered a further examination. When new soundings were taken, it was found that there was no rock. The original chart was in error, or had a fly speck in the critical position. No objection now remained and the Grand Trunk Pacific announced their selection of Kaien Island.

To complete their possession of the necessary land on the island it was obligatory that the Railway procure the western portion of the island which was an Indian reserve for the Metlakatla natives. To purchase it from the Indian Department of the Dominion Government required the consent of the Provincial Government, and this gave Sir Richard McBride, the premier, a chance to do some further negotiating with the Company. In the original agreement for the construction of the railroad there was no undertaking that construction should proceed from both ends simultaneously, and the Grand Trunk did not show any inclination to get started. In fact, Mr. Hays was trying to get further land concessions from the Provincial Government along the proposed right of way, which, if granted, would have amounted to about eight million acres. Sir Richard McBride stood firm, refused any further land concessions and, in return for his agreement in the sale of Indian lands, required that work should start immediately from the western end. He won his point and work started in the summer of 1907.

Locating the railway through the coast mountains was a difficult task. Two routes were considered: one left the Bulkley Valley at Telkwa and, proceeding up the Telkwa river, crossed over to the headwaters of the Zymoetz or Copper River and descended that valley to the Skeena; the other ran right down the Bulkley River to the Forks of the Skeena and proceeded on down the Skeena River. The first of these routes was preferred as it was eighty miles shorter, but the second was the one finally chosen as the Provincial Government wanted to service the mining areas and agricultural land around Hazelton and up the Kispiox Valley. It was also pointed out that north from Hazelton was the natural route for a branch line to Dawson in the Yukon.

Some really difficult engineering problems were met in the

line down the Skeena. It is said that twelve thousand miles of trial lines and surveys were run, before the one hundred and eighty miles of track were finally laid.[4] While this work was proceeding, construction was started on a branch line to Kitamat, which could only have been done for two reasons. A start had to be made from the western end, and, as already mentioned, the Grand Trunk Pacific had purchased the charter of the Pacific Northern and Omineca railroad, which charter required that a certain amount of work had to be done before the company was entitled to the concessions under the charter. Certainly the work done by this first contract did not make any contribution to the final railroad as it was on the opposite side of the river.

The contract for all the construction of the Grand Trunk Pacific was awarded to the firm of Foley, Welch and Stewart, who sublet it to individual contractors. This firm operated under several names, one of which was Foley Brothers, Larsen & Co. Here we find the name of the man who figured so largely in the original negotiations for the townsite on Kaien Island, and in the proceedings of the special committee of the Legislature, it was pointed out that Larsen was a personal friend and business associate of Mr. Foley. It would seem therefore that Mr. Larsen accomplished his purpose of making a favorable impression on the Grand Trunk officials by obtaining their land for them at a nominal rate.

Construction of the Skeena River portion of the road was a stupendous undertaking. Mr. C. C. Van Arsdoll was the engineer in charge and the work was sublet by Foley, Welch and Stewart to small contractors, who in many cases went broke. Camps were set up every two miles, and in order to keep them stocked with supplies water transportation was used. The contractors employed a number of river steamers for this purpose, the "Contractor", "Operator", "Conveyor", "Omineca" and "Distributor". Pat Burns, of meat packing fame, put on the "Skeena". Fresh meat was supplied by driving cattle from the Bulkley Valley to a point just below Hazelton where a slaughterhouse was built. There the cattle were butchered and the meat put in cold storage units spaced at strategic points down the river. The camps cost between two thousand and six thousand dollars to construct. Provisions and supplies for these camps during construction totalled over four million dollars. The river boats represented an investment of two hundred thousand dollars, and, all in all, the contractors had expended six and a quarter million before a sod of earth was turned.

Practically the whole stretch of line required rock work,

particularly in the lower sixty miles. The explosives used were manufactured in Prince Rupert Harbour, at a plant on Wolf Island. This was essential as transportation of explosives up the coast by steamer was an involved process and the amounts used were tremendous. An explosive known as "Virite" was made as well as dynamite and black powder, and the owner of the plant was a Mr. E. A. LeSueur with a Colonel F. E. Leach in actual charge. In the short distance between Prince Rupert and Aberdeen, over two million shots were fired and it was quite common to have from twenty-five hundred to five thousand dollars' worth of explosives in one blast. By the time the line had reached Kitselas Canyon, ten million pounds of explosives had been used. The cost of this first hundred miles of grade was eighty thousand dollars per mile before any track was laid.

The problem of procuring and holding labourers presented serious difficulties also, as there were other opportunities for work available during the summer, which offered the men higher remuneration. Wages were raised to three dollars per day without success. Under these trying conditions progress naturally was slow and the line to Kitselas was only graded by March 1910. No track had yet been laid. The bridge from Kaien Island to the mainland which had to cross strong tidal rapids (Zenardi) was another engineering problem. This bridge was completed in July 1910 and with the first work train across the bridge on July 31st, the laying of track proceeded rapidly. In the meantime, construction was proceeding steadily from the East, and in the summer of 1910 Van Arsdoll moved his headquarters to New Hazelton, a point adjacent to the old Indian Village of Hagwilget.

While the work was going on below Kitselas, progress east of the canyon also was steady. The two sections were separated by the rugged canyon walls, where three tunnels had to be blasted out before the track could be laid. These were completed in January 1912. In the meantime, with so much construction taking place around the canyon, this was the logical place for a community to start. It was, of course, a point of call for the river steamers, and often they were unable to ascend the river further. A few settlers had already taken pre-emptions in the area—notably Thornhill, Stuart, Bostet and Durham—and on the south bank of the river, just below the canyon, was the Indian village of Kitselas. Adjacent to, and mingling with, this Indian village a white settlement grew up with the coming of the Railway. C. W. D. Clifford was the moving spirit and he got a hotel and a store started, the latter under the care of Mr. Patterson. The hotel was the rendezvous for the men working on the railroad, as its liquor license was the only source of alcohol available to these men. Perhaps we should say, it was supposed to be the only source. W. J. O'Neill tells a story of those days—[5]

"During the Railway construction on the Skeena, Constable Tom Parsons, who in later years became Top Dog of the B.C. Police Force, policed the territory around Kitselas and Kitsumgalum. He was getting complaints from the contractors building the long tunnels at Kitselas Canyon. They complained about an Indian girl visiting the camps and putting the gangs on a spree and disorganising the crews. One night the Constable, with the aid of a Deputy, crossed the river and raided the camps and brought the lady in question back as a prisoner. She was locked up in the little two by four Skookum House at Kitselas, and committed for trial. Two J. P.'s sat on the case, Mr. Charles William Digby Clifford, the local Kitselas law man, and the Rev. Canon Marsh who was called in from Kitsumgalum. The charge was read by Tom and she was asked if she was guilty or not. The comely maiden had nothing to say; she stood there with a stolid face, as if it was all Dutch to her.

"After repeated tries to get her to understand, with no response, Mr. Clifford tried Chinook on her, with no results. Canon Marsh, who hailed from the prairie Provinces, opened up in the Cree language, with no response; just the same stolid stare. No savvy! They tried Pidgin English, then Canon Marsh resorted to the Blackfoot lingo, with the same results. Just didn't know nothin'!

"It became evident to the two wise men that she was either deaf, dumb, or completely lacking in intelligence. After having a confab with each other, she was told that they had no alternative but to fine her twenty-five dollars. The maiden pulled a well-knotted handkerchief out of her pocket, and after untying several knots, exposing a good-sized bank roll, she peeled off a couple of tens and a five, threw them on the table, and said in perfectly good English, 'Thanks, Gentlemen, it was a mere bagatelle.' It turned out that she was a graduate of one of the mission schools."

After an outbreak of smallpox amongst them, the natives decided to move their village, and they crossed the river and occupied a site a short distance further down. This was known as New Town. The railroad eventually placed their station at that point and called it Van Arsdoll, after the chief engineer. The days of Kitselas were numbered, for as soon as the railroad reached Hazelton, the river boats were withdrawn, and the construction crews having moved on, there was no one left to patronise the town's facilities. Today, no trace remains of the village of Kitselas. On the railroad side of the river a small band of Indians still occupy "New Town". The name, Van Arsdoll, has been dropped and once more the village is called Kitselas. Even the railroad has accepted the inevitable and "Kitselas" appears above the station platform.

Above the Canyon another station was erected and this was called Usk. There had been no one living there previously, but the inevitable store and hotel soon appeared. A few settlers gathered 'round, and we note such names as Alger, Bethuren and Skinner. Across the river they built a sawmill which delivered its lumber to the railroad by means of an aerial tramway.

The Skeena section of the railroad was laid on the north side of the river, while the Bulkley portion was located on the south side. The crossing of the river was to take place at Kitseguecla, and this required the building of a bridge nine hundred and thirty feet in length. It was only a little longer than the one required to bridge a deep gulch adjacent to the townsite of Sealy, ten miles further up the Skeena, which was nine hundred feet long and one hundred and eighty feet at its deepest point. These two structures delayed the track-laying for some time.

By March 1912, trains were operating as far as Skeena Crossing and, through an arrangement with the Hudson's Bay Company, it was possible to buy a through ticket to Hazelton. In August of that year the first train reached Sealy. The following year the tracks were laid through the Bulkley Valley and on to Burns Lake, and on April 7th 1914, east and west met near Fraser Lake and the last spike was driven. The first through train reached Prince Rupert on the 8th of that month.

Throughout the western construction the railway was bedevilled with townsite problems. The Grand Trunk Pacific Development Company was the child of the Railway, incorporated to hold and sell land, but often it appeared that it was in direct opposition to the best interests of the railroad. In the upper Skeena and Bulkley areas, townsite rivalry reached its peak.

At the Forks of the Skeena, Hazelton was the only populated center, but, unfortunately, it was located on the opposite side of the river from the railroad. How it should be served gave rise to a heated controversy. The flat ground adjoining the Indian reservation of Hagwilget was particularly suitable for a townsite and this was the point at which the road from Hazelton crossed the Bulkley on a suspension bridge which had been erected some years earlier by the Government for the traffic into the Bulkley Valley. The Indians, too, had their bridge across the Bulkley Canyon at this point.

Two adjoining parcels of land were picked up and promoted by rival interests. Robert Kelly of Vancouver, of the firm of Kelly Douglas and Company, owned one, and W. J. Larkworthy, a Hazelton merchant, and his associates owned the other. The latter called their townsite Larkton, while the former called his New Hazelton, and advertised it as the Spokane of Canada. Both groups put their lots on the market with good success, as the majority of the Hazelton citizens felt sure the railroad would place their station in that neighbourhood.

In the meantime the construction crews had established their camps a few miles below the Forks and the townsite of Ellison was put on the market. It was called after Price Ellison, the Provincial Minister of Lands, but later was known as Sealy, named after the hotel proprietor of that name, J. C. K. Sealy, of Hazelton. Traffic for Hazelton disembarked at this point and proceeded by wagon road to the Forks, crossing the river by canoe ferry to Hazelton.

The Provincial Government seemed to favor this route for servicing the old town and showed no inclination to assist in developing the townsite of New Hazelton. This is not remarkable, as in those days of political patronage, one would hardly expect a Conservative Government to co-operate with one of the prominent Liberals of the Province in the person of Robert Kelly. The canoe ferry was far from being satisfactory, so the Government gave a charter to R. S. Sargent of Hazelton for a ferry and this was built and placed in operation in 1913. It also proved unsatisfactory, as it could not operate during low water, so the Government built a bridge to replace it that same year.

New Hazelton, meanwhile, was struggling for its existence. Kelly's company was determined to make its townsite the hub of the District, particularly for servicing the mines which were exceedingly active in the mountains of the immediate vicinity. The original bridge across the Bulkley, which had been built by the Government, was narrow and, owing to its position low down in the canyon, had a very steep approach to both ends. A team of horses could barely get across, and the steep hills made heavy loads impossible. To alleviate this situation and to make the route to New Hazelton attractive to the mining companies, Kelly undertook to put in a high level bridge across the Bulkley at the site of the old Indian bridge. This was built by an English firm, Craddock & Co., and was completed in October 1913. However, it was not usable as there were no roads linking it with the existing highways, and the Provincial Government showed no interest in providing them. Kelly had to build the roads as well, to get his bridge in operation.

130

Several hundred people had now settled in New Hazelton and the railway ran through the town, but there was no station. As a matter of fact, the Grand Trunk showed no inclination to place a station there, but was planning a station a couple of miles to the westward, directly opposite the old town of Hazelton. A new townsite called South Hazelton was started at this point and the townsite of Sealy was abandoned, holders of lots in the latter being given lots in the new townsite. Traffic for New Hazelton was put off at South Hazelton and the trains were run empty up to New Hazelton to be turned around on the Y at that point.

The New Hazelton citizens were rightfully indignant and appealed to the Board of Railway Commissioners who ruled in their favor and instructed the Railway to build a station in the new town. The opposition carried the appeal to the Supreme Court, who referred it back to the Commissioners and again the Railway was ordered to put in a station at New Hazelton. This was finally done and the town appeared to be established, with a promising future.

However, the station at South Hazelton and the bridge across the mouth of the Bulkley enabled the old town of Hazelton to maintain its existence and some of its prestige. The mass migration to New Hazelton which Kelly and Larkworthy envisaged did not occur, and bitter rivalry between the two communities broke out and persisted for many years. New Hazelton started out with great pretensions and during construction days it was a lively place. Amongst other evidences of a thriving community, it boasted a bank, which was designed primarily to handle the payrolls of the railway. With many questionable characters employed on the road construction, it was not surprising that the little bank in the wilderness excited the cupidity of some; and on November 11th, 1913, five masked men entered the bank, and after shooting the bank clerk, Jock McQueen, in the head, escaped with seventeen thousand dollars. The bank clerk recovered, but the money was not found. The following April, on a beautiful spring day, the manager of the Bank was out on the sidewalk talking to a friend, when seven men entered the Bank. The manager thought he heard sounds of confusion in the building and went to investigate. He was met by an armed robber at the door who fired a shot at him but missed, and the manager and his friend then ran down the street to rouse the populace. Several citizens rushed to the rescue, armed with whatever weapons they possessed. In the meantime, the robbers had collected the cash, and decided to make a dash for it. They were greeted by a fusillade of shots, and two of them dropped on the road. A third was badly wounded and was soon captured, but the remaining four managed to make the bush. Eventually three of them were taken, but the fourth made his escape and took with him thirteen hundred dollars in cash. The wounded man subsequently died in hospital, but the three men stood trial and were sentenced to twenty years by Judge Young. No trace was ever found of the missing man or the money.

Mining was particularly active in the Hazelton area and this was the natural resource upon which the prosperity of New Hazelton was supposed to stand. Here again, general economic conditions frustrated local effort and the new town so optimistically begun degenerated into a small collection of shacks, a small store, an inferior hotel and the inevitable Chinese restaurant. In spite of these obviously depressing prospects, the town had at least one perennial optimist in the person of Charles H. Sawle, the editor and publisher of the newspaper for the District, "The Omineca Herald". His brother, G. T. R. Sawle was, for a time, editor of "The Optimist" of Prince Rupert. For thirty years and more, "Chuck" Sawle stayed with New Hazelton and "The Omineca Herald", a voice crying in the wilderness. However, like so many of the old-timers, he was forced to retire, just when the tide seemed to have turned. He disposed of his paper to Mr. and Mrs. Tommy Fraser, and they subsequently moved the plant to Terrace, where Destiny had, at last, heard the call of the Skeena.

As the railroad proceeded eastward it was necessary to choose suitable locations for divisional points. These were set at intervals of approximately one hundred and twenty-five miles, and three were therefore required between Prince Rupert and Prince George. The first, called Pacific, was one hundred and twenty miles from Prince Rupert, and was a short distance up the river from Kitselas. Here the railroad was still in the heart of the Coast Mountains, where there was nothing to warrant the building of a town; and it remains today, what it was at first, only a railroad divisional point, with railroad yards and shops and the necessary residences for railway employees.

A much happier choice from a scenic point of view fell on Smithers, another hundred and twenty miles east, but, once again, skullduggery entered the picture. Telkwa would have liked the divisional point but it was on the wrong side of the river, and the railway would have preferred an excellent location about ten miles further east. This choice had been anticipated and the townsite of Hubert had already been established there. It was finally decided to use a straight stretch of track twelve miles west of Telkwa, and the firm of Aldous and Murray was engaged to acquire the necessary land, on which numerous settlers were already located. Strict secrecy was necessary and the report was allowed to circulate that Hubert had been chosen, and a party of surveyors was sent in to lay out a town. In the meantime, Murray had his brother in Erie, Pennsylvania, write him a letter announcing that a company was interested in a settlement scheme in the Bulkley Valley, and commissioning him to purchase land. This he proceeded to do, buying up all the farms in the chosen area at fifty dollars an acre. As soon as the land was procured, the surveyors were withdrawn from Hubert and the new townsite of Smithers was announced.

Smithers was named after A. W. Smithers, the chairman of the Grand Trunk Pacific. As a townsite it was about the worst that could be found. The only thing to commend it was the straight stretch of track. The townsite, itself, was a swamp, and the men who cleared it had to work in gum boots. The contract for the clearing was given to Wiggs O'Neill who sublet it to individual contractors, as he was busily engaged in operating the Gitekshan on the Bulkley River for the construction camps. Although the land was drained, the subsoil was composed of layers of quicksand and clay, and foundations could only be laid by driving piling—in some cases one pile on top of another. Water was obtained by sinking sand points and pumping, but the Railroad required a large amount for their roundhouse, and attempted to sink a well. Cribbing was placed in position to line the results of the first day of digging, but when the crew came on duty the next morning, they found the cribbing floating on the surface again. The project was finally given up and a small lake nearby was dammed and the water piped in.

The business section of the town today is in the same plight. The town is supplied by water pumped out of the Bulkley River, filtered and chlorinated before use. Laying water mains was a difficult problem in the same quicksand and the town has yet to tackle the task of trying to put in sewers. Fortunately, the residential portion of town is located on slightly higher ground and building there is a little easier. In spite of several disastrous fires, the town is slowly growing and becoming the center of a prosperous dairying industry. It is beautifully situated at the foot of Hudson's Bay Mountain, and nearby Lake Kathlyn has become a popular summer resort for the local residents and many commuters from Prince Rupert. With the development of Smithers, the nearby town of Aldermere disappeared.

There is only one other community on the railroad in the Bulkley Valley worthy of report. The land around Pleasant

Valley was taken up for a townsite and a contest was run in the newspapers of the District for a suitable name for the new town. In December 1910 the contest closed and the name Houston was picked. It was chosen in honor of the first newspaper man in Prince Rupert, John Houston. Again the vision immeasurably surpassed the reality, and for years there was only a small community at Houston. Aside from the few settlers, a lumber mill provided the only activity. Today it is enjoying a measure of prosperity due to the increase in lumbering and the fertile land of the valley is a potential source of permanent prosperity.

With the new settlements and the building of roads, the lot of the pioneers rapidly improved. The little villages developed their own individualities, and community spirit and good-natured rivalry flourished. Radio and moving pictures were still in their infancy and rarely touched these remote spots, so the people were thrown entirely on their own resources for recreation and amusement. The long winter months were lightened with concerts and plays by local talent, and rival hostesses vied, through teas and parties, for the leadership of local society. The men organized hockey teams and for some years a league operated amongst the two Hazeltons and the towns of the Bulkley Valley.

In the summer, the rivalry was carried on to the baseball diamond, and a baseball game with the neighbouring town was the main feature of the sports program on the national holidays. In addition, each community had its particular celebration some time during the summer. In Telkwa, it was the annual Barbecue, when a whole steer was roasted in an outdoor pit and horse racing and bronco-busting featured the day. Smithers had its Fall Fair, and Hazelton its Flower Show. Altogether, life was good in this frontier country.

Early View of Smithers

Hudson's Bay Mountain and Lake Kathlyn

Sunset in Prince Rupert Harbour

Aerial View of Prince Rupert on Kaien Island

CHAPTER FOURTEEN

Prince Rupert

The present-day visitor to Prince Rupert is struck at once by the spaciousness and sheltered character of the harbour. Completely land-locked, and of uniform depth, it ranks amongst the best harbours in the world. Along its eastern shore on Kaien Island lies the City, backed by two low mountains, Oldfield and Hays. The former was named in 1867 after Captain Oldfield of H.M.S. "Malacca"; the latter after Charles M. Hays of Grand Trunk fame. The western shore of the harbour is generally low except for Mount Morse which dominates the upper end of Tuck Inlet. Toward the harbour mouth the western shore is composed of a number of islands through which wanders Venn Passage. At night, looking westward from the City, the lights of the old village of Metlakatla may be seen twinkling between the islands from their position at the western end of the passage. Over these islands, too, during the long summer evenings, the sun sets in a path of gold, leaving a flaming sky of brilliant yellows and crimsons—sunsets that are unexcelled for beauty, and leave the watcher on the hills of the City uplifted and enthralled by the magnificence of the northern sun.

To Metlakatla, on May 7th, 1906, the steamer "Tees" brought the first party of men and material for the new city.[1] J. H. Pillsbury was the engineer in charge of the group and he was accompanied by A. E. Hill and W. A. Casey, as engineers, and John Leggatt and W. E. Edgecomb as carpenters. They were fortunate in finding a steam launch, the "Constance", available, and they hired its Captain Robinson to take them across the harbour to the proposed site.

The first construction work was commenced on May 17th with the building of a tool shed, and the erection of some tents for living accommodation. The next day Mr. Pillsbury began the survey for the docks and Company houses. As soon as the camp was established they started clearing the foreshore for the building of the wharf, and soon the first piles were driven. The pile driver was rented from George Cunningham and was not a very efficient machine. Nevertheless, the work proceeded and the wharf was completed on time, on July 1st. This was followed by the erection of the Company building for offices and then the cutting of a road straight up into the wilderness from the wharf. This road was called Center Street, and it consisted of a narrow wooden sidewalk with hand railings, and short branch walks running off to buildings which soon sprang up along either side. The grade was rather steep, so the sidewalk was equipped with a narrow gauge railroad up which a car could be pulled by a donkey engine at the top, for the movement of supplies and heavy equipment.

So far, Prince Rupert was a name only.[2] The Grand Trunk Pacific owned the land on Kaien Island, but no move had been made to lay out a townsite or dispose of land. Some essential services were immediately needed in the new community, and to supply them the Company granted permission to certain individuals to set up temporary shelters to house their activities. Thus we find a bank, The Canadian Bank of Commerce, a drug store operated by Dr. Reddie, the United Supply and Contracting Company dealing in hardware and lumber, the Kelly-Carruthers Supply Company dealing in general merchandise, L. Morrow and Company who ran a meat market, a barber shop run by Harvey Creech, and two physicians, Dr. J. G. McKay in general practice and Dr. E. Tremayne who moved over from Metlakatla to be the Company doctor. In addition, the Anglican Church had been permitted to put up a hall, but the Presbyterian minister had not been allowed to build. The law was represented by William H. Vickers who served as constable for the Skeena District, also deputy mining recorder, health inspector, deputy game warden, justice of the peace and notary public. All the other inhabitants of the town were employees of the railroad or the contractors, and since there were no hotels or restaurants, the travelling public were repeatedly warned to stay away.

However, you can't keep people away from what appears to be a sure source of steady employment and a gold mine for speculation and investment, and in spite of the restrictions the people did arrive. They got around the regulations by the single procedure of filing a mineral claim. This was done by a John Knox. He allowed his friends and others to erect temporary buildings on the claim and thus sprang into being the community of Knoxville, a thorn in the flesh to the Grand Trunk Pacific.

One of the early arrivals who was particularly unwelcome was John Houston, an energetic newspaper man. He took refuge in Knoxville and proceeded to publish a paper called "The Empire", the first newspaper in Prince Rupert. Houston had three particular antipathies. He had no use for the Federal Government of the day, the policy of the Grand Trunk Pacific, and Oriental labor. In each issue of his paper he waxed eloquent on all three subjects. He ran afoul of the Railway right at the first, as the Company refused to allow him to ship in a press, and when it arrived they locked it up in the warehouse on the dock. The editor immediately appealed to the local constable, who broke the lock on the door and released the press. Willing hands carried it up Center Street and deposited it in front of the Provincial Police office. A tent was placed over the press and "The Empire" issue of September 21st, 1907, was published, after the type had been set in the Police office. This is probably some kind of record for publication, and is thus described in the paper—"The type is set in the provincial police office; the press work is done in a 10 x 12 tent pitched in the middle of Center street; the paper and ink is stored in Kenneth Munro's warehouse on Rupert road; the copy is penned in the sleeping apartments of the government telegraph operator."

There was still no sign of a townsite, but in October 1907, the work of clearing land started. It was let out to individual contractors in blocks at a contract price of one hundred and twenty dollars an acre. While this was going on the construction of docks and warehouses was proceeding and as the land was cleared more temporary buildings were erected. The inevitable sawmill had been started out at Seal Cove, a bay at the northwest point of Kaien Island, and there much of the lumber was cut. It employed a large number of Japanese workmen, and this was one of the bones of contention which received a weekly gnawing by John Houston.

By the time the lots were all cleared and surveyed in May 1909, the town had acquired one thousand inhabitants and one hundred and fifty businesses. Three-quarters of these were located on the mining claim of John Knox and John Houston, although there were one or two other mining claims as well. These claims were located on the portion of the townsite which was Indian reservation, and therefore were not under the jurisdiction of the Grand Trunk Pacific until they acquired the land. Knoxville, therefore, was the principal community. The Company buildings grouped around the docks were known as Baconville, named after the Grand Trunk Pacific Harbour engineer, Mr. James H. Bacon, and the remainder of the settlement, Vickersville, was named after the provincial police constable. The city lots were put on sale in May and June of 1909, and thus with the establishment of an official townsite, the old divisions disappeared. In fact, most of the land concerned was blasted into the air, as the railroad yards were levelled along the waterfront.

With the passing of Knoxville went the most colorful figure of those early days in Prince Rupert, John Houston. He closed his doors and disposed of "The Empire", moving on to newer frontiers. Prince Rupert was getting too civilised for him. He later started a paper in the town of Prince George. "The Empire" was taken over by Sam Newton, who operated it for many years as one of the two leading newspapers of the City, and the recognized mouthpiece of the Conservative Party.

The town lots sold rapidly and permanent buildings mushroomed over night. As in most boom towns the prices were inclined to get out of hand and ranged from fifty dollars to six thousand dollars per lot. Everywhere was a sense of urgency. Citizens' committees were organized for telephone, for waterworks and for electricity, without waiting for the passing of the Act of Incorporation of the City, which was even then before the Provincial Legislature. The Bill of Incorporation was sponsored by the Attorney General, Mr. Bowser, and eventually bitterly attacked by the local member, Mr. William Manson, who was a member of the Government but opposed to the terms of the Bill. The citizens wanted the Act of Incorporation to retain for the City all rights in public utilities, so that they might exclude speculating companies who already were clamoring for the opportunity of supplying the City with its fundamental requirements. The first electric lights in the town had been supplied by the B.C. Tie and Timber Company from their plant at Seal Cove, and a very primitive installation of street lights was the result. Unfortunately the plant was burned out and the company went bankrupt. Nevertheless, the Incorporation Act made it obligatory that the City should purchase the remains of the light plant with the poles and wires, in situ, at an arbitrated figure. It is not to be wondered at that the Act, which should have been welcomed, was, in fact, strongly criticized on all sides. It finally passed the Legislature on March 3, 1910.

The first City elections were held in May of that year, and they aroused the partisan feeling one would expect. A second paper, "The Optimist", had made its appearance and the two mayoralty candidates received the backing of the two rival papers, cutting completely across recognized political lines. William Manson, the sitting member, was supported by "The Optimist", and Fred Stork, a Liberal and a hardware merchant, by "The Empire". While the contest was spirited it was not bitter and it was enlivened by the wit and humor of the candidates.

G. R. T. Sawle, the editor of "The Optimist", parodied the story in the following manner:—

GENESIS OF PRINCE RUPERT
Being the first epistle of Bill to the Electors

Chapter One

And it came to pass that the Moguls of the Grandtrunk sought an outlet upon the Pacific Ocean.

And they raised the wind and established a city; and the city grew; and the blindpigs waxed fat, and were killed off.

And the tinhorns prospered.

And certain among the fat men of the city became ambitious, and they spoke among themselves on the plankstreets and in Dennyallen's and they brought forth many words at the public meetings.

And they drew up a bad bold charter.

And they embarked upon the waters and set their sails for the city called Victoria, bringing with them this charter.

For in this city dwelt the wise men; and also the attorney general.

And the rulers of the country did receive their correspondence at the Union club.

And when the travellers had set foot upon the shore they proceeded to the seat of government.

And they kissed the foot of the attorney general.

And a great rage against the City rose within him, and he fell upon the charter with great gusto.

And he more than fixed it.

And he mutilated the clauses.

And he took from them by stealth the city's assets, and he loaded upon the city liabilities and copper wire. And the delegates were chastened in spirit. And there was nothing doing.

And they re-embarked and returned from whence they came, and the people wailed in the city and peace was not in them.

Chapter Two

And it came to pass that the people sought to choose from among themselves, the rulers of the city.

And a great rain fell and washed the conscience of many people so that they became clean, and lo! there came forth many who would be rulers, where few only could be chosen.

And the people spoke among themselves again, saying, "Let us have a public meeting."

And lo! there were none who would dig down for the rent of the theatre.

Chapter Three

But when this thing had been adjusted, the people met together.

And there were many of all nations.

And Vernonsmith, the Mansonite, was chairman of the meeting.

And he called upon the people in a loud voice to send forth their wouldbes.

And one arose and spoke the name of Manson, and lauded him with cause and put him in nomination.

And another spake to the great multitude and said, "Here is Manson, the elder, Hath he not found favor once in the eyes of the electors, and am not I, Georgemorrow, his right hand? See therefor ye support him and make for me my seventeen hundred pieces of silver to put in the Unionbank."

And the Conservatives and others applauded and there was much uproar and tumult.

And another spake saying, "Here is Stephens of the Board-oftrade. Have they not put upon the waters the Henriette to provide efficient mail service, and have they not put the postoffice in the hollow where the multitude may see it, when they know where it is? Let us therefore support Stephens."

And there was much silence.

And there arose Quinlan, the extractor, and he spoke saying: "Lo! am I not the president of the great conservative association? and have I not the promise of a full score votes? Yea, verily, shall I go to the post before my platform falls and my voters are struck off!"

And the multitude applauded and he blew up his chest and peace fell upon his shoulders.

And he extracted a cigarette and departed from the platform.

And one arose and spake the name of Bowser, the Attorney-general.

And the name was as a hissing scorn and even Harryevans, he whose roar is like the murmur of a thousand brick, mocked him gently, saying, "To the pines for him, yea, even unto the Cedar of Lebanon."

And they all mocked him.

And there arose among the people, a princely merchant, clad in much tunic and a sword.

And beneath his thumb he bore a ticket.

And he reasoned among the voters for their ballots. And he promised to keep that ticket in his hands.

And he foretold a whitecity and much efficiency, and a new postoffice close to his dwelling place.

And they questioned him and argued with him.

And they said unto him at last, "Go thou, and show unto us, for we come from a far country, yea, even from Missouri."

And there was nothing doing."

And so on!

The citizens went to the polls on May 19th and a thousand cast their ballots. Fred Stork was elected as the first Mayor with a majority of one hundred and four votes. His council was composed of Messrs. F. Mobley, A. A. McIntyre, T. D. Patullo, W. P. Lynch, A. R. Barrow, V. W. Smith, J. H. Hilditch and G. R. Naden, elected in that order.

A tremendous task awaited the new council. They had been shouldered with the responsibilities of a townsite for a city of fifty thousand, and the enthusiasm of the day gave them no reason to suppose that this estimate might not be realized. Their planning, therefore, had to be on the grand scale and they rose to the occasion. A temporary water supply had been established on Hays Creek, a small stream that flowed through the eastern part of the city, and the Provincial Government had commenced the construction of a reservoir on the top of the highest hill in the town, known as Acropolis Hill. This was to be turned over to the new city council, together with the debt incurred in its construction. The supply of water was totally inadequate, and it was obvious that some better source must be found immediately. This situation had been anticipated by the Prince Rupert Light and Power Company who had applied for water rights on Shawatlans Lake, on the mainland nearby. However, the Government had reserved for the City, the rights to water from Woodworth Lake which emptied into Shawatlans, and the city council decided the Woodworth supply was the more desirable since it could be obtained by gravity. Immediate steps were taken to make it available.

The need for electricity was another urgent problem. It had originally been supplied by a company which went bankrupt, and, as we have noted, the city was bound to take over the plant which had been practically destroyed by fire. A steam plant was ordered as a temporary measure, but there were outside companies who were anxious to get the franchise to install hydro power.

Before the incorporation of the city, a group of citizens had begun the organization of a telephone company and this was turned over to the city as soon as the council was set up. The installation was under the supervision of Mr. Ernest Love, who remained in charge until recent years.

Construction of roads and sewers constituted a major problem. The ground was exceedingly hilly and the road grades had been arbitrarily set by the Grand Trunk in the initial survey. Temporary plank roads had been built, in many places elevated many feet in the air to bridge the numerous gulleys. To get down to grade on some streets whole hills of rock had to be blasted out, and on others tremendous rock fills were dumped into the almost bottomless muskeg. Sewers presented the same necessity for blasting to open up the ditches. Immense sums of money had to be obtained and the inevitable high rate of taxation was a heavy burden on the relatively small number of taxpayers.

Last, but not least, a cemetery had to be provided, and following the lead of the Roman Catholic bishop, who obtained a site in the western portion of the city, known as Fairview, the council obtained sixty acres adjoining for the city cemetery. In the earlier days, the cemetery had been located on a small island across the harbor, and the local undertaker, Frank Hart, who also ran a furniture store, had to organize marine funerals. There are many stories told of this man, one of which suggests that his natural thrifty nature inspired him to reclaim the coffin after the funeral party had retired from the island, and before he had closed the grave. He is also supposed to have figured in a midnight escapade which had its humorous side. Frank was called one night to collect a body from a cabin at the end of a long board walk. He took with him as a helper a man whose brawn was superior to his mental powers. After seeing the corpse safely loaded on his helper's back, Frank hurried ahead with the only lantern to get the medical health officer, leaving his assistant to find his way in the dark on the wet and slippery sidewalk. The inevitable happened; Joe slipped and rolled down the bank, losing his burden in the process. He got up and groped around until he found his passenger, struggled up to the walk and eventually reached the undertaking parlors. There he deposited his burden on the slab and wended his way homeward. Hart returned a few minutes later with the doctor, who, after a cursory examination said, "This man's not dead! He's drunk!" Now Hart knew a stiff when he saw one and he had to admit the doctor was right. Where was the corpse? He hastily questioned his helper and then set out with his lantern to solve the mystery. Where Joe had fallen he found the body lying in the ditch! Joe had picked up a drunk who had had the same difficulty negotiating that particular stretch of slippery walk as he had had.

When the city council finally adopted their budget for the first year's work it totalled one hundred and forty-nine thousand dollars and they set a mill rate of fifteen on land with no tax on improvements. This budget included twenty-three thousand dollars for a city hall.

The year 1910 was a fruitful one for the embryo city. Besides the incorporation of the city and the strides made in organizing the public utilities, two important industries made their appearance. Old Country interests began the construction of the Canadian Fish and Cold Storage plant at Seal Cove, a plant which was destined to be the largest cold storage plant, devoted entirely to fish, in the world. It was the forerunner of the halibut industry which eventually played such a large part in the economic life of the city. The Grand Trunk Pacific, this same year, obtained a subsidy from the Dominion Government for the construction of a Drydock and Shipyard. Preliminary surveys were started that fall for a plant capable of handling ships of twenty thousand tons—an important development, for at that time the drydock at Esquimalt was the only other establishment of the kind on the British Columbia coast. It was a year of accomplishment, including as it did the building of the first permanent school and the General Hospital. The citizens were enthusiastic, and all public issues were hotly debated. By this time there were three daily papers in town—the original Empire, the Prince Rupert Optimist, and The Journal. The first and second were keen rivals and spent a great deal of their editorial space berating each other or the members of the city council.

Probably the most important accomplishment of that first city council was the tax agreement with the Railway. The Grand Trunk Pacific objected to paying taxes on their land in the townsite, and were horrified and indignant at the assessment figure of seven million dollars which represented their holdings. They suggested that they should be granted exemption from taxation, since the railroad made the town; but they would be willing to pay five thousand dollars per year for twenty years. The city council stood firm, and it was not until the end of the year that the Grand Trunk Pacific eventually offered to give certain lands and other perquisites to the City, if the council would agree to reduce the assessment to two million dollars, which assessment would be in effect for ten years.

The following year Fred Stork declined to run for mayor and William Manson was elected. He was still the member of the Provincial Legislature for the District, so he had to fill both offices and received considerable criticism as a result. This second council was notable for its acrimony. Every meeting was a hotbed of controversy and the center of the storm was inevitably Sam Newton, the fiery editor of The Empire, who had been elected as an alderman. No one on the council was immune from his attacks, but Alderman Hilditch was the principal victim. Large sums of money were now being spent and the temptation to share in the spoils was too much for many of the councilmen. Petty graft was rampant, and was freely referred to by its proponents as patronage. In spite of this atmosphere, the council did accomplish a great deal. Two important issues, the water supply and the Grand Trunk assessment, were brought to a successful conclusion. A bylaw was passed for five hundred and fifty thousand dollars to develop a water supply from Woodworth Lake and also a hydro-electric plant from the same source. The Grand Trunk Assessment was finally settled by an agreement which called for an annual payment of fifteen thousand dollars for ten years as taxes, and the deeding of numerous park sites and other lands to the City.

The grading of the city streets proceeded apace during 1911. It was a difficult job with a tremendous amount of blasting required to move the rock. It is amazing to read in the papers of those days the repeated accounts of wholesale damage to life and property, and it is literally true to say that no one knew when he might be blown up. The men in charge of the powder were often criminally careless and seemed to have no idea of the extent of the blast they were about to set off.

One of the worst examples of this carelessness was the storing of seventy-five sticks of dynamite with caps attached in a case in the corner of the local blacksmith shop—a nice quiet place! The blacksmith knew it was there, but it had sat harmlessly in the corner for weeks and he had paid no attention. One morning, while working at his anvil, he noticed a spark sail through the air and land on the box of powder. He grabbed his assistant's arm, rushed through the door, and tore off down the street. He had just reached a safe distance when, with a roar and flash of flame, the blacksmith shop soared into the air and was scattered over the surrounding countryside. Nothing was left but a hole in the ground. The neighbouring Central Hotel was a shambles. One guest, asleep on the side nearest the blacksmith shop was awakened by the blow he received as his head hit the floor. He had been lifted bodily out of bed. Every window was shattered and the dining room littered with broken crockery. Other buildings in the neighbourhood fared similarly. Over a thousand windows were broken.

On another occasion a guest was eating his breakfast in the dining room of one of the hotels, when a blast outside sent a shower of rocks through the window, many of which came to rest on his table. It is recorded that such an everyday occurrence disturbed him not at all. He merely remarked to his waitress, "I asked for bread, and you gave me a stone!"

When the site was being cleared for the City Hall, the first blast was a big one. The nearby building of the Mack Realty Company was thoroughly wrecked. No one was hurt, and Mr. MacLaren, the proprietor, remarked, "Although wrecked ourselves, we are not any the less able to insure others against accidents to their buildings from fire, blast, or any other cause."

As usual, labor troubles beset the new council. The going wage in 1910 was thirty-seven-and-a-half cents an hour. The men wanted forty-five cents, and the civic election of 1911 was fought partly on this issue. The men who were elected had come out in favor of the increase. Early in their year of office, the council had been approached by the workmen, and the former had gone on record as approving the forty-five-cent wage and immediately instituted it for all civic employees. The road contracts, however, had been let on estimates based on the old wage scale, and the contractors could not pay the increase without endangering their finances. At any rate, they said they couldn't! Dissatisfaction amongst the labourers steadily mounted, and their organization, the Prince Rupert Industrial Association, finally called a strike. The contractors replied by bringing in fresh men from Vancouver, but these men immediately joined the strikers. Work was at a standstill for some weeks and tension reached the boiling point. The action of the Council in asking the Government to have the cruiser H.M.S. "Rainbow" stand by didn't help matters any, and in the midst of the controversy, McCarvill, the Chief of Police, resigned. The council appointed as his successor, William Vickers, a fortunate choice, as he was able to cope with the climax when it came.

The council refused to amend the contracts, and the contractors refused to give in to the strikers. In fact, the contractors continued to try to obtain men as scab labor, and finally, with Chief Vickers' assurance of police protection, one firm, McInnis and Kelly, got a crew started in their cut on First Avenue. The P.R.I.A. held a meeting, and then, marched in a body to the cut. The police, strengthened by the addition of many of the citizens whose sympathies were now with the contractors, stood in position to protect the gang at work. Rocks started to fly and eventually revolvers came into play, used at first by the strikers and then by the police. Sergeant Phillipson of the police was hit a glancing blow on the forehead by one striker's bullet and one of the strikers slumped to the ground with a bullet in the abdomen. Hand to hand conflict ensued, and slowly the strikers were forced back and eventually were dispersed. Thirty arrests were made, filling the local gaol to overflowing, and the back of the strike was broken. Thus passed into history the "Battle of Kelly's Cut". Some of the men were later released, but the ringleaders were tried in Vancouver and sentenced to prison terms from six months to three years.

Out of those two councils came three men who figured largely in the affairs of the City and District during the ensuing years. Fred Stork, the first mayor, later ran for the Federal House as a Liberal and held the seat for a number of years. T. D. Patullo, an alderman on the first council, was later mayor of the City in 1913, and subsequently was elected to the Provincial Legislature. He held the seat for twenty-five years, and during that time was Minister of Lands and later Premier of the Province and leader of the Liberal party. Finally, Sam Newton, who, as we have already mentioned, was editor of The Empire, became an alderman in 1911, mayor in 1912 and again from 1923 - 27 inclusive was Chief Magistrate of the city.

Those were stirring days in Prince Rupert and unbounded optimism was the order of the day. It is true that at times the money markets of the world did not seem to share the enthusiasm, but the City borrowed from the bank and always managed to dispose of its Bonds eventually. The first cloud on the horizon was the defeat of the Liberal Government at Ottawa, on the issue of Reciprocity, although the Conservatives continued their support of the Grand Trunk Pacific. Then Charles M. Hays, known as "The father of Prince Rupert", lost his life in the sinking of the "Titanic". It is impossible to estimate the far-reaching effects of his sudden passing, for Hays had never recorded his plans in detail, and no one knew the course he intended to pursue. Certainly the Grand Trunk Pacific Railway and the City of Prince Rupert were entirely the children of his brain and he had repeatedly forecast an important role for both in Transcontinental and Pacific trade. With his death, the inspiration was gone, and it was a difficult matter to find someone who could adequately replace him as President of the Railway.

In 1914 came the First World War and like many other communities Prince Rupert and the Skeena Valley responded by sending the flower of their young and middle-aged manhood to Europe. Many of them failed to return, and the loss of so many of the best citizens, augmented by the ravages of the Flu epidemic of 1918, had a stagnating effect on the economy of the District.

The clouds continued to gather, for in 1922 the Grand Trunk Pacific Railway and the rival road, the Canadian Northern, got into financial difficulties, and finally the Dominion Government took over both of them, and amalgamated them to form the Canadian

National Railways. This resulted in the Pacific Coast terminal of the main line being located at Vancouver, and the line from Jasper to Prince Rupert was relegated to a branch standing. Talk of Pacific freighters, subsidiary industries, Railway Hotels, and kindred subjects was now confined to the determined citizens of Prince Rupert, and found no response from the politicians in Ottawa. It is true that an occasional sop was thrown to the local electorate, and in 1920 a Government-owned grain elevator was built, but except for a short flurry of shipping, it was used for storage purposes only.

Following the war, in the rush to replace ships lost in the conflict, orders for the building of ten-thousand-ton freighters were received by the local drydock and shipyard, and the "Canadian Scottish" and the "Canadian Britisher" were launched and commissioned in 1921. The prosperity attendant on these activities was short-lived and when the Depression of 1929 struck it completed the devastation of the City's hopes. A population of approximately six thousand found it impossible to support the financial burden of the debt-ridden city structure, especially since the tax revenues were considerably reduced at this time. Owing to the world-wide depression, much of the property held by outside interests reverted to the city for non-payment of taxes.

The climax was reached in 1933 when the city finally went bankrupt and the Provincial Government appointed Mr. Bracewell as Commissioner to administer the affairs of the town. Mr. Bracewell was followed by Mr. Alder and then by Mr. Mathieson; and by dint of spending the absolute minimum in city maintenance and by refunding the city debt at a lower rate of interest, the city's finances eventually reached solvency and municipal government was once more established in 1943. In the interim, the Second World War had broken out, and American and Canadian forces were stationed in large numbers in the area. The prosperity which ensued contributed materially to the city's recovery.

During these lean years Prince Rupert became indeed a fishing village. With the exception of the payroll of the Railway which was now operating at a basic minimum, the economy of the people was associated exclusively with fish. The halibut fisheries of the north coast had begun long before the days of Prince Rupert, when American companies began to exploit the fishing grounds of Hecate Straits, and built a fish packing plant on Eddy Pass. The Canadian Fish and Cold Storage Company pioneered the halibut fisheries in the city, but they were soon followed by other companies and individual fishermen. The first method used for obtaining halibut was that of the steam trawler, but individually manned schooners introduced the dory and hand lines, and later the power gurdy. So rapidly did the halibut fleet expand, and so plentiful was the supply of fish on the continental shelf, that Prince Rupert became the home port of the foremost halibut fisheries in the world, and the annual landings would total twenty million pounds. To care for this harvest, additional cold storage plants were built and in the early thirties when the price of halibut reached a low ebb, some of the fishermen formed a co-operative association for their own survival. This organization, after its first few years of hazardous existence, has become one of the largest industries on the City's waterfront. With a cold storage plant second in size only to the Canadian Fish and Cold Storage Company, it processes both halibut and salmon, and like the other company has its own reduction plant to handle waste products and herring.

The close proximity of the mouth of the Skeena River brought the city early into the salmon fisheries. A salmon cannery and a reduction plant for waste were both built in the harbour and contributed to the livelihood of many of the citizens.

Reference has been made to the struggles of the infant city to obtain adequate electric lighting. It started with a steam plant which utilised the boilers of the original B.C. Tie and Timber Company at Seal Cove. The hydro power rights on Shawatlans and Woodworth Lakes were owned by the Prince Rupert Power and Light Company and the city purchased these rights from the company for fifteen hundred dollars. They then combined hydro development plans with those for a water supply from Woodworth Lake and eventually built a power house below the dam to supply the city.

In the meantime, the Tsimpsean Light and Power Company had the power rights for Khatada river. They joined forces with the Prince Rupert Power and Light Company to form the Prince Rupert Hydro-electric Company and to strengthen their hand procured the power rights on the Big Falls on the Ecstall River. This new company still tried to interest the city in a franchise to supply light and power, arguing that the needs of industry would soon exceed the limitations of the city's own installation.

A number of Prince Rupert business men, optimistically envisaging a rush of industry with the completion of the railroad, procured land on the mainland adjoining the railroad right of way where it crossed over from Kaien Island. Here they laid out Port Edward townsite, and hastily cleared the land for Prince Rupert's industrial suburb. The Prince Rupert Hydro-electric Company immediately acquired waterfront property and proceeded in 1912 to build a power house, in which they proposed to install diesel engines to generate electricity until their hydro developments at Khatada could be brought to fruition. The townsite was put on the market and sold in March 1913, but the town and power house both "died a-borning", and today the reinforced concrete building still stands, a monument to frustrated speculation.

The suggested shortage in power did in fact occur and in 1929 the city gave the franchise to the Northern B.C. Power Company, a subsidiary of the Power Company of Canada. The new company purchased the city's plant and undertook to develop a hydro-electric plant at Big Falls on the Ecstall River. It was completed in 1939, a dam and power house being erected on the Big Falls capable of generating six thousand horsepower, and the high tension line was run down the east bank of the Ecstall, across the Skeena on towers, and thence into the city through a pass in the mountains. The new plant was capable of expansion, and the city was thus assured of adequate power for its present needs, and for the use of the industry which the Power Company assured the city it was prepared to induce to come into the District. Once again hopes were blasted, for no industry arrived, and it is small wonder that, one by one, the old-timers shook their heads, disposed of their holdings in the bedevilled city and retired to the "sunny south".

CHAPTER FIFTEEN

Fisheries

Of first importance among the natural resources of the Skeena are the fisheries. Although supplanted in recent years by his flathead cousin, the halibut, from olden times the salmon was king. Year after year, the cycle of life was repeated, and the streams and lakes of the upper river came alive with struggling salmon. So bountiful was the supply that the Hudson's Bay Company, as we have noted, invaded the Skeena Basin for the prime purpose of obtaining a reliable source of salmon for food. They had frequently found the runs on the Fraser a failure, due, probably, to the fact that the main run of fish on the Fraser spawned in streams farther south.

There are several types of salmon running up the Skeena— the Spring (Oncorhynchus tshawytscha), the Sockeye (O. Nerka), the Coho (O. Kisutch), the Pink (O. Gorbuscha) or Humpback, and the Dog Salmon (O. Keta). All five have always been taken commercially, but in the mind of the canner, salmon means sockeye.

As early as 1878, when the first cannery was established at Skeena-mouth, an effort was made to capitalise on the silver hordes of the Skeena. For many years the fishing was done with gill nets from Columbia river type sailing boats, and the bulk of the fishing was done in the lower reaches of the river. With the advent of the gasoline engine, the style of boat changed and the fishing area was extended, until now the fisherman ranges out to sea as far as the Queen Charlotte Islands, to meet the homing salmon.

Government regulations, adopted to conserve the fish, have reduced the number of days in the week when fishing may be carried on, and have gradually pushed the up-river fishing boundaries down toward the mouth, thus indirectly contributing to the movement of the fishermen out to sea.

In addition to the use of gill nets which have changed little through the years, the fish are taken now by seine and troll. Canning methods have shown the greatest evolution. In the early days of the fishing industry the work was done largely by hand,

Prince Rupert — 1909

Road Building in Prince Rupert

Kitimat — Plant and Docks

—Courtesy of Alcan

—Courtesy of Wrathalls Photo Finishing

Columbia Cellulose Company Plant on Watson Island, Port Edward

and in this Chinese labor played the predominant role. Cans were made at the cannery before the season started. They were punched out of sheet tin by manually operated machines and soldered. Cooking methods also were primitive. The filled cans were wheeled into large ovens, or retorts, where they were cooked by steam. Two sessions were necessary, as the air had to be released from the can by perforating the top which then had to be resoldered, and then the final cooking took place. The finished product was protected by a heavy coat of lacquer and then gaily bedecked with a gaudy label.

Today the fish are handled largely by machine, and by sealing the cans in a vacuum the necessity for perforating the cans during cooking is avoided. With the modern tin, lacquering also is unnecessary, but the gaudy label still catches the eye of the shopping public. Modern methods enabled the companies to handle larger amounts of fish in fewer establishments, and gradually the numerous canneries at the mouth of the river amalgamated into groups out of which one cannery, strategically placed, operated, while the others were allowed to disintegrate.

At the height of the industry there were eighteen canneries operating. Along the Slough there were five—Inverness, North Pacific, Sunnyside, Cassiar and Dominion, and on the outer side of Smith Island was Oceanic Cannery. In the main river Aberdeen and Haysport were located on the north bank, Alexandria and Balmoral on the east shore of the Ecstall River; A.B.C. Packing Company, Skeena River Commercial Company and R. Cunningham and Son had canneries at Port Essington; and further down the south shore in this order, were Carlisle, Claxton and Standard canneries. Then across the mouth of the river on the shore of Porcher Island was Humpback Bay; and in Porpoise Harbour, hard by the mouth of the Slough, was Port Edward Cannery.

Ultimately these individual units became grouped into three large companies. Only two retained, and still retain, their individual character. Inverness throughout the years remained the property of J. H. Todd and Sons; and Cassiar is still operated by the Cassiar Packing Company. All the canneries in the main river have been abandoned, and today are marked only by a few old piles and disintegrating buildings. The three companies which rose from the ruins are the B.C. Packers Ltd., the A.B.C. Packing Co., and the Canadian Fishing Co. Of these, the B.C. Packers still operate Sunnyside Cannery, and the A.B.C. Packing Co., North Pacific, while the Canadian Fishing Co. have concentrated their activities in Prince Rupert. Port Edward Cannery, after a start as a plant owned by American Interests, is now operated by

Nelson Brothers, a comparative newcomer on the Skeena. So the canning industry, which originally started on the Slough, is once again confined to that small strip of the river.

To follow the salmon in their passage is to see the river in a different light—as a mother welcoming home her brood, and yet, withal, a woman fickle—now wooing with deep pools and sluggish current, now rejecting with thundering cataract and savage waters over jagged rocks. Only the strongest survive, and as if the moods of the river were not hazard enough, along its banks are the Indian fishermen, taking their toll with spear, net and trap; or in shallows the lumbering bear, who, with the amazing speed of his lashing forepaw, whips the unsuspecting salmon on to the bank behind him. Indeed this denizen of the woods is one of the most destructive enemies the salmon has, for he is a gourmand and relishes only one bite from the back of his victim, which he then leaves on the bank, while he wades the stream for more. Behind the salmon comes the hair seal, pursuing his prey as far up the river as Hazelton and even into some of the lakes; while overhead the soaring eagle awaits his chance to pounce on the fish that wanders into the shallows. Amazing that any fish at all reach the spawning grounds, let alone the thousands that finally win through!

Spawning takes place on both lake and stream, but on the former only when there is a shortage of suitable stream beds. Then the gravelly shores of the lake will be used. Primarily the lake is the depot where the adult fish rest from their up-river struggles until they are fully matured and ready to spawn; and where the progeny of that spawning have their home for the following year.

There are two types of lakes on the Skeena watershed:[1] one, the shallow, relatively warm body of water which is free from sediment and rich in vegetable and animal growth; the other, the deep cold lake burdened with glacial silt and comparatively low in animal and vegetable life. Fortunately for the salmon, the first class predominates and the number available would assure the fry of unlimited feed were they the only ones interested. In the same lake, however, we find chub, white-fish and Kokanee using the same feed, and, of course, the fry themselves are fed upon by lake, rainbow and cutthroat trout and squaw-fish, all of which are found in plentiful supply. The cold deep lakes of the second class are not well supplied with food for the fry except in small areas along the shore, and they serve only as connecting links to suitable tributary streams beyond.

As the sockeye wend their way up stream, the first divergence is to Kitsumgalum and Lakelse Lakes. Each of these represents one of the two classes, which is rather remarkable, since they lie in the same valley and are only a few miles apart. Kalum Lake is deep and cold; in fact, parts of its bottom are below sea level, and while it is much larger than Lakelse, the salmon population is only about one quarter of the latter. Lakelse, on the other hand, is an excellent example of the first class of lake, being shallow and of moderate temperature. It is well supplied with feed and supports a large run of salmon. It has the usual collection of other species already mentioned except the Kokanee and Rocky Mountain whitefish, which have not been reported.

When the Kitwanga River is reached, there is a further deflection from the main migration, but one of rather insignificant proportions, as the Kitwanga Lake is not particularly suitable for spawning. The fish, after a sojourn in the lake for maturing, apparently drop back into the Kitwanga River for the actual spawning. This lake is the first to show the presence of the Kokanee, or small sockeye salmon, which completes its life cycle in the lake.

At the Forks of the Skeena, the main division of the run takes place, by far the larger portion proceeding on up the Skeena. There is a substantial run, however, up the Bulkley and these have a strenuous time of it, struggling through the canyon for twenty-five miles until the falls at Moricetown is reached. This obstruction is much too high for the pink salmon, which do their spawning in the small streams below, but the sockeye struggle over it and make their way to the Morice River. For some reason yet unknown, the great majority of the salmon which reach this point choose the Morice rather than the much more slowly moving Bulkley. For sixty or seventy miles they battle their way up the Morice which, although free from water-falls, is studded with rapids, log jams and canyons. Morice Lake, like Kalum, is an example of the cold, deep, heavily-silted glacial lake, and is not conducive to spawning. It merely serves as a passage for the fish, pressing on to the two main spawning areas on the Atna and Nanika Rivers.

The main run of fish up the Skeena heads for Babine Lake, and here, for many years, the Dominion Government operated a hatchery. At the present time, on the upper end of the Babine River, there is a counting fence over which all the fish must pass, so that it is easy to determine the number of sockeye which succeed in reaching this stage of their journey. Their trials, however, are far from over, for their immediate passage after leaving the counting shute, is through narrow Nilkitwa Lake, which is really an expansion of the Babine River, leading into Babine Lake proper. Here the interior Indians congregate and net the fish for their winter food. As many as forty thousand may be taken in this way for smoking and drying.

Babine Lake is a large body of water, deep and cold, and its importance as a spawning area is derived mainly from the excellent spawning streams entering it. Chief of these are Morrison Lake and River, Fulton River and Pinkut or Fifteen Mile Creek. The adult fish arrive in the lake after a trip of approximately thirty days from the sea, and remain in the lake for another month. They then ascend the streams and spawn and die, this period covering approximately two weeks. The eggs hatch by February of the following year, and the embryos lie in the gravel until May or June when they are washed down into the lake by the spring floods. Here they spend a precarious existence, the prey of lake and rainbow trout, and fighting for food with the Kokanees, chub and two types of whitefish, for in this lake the eastern variety is present as well as the Rocky Mountain whitefish. When the ice leaves the lake the following May the sockeye parr, now a full year old, school up and leave the lake, travelling down the river to their unknown destination in the Pacific.

The remainder of the migrant sockeye head for three main spawning areas. The first of these is the Kispiox River which leads westward to a group of lakes bearing the interesting Indian name of Lac-da-dah, otherwise known as the Swan, Chub and Stephens Lakes, and doubly interesting since they lie within a few miles of the Naas Valley and along the trail leading from the Cranberry River to Kispiox—the old Grease route. The second area is Bear Lake which lies in the northeastern portion of the Skeena basin and closely approximates the Driftwood Valley, which empties eastward into the Fraser. The third area is composed of the group of lakes draining into the Sustut River, which river, incidentally, receives the Bear River from Bear Lake. All these lakes fall into the first category, being quite shallow, except Swan Lake which might be termed intermediate. They lie in relatively inaccessible country and are seldom visited. Bear Lake is the only one where there are any permanent dwellings and at this point—the site of the original Fort Connolly—there is a small Indian village of about thirty inhabitants and an independent trader, Mr. Carl Hanawald.

To sum up, while spawning is general throughout the Skeena tributaries, the important sockeye ground is in the Babine Lake, and the future of the fishing industry on the Skeena will depend on the maintenance of that area. In 1951, a disastrous slide occurred along the Babine River seriously obstructing the passage of the salmon. Fortunately it was quickly discovered and as quickly dealt with by the Dominion Government. Temporary measures were taken to assist the fish over the obstruction, and meanwhile a road was cut in from Hazelton to the site of the slide, so that heavy machinery and supplies could be introduced. In short order the slide was cleared and the flow of fish was again unhampered. For one or two years, however, the runs representing the offspring of the 1951 run will be much depleted.

CHAPTER SIXTEEN

Forest Industries

Although of minor importance in the early days, the forest products of the Skeena have rapidly come to the fore since the Second World War, and now rival the Fisheries for first place in the economy of the District. Along the coast and inland over the western slopes of the Coast Mountains, the mild, moist climate of this region produces a luxuriant growth. So densely do the trees grow, that travel by land is virtually impossible except on established trails. Hemlock, Spruce, Balsam and Cedar predominate, and along the lower Skeena there is a considerable stand of Cottonwood. In all, there are over two million, six hundred thousand acres of timber in this area.[1]

The Upper Skeena, Babine and Morice River area comprise another four million acres of forest land. Here the same trees are found but in very different proportions. Cedar is relatively rare and Lodgepole Pine appears in greater quantity. Spruce and Balsam are still plentiful and Hemlock is found in large stands on the Upper Skeena only. On the Babine, Cottonwood again enters the picture.

The early settlers, like the Indians, used the trees for their habitations, either as rough logs, or handsawn boards. Cedar, because of its straight grain, was split with wedges to form planks and shakes. The first sawmill was established by Duncan at Metlakatla, and other mills followed at Port Essington and Georgetown, just south of Port Simpson, and up the river at Kispiox and Minskinish. These mills, however, were small and did not adequately supply the needs of the district, so that lumber was brought up from the southern coast. In most cases, these early mills were operated by water power. Later on, steam plants made their appearance and the lumbering industry slowly expanded, new mills appearing up the Skeena and Bulkley as the communities developed.

With the coming of the railroad a new use for timber was introduced—the production of poles and ties. Trees suitable for this purpose were found on the upper Skeena, and the new industry thrived all the way from Kitwanga to Houston. The development of this industry was largely the work of one man, Olaf Hanson.

Olaf Hanson was born in Tannas, Sweden, and he emigrated to the United States when he was eighteen years old. After a short stay south of the border, he moved north into Alberta in 1904, and settled near Stoney Plain. As the Grand Trunk Pacific pushed its way west, he got work with the railroad cutting ties. It proved profitable and he decided to follow the railroad west. He walked the right of way across the mountains until he came to the Skeena, and there set up in business. He formed the Hanson Lumber Company with headquarters at Prince Rupert, and a branch office in Smithers, and took the contract for cutting all the poles and ties for the railway company, subletting the contract to individual operators. The ties were taken by road to the railway, but the poles were spilled into the Skeena in the spring and trapped by a boom placed across the river at Cedarvale. Here they were hoisted out of the water and stacked beside the railroad for loading on flat cars. The pole and tie business is still a profitable enterprise, and in 1954 resulted in the production of forty thousand hand-hewn ties and two million feet of poles and piling.

Mr. Hanson became a prominent citizen of the north. For thirty-two years he was the Swedish Consul, at first for the whole of British Columbia and later for the northern part of the Province. In 1930 he was elected Liberal member for the Federal House and served in that capacity for fifteen years, being re-elected twice. With his retirement from politics, he was considered a likely appointee for the next vacancy in the Senate, but his health failed and he died in 1952, at the age of seventy.

With the conclusion of the Second World War, there was a great demand for lumber, and small mills, in most cases powered by gasoline motors, blossomed out all along the Skeena and Bulkley Rivers. The boom has continued unabated, and in 1954 there were one hundred and eighty mills in the area which cut a total of nearly eighteen million cubic feet of sawlogs. This was exclusive of the Forest Management License, which produced another six million, seven hundred thousand, for a grand total of twenty-four million, four hundred thousand cubic feet.

During the same postwar period, another use for timber was developed on the lower Skeena. The Columbia Cellulose Company, interested in manufacturing high grade alpha pulp for textiles, approached the Provincial Government for a timber reserve. The deal, which was ultimately consummated, marked a new departure in the handling of the timber resources of the country. The Government issued a Forest Management License covering six hundred thousand acres in the Skeena and Naas Valleys and the adjacent coast. It is estimated to contain three billion cubic feet of timber.

There are four main objectives involved in Forest Management as outlined by the Provincial Government. They are—
(1) To regulate the annual cut from the forest, so that it balances the yearly growth.
(2) To improve the forest crop by silvicultural treatment.
(3) To keep the forest land productive at all times, reforesting if necessary.
(4) To protect our forests from fire, insects and disease.

The Columbia Cellulose Company are able to use approximately ninety percent of the timber in their reserve. Since they must log off their land completely, to permit of regrowth, the remaining ten or twelve percent, which is composed largely of cedar, has to be disposed of in the open market. At the present time, this timber is being shipped to the southern part of the Province, an economically unsound procedure. There is, therefore, an opportunity for the establishment of a large mill somewhere in the neighbourhood of the Pulp Plant, to utilize this large quantity of good quality cedar.

Cottonwood is another log which is not particularly suitable for pulp, although a small proportion may be used. It is used extensively in the production of plyboard, and Skeena River cottonwood logs have been shipped in recent years to the plywood mills at the mouth of the Fraser River. Before the war, one or two trial shipments were made to the Orient, for the production of matches.

As long as the demand for lumber exists, the future of the industry in the Skeena area is assured. The supply, under modern methods of forest management, is unlimited; the means of transportation by road, rail and water is now adequate; and overseas markets are being developed, with export through the Port of Prince Rupert. All indications are that forest products will continue to make a large contribution to the development of the economy of the District.

CHAPTER SEVENTEEN

Mining[1]

The mountains of the Skeena Valley are highly mineralized, but, so far, the veins discovered have been small, although occasionally of rich deposit. For this reason, mining activity has always been sporadic, production depending on the height of the world market for that particular metal. With the exception of the Silver Standard, no large body of ore which would permit of long term development has been discovered.

The earliest activity in this sphere was placer mining and gold was discovered on several creeks—Lorne, Chimdemash, Fiddler and Kleanza. These streams were worked from time to time and Lorne particularly had quite a rush. The early newspapers claimed that approximately two million dollars' worth of gold was taken out of Lorne Creek but the official Government estimate is seventy thousand. It was extensively worked by the Dry Hill Hydraulic Mining Company in recent years but with indifferent success. Placer mining is still being carried out on the Kleanza. In addition there has been gold in small quantities found on Philips and Porcupine creeks, and up the Kitseguecla River; and Douglas Creek on Kitsumgalum Lake has been a small steady producer for many years.

Until the present, mineral deposits have been found mainly in two areas. The first discoveries were in the region of the Kitselas Canyon and the first claim was filed in 1893. This was followed by a rush of claims and the development work on some of the properties resulted, as has been mentioned, in opening up the country toward Kitamat with trails. The mineral deposits were gold, silver and copper, and some of the showings were quite rich, but no large body of ore was brought to light. No real production occurred but several companies made initial shipments of hand picked ore. In two cases small mills were installed and production went on for a time. One of these, the Columario mine, is on Kleanza mountain. The company installed a complete mining plant and a flotation mill with a capacity of seventy-five tons. This plant operated only for ten months in 1934-35. The Cordillera Mine on Kitselas mountain also was developed to the point where a small amalgamation mill was installed which in 1921 produced some gold, silver and copper.

There are several hundred properties in the Terrace-Usk area and the region has been only partially prospected. None of the present discoveries appear to be too exciting, but undoubtedly the possibilities of a great mine in the district exist, and such a discovery may yet be made.

The second area is the mountainous country in the vicinity of Hazelton. Hazelton lies between two big and rich mineral belts. That to the south covers Rocher de Boule mountain, and the prevailing ore is high grade chalcopyrite with good gold values. To the north are the Glen, Four and Nine Mile mountains and these are covered with good outcroppings of lead and silver. The most important mine on Rocher de Boule was the mine of the same name, and it was developed to the production stage in 1914 with the installation of a hydro-electric power plant and an aerial tramway to transport the ore to the railroad. The outbreak of war, however, brought mining activity to a standstill. The other important mine on this mountain was the Red Rose. In addition to the usual gold-copper showings, this mine has a low value of Tungsten, and in recent years has been operating under contract to the United States Government. This contract has now been terminated and the cost of producing the Tungsten is such that it cannot be profitably marketed at the present world price. The mine has therefore shut down again.

The deposits of silver and lead occurring in the mountains of the Babine range have so far proven to be the only ones commercially productive. In fact, the first shipment of ore from the District was made from the Harris Mines in that area, in 1913.[2] This was followed by a much larger consignment from the Silver Standard and the latter has been the one consistent producer in the Hazelton area. At the present time it is the only one in operation.

Here again, prospecting has only scratched the surface. The upper Skeena, in which a mine at Kisgegas was once developed, offers a tremendous area of unexplored territory. The same condition prevails in the presently known properties as existed in the Terrace area, namely, small concentrations of relatively rich deposits. The discovery of a large body of ore is still possible, and the whole Skeena Valley is well worth prospecting.

To the eastward, the Hudson's Bay Mountain almost duplicates the picture at Hazelton, and here the Duthie Mine has been operating intermittently for years.

Throughout the whole Skeena district there is to be found

a scattering of coal deposits. These are mostly concentrated in the region around Telkwa and the Hunter basin, although occurring in some quantity also up the Kitseguecla River. The Telkwa Coal Mines have been in production since the coming of the railroad but the output has never been adequate to supply all the needs of the district. After the war the demand for coal for the Columbia Cellulose plant at Port Edward stepped up the shipments from the mine at the expense of the local needs. Now the pulp plant is changing over to oil and as the railroad gradually becomes dieselised, the outlook for further coal production is not too bright.

Two further mineral deposits should be mentioned. In the valley of the Kwinitsa creek a surface oozing of brine was discovered and investigated by Mr. D. C. Whiteford. Test holes were bored and at a depth of two hundred feet a bed of rock salt was encountered. Some attempts were made to develop this discovery to economic production, and a small plant with evaporating pans was established, but salt was never produced in commercial quantities. The analysis of the brine showed a mixture of Sodium Chlorite, Magnesium Sulphate and Calcium Chloride totalling 3689 grams per gallon. Since sea water is 2346 grams per gallon, this does not represent a very great concentration, and indeed it is probable that the salt bed is derived from this source, as Kwinitsa is the upper limit of tidal flow, and at one time this portion of the Skeena valley was undoubtedly an arm of the sea.

Up the Ecstall River, near the confluence of Johnson Creek, is a large deposit of iron and sulphur, upon which considerable development work has been done. A large body of ore has been blocked out and it seems likely that eventually this mine will go into production. The location is not very far from salt water in Douglas Channel, and the proximity of cheap power at Kitamat is expected to make possible the establishment of a smelter.

CHAPTER EIGHTEEN

Hunting and Fishing

This is the last large area of relatively unexplored country in the West, where game and sport fish abound. The scarcity of roads has kept it virgin territory for the hunter and fisherman. With the building of the highway and the popularity of the aeroplane, the situation is rapidly changing.

In the early days, the larger game animals were very scarce, and even deer were hard to get. Recently the moose has been working his way westward until he has reached salt water at the head of one or two inlets, and on the Skeena is commonly seen as far west as Kwinitsa. Moose occur in large numbers on the central plateau, particularly around Babine Lake, so much so that the road running from Topley to Babine has been called the "Slaughter-house". Hunters walk the road in the morning and evening and seldom fail to get at least one moose crossing between the meadows on either side. In the winter, the animals congregate in the willow patches along the Bulkley Valley and the passenger will soon get tired counting the moose to be seen from the window, through the leafless trees, as his train winds slowly along the valley floor.

Deer are of the mule tail variety in the up-country, while along the lower reaches of the river, the coast deer may be found. As the Game Department has instituted a campaign for the extermination of wolves, the deer population should increase; but even now, they are plentiful in certain districts, notably from Telkwa to Houston.

Since this is a mountainous country, goat and sheep abound; the former on the mountains of the Coast Range, the latter further inland, for example on the mountains of Babine and the Hunter basin. In the same region, grizzly bear are found while black bear are numerous all along the river, particularly in the fall when the salmon are running.

Procuring sheep, goat and grizzly requires considerable preparation and a fairly strenuous trip. For years, guides with well-equipped pack trains have been available at Hazelton, and more recently at Smithers and Telkwa. An enquiry directed to the local Game Warden will always bring forth a list of licensed guides.

In the realm of smaller game, the most popular pursuit is grouse-hunting, grouse being plentiful all through the Skeena District. On the lower levels willow and spruce grouse are found, while on the mountains the blue grouse is obtained. The latter is a wonderful game bird, weighing as much as or more than a good sized chicken.

The Skeena is not particularly noted for an abundance of ducks and geese as it lies slightly west of the main fly-way. Nevertheless, there is good flight shooting on Babine Lake in the fall, and in the tidal stretches of the river there are flocks of birds which winter in the district.

It is in sport fishing that this region particularly excels. Any type of fishing can be obtained in sufficient quantity to delight the heart of the most ardent angler. Around Prince Rupert and the mouth of the river, deep sea trolling for salmon is popular for nine months of the year, spring salmon and cohoe being caught in this manner, in season. When the cohoe are running they can be caught on spinning gear from a position on the shore around the mouth of the creeks, using a golf tee spinner. Such cohoe streams as Cloyah creek ten miles out of Prince Rupert on the main highway then become the mecca for young and old alike, as they swarm over the rocks, right beside the road, and cast their lures into the schools of fish waiting to ascend the creek. This same creek is a popular place to take steelhead trout during the late winter and early spring, although the best fishing for steelhead is found up the Skeena itself. Two tributaries of the Skeena are outstanding—the Copper River near Terrace, and the Kispiox River above the village. In 1954 the world record steelhead was taken from this latter stream. On the Bulkley, the Morice River is equally famous for its run of steelhead, and local sportsmen take the fish in this river on the fly.

Trout fishing can be enjoyed everywhere in the district. In the lower portion of the river cutthroat and Dolly Varden predominate, but in the lakes, a so-called "rainbow trout" is taken which is really a young steelhead. In the lakes of the interior the true rainbow occurs, otherwise known as the Kamloops trout. This is the finest game fish to be found, and in the larger lakes reaches immense proportions, requiring heavy tackle for its capture. It is quite common to take three and four pounders on the fly, but on the troll they can be caught up to twenty pounds.

It is difficult to say which lakes are the best; they all have their local supporters. Lakelse lake and river were famous in the earliest days, and, in fact, were often called Trout Creek and

Lake. Near Hazelton, and right beside the Highway, is Sealey Lake, a rather unusual lake in that it is quite shallow and requires a skilled angler to catch the "big ones". There are many other small lakes which in most cases are over-populated with fish, and in some the presence of squaw fish spoils the sport fishing.

Without doubt the finest fishing is to be obtained on Babine Lake and its tributaries. Two roads are built into this lake. The one from Burns Lake goes to Pendleton Bay near the head of the lake, and from there it is an easy trip to Fifteen Mile Creek. Only the lower half mile of creek can be fished but beautiful three and four pound rainbow can be taken on the fly in the pools and riffles. Around the mouth larger trout can be caught on the troll. The second road goes in from Topley, but it is longer and not in as good condition. It reaches the lake about two-thirds down the west shore, right by the mouth of the Fulton River. This river is about four miles long and there are large falls where it drains out of the lake of the same name. The fishing is good at the mouth of the lake and all along the river, particularly in the pools. The writer has taken three-and-a-half-pound rainbow out of the famous Millionaire Pool on wet fly.

Similar fishing conditions are found in Morrison Lake and river on the east shore, but the finest fishing of all is obtained at the outlet of Babine Lake, where the counting fence has been put in for the Fisheries Department. Here the size of the rainbow taken is limited only by the strength of the tackle used, and even a rank amateur can catch his limit. Truly Babine Lake is the angler's paradise, and the supply of fish is so great that there is little likelihood of intensive fishing spoiling the grounds.

We have made no mention of the char which occur in these inland lakes, as they are not a very sporty fish. They stay at great depths and heavy weights on the line are required or, better still, a fine copper line. However, they can be taken on the troll up to forty pounds and are excellent eating.

CHAPTER NINETEEN

Destiny

It is an ironical fact that, whereas the First World War resulted in the stagnation of the Skeena District, the Second World War brought it into its own. The port and railroad, which in peace had been steadfastly ignored as a medium of trade and commerce, was suddenly thrust upon the national consciousness as a potential line of invasion for a determined enemy.

Even before the outbreak of war in September 1939, it had been decided to fortify the harbour of Prince Rupert, and construction had started on two forts, one on either side of the entrance to the harbour. The western one was built at Frederic Point on Digby Island, while the eastern was at Barrett Point on Kaien Island. When hostilities started, Headquarters for Prince Rupert Defences were set up with Colonel S. D. Johnston in charge, and the forts were temporarily manned by the members of the local militia, known as the 102nd Battery.[1]

Looking back now on those hectic days one wonders just what was in the minds of the military or the Government, that so much preparation was made in the area. Certainly there was not the remotest possibility that a European enemy would attempt invasion of Canada through Prince Rupert, and the main thought in the early days of the war seems to have been to have available a safe harbour for units of the British and Canadian navies. Later, when Japan entered the War the picture changed and the possibility of invasion could no longer be ignored.

At first, troop activities were confined to manning the Forts and guarding the Drydock and Shipyard, and the bridge across the Skeena at Skeena Crossing. Guards were also placed on the railroad bridge at Zenardi Rapids. Even this amount of duty was too much for the limited strength of the 102nd, and re-inforcements were sent almost immediately in a detachment of the Irish Fusiliers. They were the first of a steady flow into and out of the district of many of the Canadian regiments—Canadian Scottish, Rocky Mountain Rangers, Edmonton Fusiliers, 9th Heavy Battery R.C.A., Midland Regiment, Winnipeg Grenadiers, Sault

Ste. Marie and Sudbury and Prince of Wales Rangers. In addition there were units of the Navy and Airforce.

To supplement the work of the Forts, examination vessels were posted at both entrances to the harbour and the openings closed with booms and submarine nets. Overzealous officials and careless and defiant civilian skippers occasioned numerous "incidents" at the harbour entrances, most of which, on retrospect, were more humorous than serious. The only casualty occurred amongst the defenders in the famous "Battle of Barrett Point", which is tersely recorded in the Headquarters Diary— "A private of the Canadian Scottish at Barrett Fort accidentally fired his rifle, the bullet going through the walls of two huts, a bandolier, glass windows, folded blankets and finally lodging in the left buttock of Gunner Shelford."

Early in 1940 it was decided to build ships at the Drydock and Shipyard, and the keels were laid for two mine-sweepers. Four of this type of ship were built, and so successfully, that it was decided to continue this yard in operation. Ten thousand-ton freighters were then turned out and thirteen in all completed. Before the shipyard was finally closed two China Coasters were added to the list. To a large extent, men for this construction had to be brought in; and housing them, with their families, was a big problem. War Time Housing, a Dominion Government Corporation, stepped in and constructed four and six room houses, a whole new section of the City being thus opened up, between Hays Creek and Seal Cove. This area was named Rushbrook Heights after the pioneer missionary of that name, whose home had been built there many years before. In addition, several large staff houses for single men and a large dining hall were built.

The Airforce activity was centered in Seal Cove, where a seaplane base was hurriedly constructed by blasting a hillside into the water to make room for hangars and barracks. It was ready to receive its first flight of Sharks on December 11, 1941.

Navy development was housed at the eastern end of the Canadian National Docks, and barracks and drill hall were built on adjoining waterfront property.

This was the stage of preparedness of the Port when the attack on Pearl Harbour signalled for the entry of the Americans into the War. The discovery of Prince Rupert by the Americans would almost seem to have been an accident. There had been a steady stream of men and supplies going north to Alaska and occasionally a ship would come to grief. One such, the "Kvichak", was sunk just north of Millbank Sound and was eventually raised by a local salvage company and brought to the Drydock for repair. In January 1942, an American transport ran aground off the mouth of the Skeena River, and troops and supplies were rescued and taken to Prince Rupert. They were under the command of Lt. Col. Adams, and this officer remained in the city while his ship was floated, repaired at the local Drydock and sent on its way. He must have been impressed with the possibilities of the Port as a point for trans-shipment to Alaska for during the next month the American Government decided to make a trial use of Prince Rupert for the shipping of men and materials to their northern territory. Col. Adams was appointed U.S. Port Commandant.

As usual, the Americans, once their mind was made up, moved with despatch. The Ocean Dock was enlarged to twice its size, and a huge warehouse constructed adjacent to the dock. To house their numerous employees and troops, a large area on Acropolis Hill was obtained from the City and there a small town consisting of barracks, mess halls and large recreational hall was laid out. Office space was eventually obtained by constructing a large administration building on waterfront property close to the warehouse.

This activity in the city was only the beginning. The American Army took over the townsite of Port Edward, and there built a town for some three thousand troops, thus forming a staging area for the passage of troops to and from Alaska. Watson Island, close by in Zenardi Rapids, was used for an immense ammunition dump, and this required the building of large docks for the accommodation of ocean-going freighters.

While this was going on the Canadian Government had not been idle. The entrance of Japan into the War had necessitated the development of defences along the Skeena Valley, and a brigade of troops was posted along the railroad from Prince Rupert to Prince George. Brigade headquarters were established in Terrace on June 1st, 1942, with Brig. Hodson in command, and an armoured train was used for communications. The Airforce also moved in and airfields were constructed at Terrace, and Smithers, and an emergency strip at Woodcock on the banks of the Skeena midway between the two.

Rapid communication between the various units was still dependent on one railway line which could easily be, and frequently was, disrupted by slides, floods and derailments. In March 1942, the two Governments decided to build a highway along the Skeena as a joint Defence Project. They had already embarked on a similar scheme for a Highway to Alaska, north from Edmonton, so it was a natural development. The Skeena road was already in existence as far west as Cedarvale, although much of it was nothing more than a wagon road, and there was a bridge across the Skeena at Terrace. Contracts were let to civilian companies from Ontario and British Columbia and the work pushed forward as rapidly as possible. It was a major undertaking, however, and the stretch from Prince Rupert through the mountains to the Skeena Valley was heavy rock work. It was completed and officially opened on September 4, 1944.

With the end of the war all military activity faded away as quickly as it had come, and the American personnel returned to their homes with a haste which belied their protestations of regret at having to leave such a hospitable country. The buildings and installations were not so easily obliterated, and through international agreement they passed under the control of a Dominion company, the War Assets Corporation. The citizens of Prince Rupert suddenly found themselves in peaceful possession of their city once more. The war years had seen it change from a town of six thousand inhabitants to one whose maximum population, estimated at the height of activities, was in the neighbourhood of twenty thousand. While there were certain disadvantages such as damaged roads, and while the now elapsed life span of waterworks and sewers had resulted in a deplorable condition in both these utilities, there were a number of assets to be noted too. Many of the buildings and installations were of a permanent nature and were now available for peace-time use. The enlarged ocean dock, the seaplane base, the Military Hospital, the Y.M.C.A. War Services building, the American Administration Building, an elementary school and the hundreds of homes built for Drydock workers, all fitted into the civilian set-up. With the exception of the permanent military establishments, the remaining military buildings, all of lock-stave construction, were removed and shipped away. Thus, in short order, all traces of the military camps were removed.

This same dismantling occurred at Port Edward and Watson Island, except for the large docks and railroad sidings, and it looked for a time as though nature was going to be allowed to sweep in and cover the scars of war-time activity.

In the hinterland the chief asset was the gravel road which now extended continuously from Prince Rupert to Prince George and so connected up with the roads of the continent. This road was eventually turned over to the Provincial Government, and now forms part of the Provincial system of roads. It was far from being up to first class standards but, nevertheless, was quite passable for most months of the year. When its reconstruction, which is now proceeding, is completed it will rank as one of the finest scenic routes on the continent. Military buildings, which shortly fell into civilian use, were left standing at Terrace and well-equipped airfields at Terrace and Smithers were turned over to the Department of Transport.

It was inconceivable to the citizens of the area that all these assets should be allowed to go to waste, and Boards of Trade and Chambers of Commerce immediately began to explore possibilities. In some cases local organizations and groups took advantage of the opportunities, and in Prince Rupert and Terrace, Civic Centre Associations obtained and operated recreational facilities. The Civic Centre at Prince Rupert is the finest of its type in the Province. The American Administration building in Prince Rupert was saved by a group of public-spirited citizens who purchased it for conversion to a much-needed apartment house. Military hospitals were turned to profitable account by various agencies, instead of being torn down. The one in the City of Prince Rupert was used as a welcome addition to the local civilian hospital. A large hospital built for the Airforce, just outside the city limits at Miller Bay, was opened for Indians with tuberculosis, by the Department of Indian Affairs. In Terrace, the military hospital was taken over by the Provincial Government and operated as a mental home for elderly people.

The greatest peacetime conversion, however, was the purchase of the Watson Island installations by the Columbia Cellulose Company, a subsidiary of Canadian Chemical and Cellulose Company of Montreal. The establishment of this company in the north was dependent on procuring a steady source of suitable timber for pulp purposes. This was guaranteed by the issuance, by the Provincial Government, of the first forest management license in the Province. This license covers a large belt of timber in the Skeena and Naas Valleys and adjacent coastal lands, containing six hundred thousand acres. The predominant trees are hemlock, spruce and balsam which are used for the production of high alpha pulp, and the principle of the forest license is that, each year, only an amount equal to the annual growth is logged off, so that the supply of timber will never be depleted.

The Columbia Cellulose Company built a forty million dollar plant on Watson Island, using the facilities left behind by the Americans, including the thirty-seven hundred feet of dockage. It was opened on June 11, 1951 and produces three hundred and seventy tons of pulp a day. The woods activity centers largely in the Terrace area, and a road is being built up the Kalum Valley to the west of the lake, to extend eventually into the Naas Valley. With seven hundred men employed in mill and woods, it is easy to imagine what this has done for the economy of the City of Prince Rupert and the town of Terrace. The permanent payroll in Prince Rupert has stabilized the economic life of the community and was one of the principal factors in maintaining occupancy in the many houses built for the Drydock workers. In fact, the postwar population increased so much that these houses were not nearly adequate, and a further low cost housing project was necessary to produce an additional fifty homes.

In Terrace, the military buildings were taken over by the Columbia Cellulose Company, and over night the village found itself booming. Property values soared and the town became a hive of industry. The boom, however, soon settled down to a steady growth, which was strengthened by the neighbouring development of Kitimat and the Alcan project.

The Aluminum Company of Canada power development is primarily concerned with the Fraser River, not the Skeena, since it gets its water from the lakes of Tweedsmuir Park which drain into the Fraser via the Nechako River. The utilization of this power required a townsite with rail and sea connection, and Kitimat was finally settled upon as the only place within reach of the power lines.

Much has been written about this five hundred million dollar development and only a short description is needed here. Briefly, the project involved damming the Nechako River and making one large lake of the Tweedsmuir chain. This was accomplished by an immense earth fill in the valley of the Nechako, known as the Kenney Dam, and with its completion the waters of the Park began to rise. In the meantime, a ten-mile tunnel was cut through the Coast Range of mountains, emerging in the Kemano River valley, thus diverting the impounded water down this stream to the ocean. Here a power house was blasted out of the mountainside, and the power lines were carried from this point across another mountain to the town of Kitimat.[2] This power development has a potential of two and a quarter million horse-power, but only a little less than one quarter is being used at the present time. The aluminum smelters and the City of Kitimat are being built on both sides of the Kitamat River, using the water-front across the bay from the old Indian village, and extending for several miles up the valley. This has been a tremendous under-taking which has caught the imagination of the whole country, for it was proposed to take an area of virgin forest and there build a city which would eventually house fifty thousand people.

The building of the dam, tunnel, power house and trans-mission line was undertaken by the Morrison Knudsen Company, and work started in February 1951. Kitimat Constructors—a combination of eight contracting firms from the southern part of the Province—had the task of clearing the land and building the town and smelter. They began in April of the same year. So great was the concentration of men and machinery, that the Municipality of the District of Kitimat was incorporated and elected its first Council just two years later; and the first ingot of aluminum was poured in August 1954. The first installation consisted of two pot lines with an annual production of 90,000 tons. Additional pot lines have been and are continuing to be added, with the objective of producing over 300,000 tons per annum by 1960.

Its impact on the Skeena will be incalculable. Already its population has passed the ten thousand mark and its growth will continue for years to come. The immediate effect was manifested in a demand for rail connection. As related elsewhere, the Provincial Government granted a charter for a railway up the Kitamat valley; and this charter was purchased by the Grand Trunk Pacific Railway. In fact, work on this line was the first activity of the Grand Trunk Pacific in the Skeena valley, although it was short-lived. Now, fifty years later, the Canadian National Railways fulfilled the objective of the original charter by building a branch line from Terrace, up the Lakelse valley, across the divide and down the Kitamat River to the new City of Kitimat. The first passenger train entered Kitimat on January 14, 1955.

A highway will not be long following the railroad. It is already in existence to the end of Lakelse Lake, approximately half of the way; surveys have been completed for the balance; and construction was started in 1956. With the entire length of the road expected to be opened in late 1957, the new city's integration into the economy of the Skeena will be accomplished.

Perhaps the most significant development of the war years, insofar as the Skeena is concerned, is the mutual awareness which one finds in Alaska and this portion of Canada. War-time traffic demonstrated the feasibility of the Canadian National-Prince Rupert route for supplying Alaska, and the people of that northern territory have evinced a lively interest in the potentialities of neighbouring Canada for producing their agricultural needs. Rapid and economical transportation is the key to the situation, and this has been supplied by the construction of loading facilities for a car ferry on the waterfront at Prince Rupert. Such a ferry service is now in operation, and the products of a pulp mill located at Ketchikan, Alaska, are regularly brought to railhead at Prince Rupert for shipment east. The route has now been established; it only remains for it to be used.

And so the Dawn of Prosperity has finally broken for the Skeena. All along its banks, lumbering has blossomed since the

171

war; mining has had a new lease on life and the prospects for the future are good; the rich agricultural lands of the Skeena, Terrace, Kispiox and Bulkley valleys are still there, waiting for the plough; industry on the grand scale has come to stay; the markets of Kitimat, Prince Rupert and Alaska are waiting to be supplied. It only requires men of vision, initiative and energy to make this the agricultural bread-basket of Northern British Columbia and Alaska. Destiny calls the People of the Skeena! Destiny calls; and must not be denied!

BIBLIOGRAPHY

Chapter One

1—Further Remarks on the Voyage of John Meares, Esq., London 1791, p. 26.
2—British Columbia Atlas of Resources.

Chapter Three

1—History of the Northern Interior of British Columbia, Morice.
2—Ibid.
3—Ibid.
4—It is very likely that this was, in reality, "oolichan grease", brought in from the Naas River fisheries and used as a medium of trade by the Tsimpseans.
5—History of the Northern Interior of British Columbia, Morice.

Chapter Four

1—British Columbia Place Names: Walbran, page 394.
2—Ibid, page 397.
3—Journal of John Wark, Memoir No. X, Archives of B.C.
4—The Apostle of Alaska: Arctander, page 51.
5—Manuscript of Charles Morrison; copy in author's possession.
6—B.C. Place Names: Walbran.

Chapter Five

1—The Apostle of Alaska. Page 22.
2—Rules as listed by Arctander in Apostle of Alaska, page 154:
    (1) To give up their "Hallied", or Indian deviltry.
    (2) To cease calling in conjurors when sick.
    (3) To cease gambling.
    (4) To cease giving away their property for display.
    (5) To cease painting their faces.
    (6) To cease drinking intoxicating drinks.
    (7) To rest on the Sabbath.
    (8) To attend religious instruction.
    (9) To send their children to school.
    (10) To be clean.
    (11) To be industrious.
    (12) To be peaceful.
    (13) To be liberal and honest in trade.
    (14) To build neat houses.
    (15) To pay the village tax.

Chapter Six

1—British Columbia: F. W. Howay, Vol. 2, Chap. 1, page 1.
2—Hunting for Gold: Downie.
3—Ibid.

4—It is more likely to have been Donald Manson, who was sent up the Skeena by Ogden in October 1832. He went up the Skeena for about fifty miles by canoe—the first recorded trip. John Wark did not come up the coast until 1835. H. B. Co. Archives B 201/a/2.

5—Manuscript of Charles Morrison.

Chapter Seven

1—Information supplied by Robert Tomlinson.

2—Victoria Colonist, March 10, 1871.

3—Ibid, April 19, 1871.

4—"Klondike Mike" was a famous freighter in the Yukon during the Gold Rush of '98 and after.

5—Victoria Colonist, Aug. 20, 1872.

6—H. B. Co. Archives B 226/b/45, fos. 178-9.

7—British Columbia Coast Names, Walbran, page 533.

8—"The Sun" of Port Essington, Oct. 12, 1907.

9—Cunningham Diaries, manuscript in archives of Diocese of Caledonia.

10—Skeena District News, Vol. 1, No. 10.

11—Wiggs O'Neill in Omineca Herald, Dec. 16, 1954.

Chapter Eight

1—Old Indian name for Bulkley River.

2—H. B. Co. Archives B. 226/b/35.

3—H. B. Co. Archives B. 201/a-9 Port Simpson Journal.

4—Peter O'Reilly, born in Ince, Lancashire, Eng., educated in Trinity College, Dublin. Came to British Columbia in 1858, was gold commissioner, Judge of County Court, Member of Legislative Council and Indian Reserve Commissioner. Died in 1905.

5—Victoria Colonist, Oct. 4, 1871.

6—H. B. Co. Archives B. 226/b/51, fo. 168 Charles to W. J. Walsh, June 26, 1880.

7—H. B. Co. Archives B. 235/e/30.

8—Original copies of this journal are on file in the Provincial Archives.

9—Appointed Indian Agent on July 11, 1889.

10—Victoria Colonist, Oct. 18, 1874.

11—H. B. C. diary from the post at Hazelton, kept by Lyons and later by Sargent. Now in the possession of Mrs. R. S. Sargent.

12—Before the coming of the Banks, the Hudson's Bay Company and Robert Cunningham issued their own currency in small denominations up to a dollar, which they used in trading. The Hudson's Bay Company coins were made from copper and Cunningham's from brass. When the practice was discontinued, the Hudson's Bay Company dumped their supply of coins in the harbour of Port Simpson. A considerable quantity of the Cunningham coins is in the possession of Col. S. D. Johnston of Prince Rupert. Both issues may be seen in the Museum of Northern British Columbia at Prince Rupert.

13—See the Trail of the Gold Seekers by Hamlin Garland—Macmillan & Co.

Chapter Nine

1—Bureau of Provincial Information. Bulletin No. 9 (1904).
2—Bureau of Provincial Information. Bulletin No. 9, page 5—extract from Bulletin No. 3 published in 1902.
3—Manuscript by Frank Dockrill—copy in author's possession.
4—"iktus"—a Chinook term meaning "belongings".
5—Several letters from F. L. Stephenson appearing in the North British Columbia News.
6—Omineca Herald—Vol. 1, No. 23.

Chapter Ten

1—T. P. Lyster Mulvany entered the Skeena area in 1901. He was employed as packer, guide and prospector etc., and became one of the best known characters of the north. His ability to tell a "tall" story added to his fame. He finally settled in Burns Lake where he became one of the leading citizens and for years was a magistrate. He is now retired but still actively engaged in writing.
2—Omineca Herald—personal reminiscences by H. L. Frank.
3—Verbal account given the author by George Little. Notes made at the time in the author's possession.

Chapter Eleven

1—History of Catholic Church in Western Canada—Morice.
2—History of Northern Interior of British Columbia—Morice.
3—Quotation from History of Northern Interior of B.C.—Morice.
4—Fifty Years in Western Canada—Ryerson Press.
5—History of Northern Interior of B.C.—Morice.
6—Translation supplied by G. Forbes, O.M.I., of original French document inserted in the oldest Baptismal Record kept at St. Augustine's Rectory, 2015 West 8th Avenue, Vancouver. Document is in Father Lejacq's handwriting and signed by him.
7—Early history in manuscript form in the library of the Bishop's Residence in Prince Rupert, loaned by Bishop Jordan.
8—AS ABOVE.
9—Since writing, Bishop Jordan has been transferred and his successor is Bishop F. J. O'Grady.
10—Biographical data supplied by Robert Tomlinson jr.
11—An account of the wedding in possession of Robert Tomlinson jr.
12—Apostle of the North—Cody.
13—History of the Diocese of Caledonia; a manuscript by Canon J. H. Keen in the archives of the diocese.
14—North British Columbia News—letters from the Rev. Mr. Price.
15—Up and Down the North Pacific Coast—Crosby.
16—Up and Down the North Pacific Coast—Crosby.
17—Up and Down the North Pacific Coast—Crosby.
18—From Potlatch to Pulpit—Pierce.

19—Manuscript in possession of the author, supplied by Mrs. J. C. Spencer.
20—Up and Down the North Pacific Coast—Crosby.
21—From Potlatch to Pulpit—Pierce.
22—Up and Down the North Pacific Coast.
23—Up and Down the North Pacific Coast.
24—Manuscript supplied by Major Poulton.

Chapter Twelve

1—H. B. Co. Archives B. 226/b/53, 58, 66.
2—Based on an article by an anonymous writer in the "Skeena District News" of 1904.
3—Graveyard Point gets its name from the grave which is there, marked by a tombstone. Recent clearing by the Columbia Cellulose Company has uncovered the old stone. It bears the name "Comahan" and the date 1873, and the stonemason's name G. Rudge. At this time George Rudge operated a stoneyard in Victoria and the monument was undoubtedly carved by him. A Port Simpson Indian called Comahan had a fish camp near this point but on the other side of the river and the victims of the tragedy were probably this man and his daughter.
4—Harvey Snow was more intimately associated with the Naas River than the Skeena. He and his wife operated a small store on the Naas for years. He is credited with having taught the Indians to build sheet iron tanks in which to boil the oolichan to extract the grease. He also introduced a seed potato which proved especially adaptable to growing conditions on the Naas and is still in use there.
5—This is probably a high estimate. Government reports estimate only seventy thousand dollars.
6—There are at least three versions of this story. In another, it was a Port Simpson Indian, a deckhand, who clambered on to the bottom of the hull as the boat rolled, and he saw the engineer's hand and pulled him out, so that both men rode on the bottom of the boat through the canyon.
7—Wiggs O'Neill in the Omineca Herald.

Chapter Thirteen

1—Canada on the Pacific: Horetzky.
2—The Making of a Great Canadian Railway: Talbot.
3—B.C. Legislative Assembly, Report of Select Committee appointed to enquire into the Acquisition of Kaien Island together with evidence and exhibits. Victoria. King's Printer, 1906. 157 pp.
4—The Making of a Great Canadian Railway.
5—Wiggs O'Neill in the Omineca Herald.

Chapter Fourteen

1—The Empire, Vol. 1, No. 4.
2—To choose a name for the Pacific terminal, the Grand Trunk Pacific conducted a country-wide contest, and offered a prize

of two hundred and fifty dollars for the winning name. Prince Rupert, the name of the first Governor of the Hudson's Bay Company, was finally chosen. Since it contained one more letter than the rules called for, the Company awarded two first prizes—one for Prince Rupert, and the other for the second choice which fulfilled the rules.

Chapter Fifteen

1—Lakes of the Skeena River Drainage, Bulletins 1 to 9 inclusive from the Progress Reports of the Pacific Coast Stations, Fisheries Research Board of Canada.

Chapter Sixteen

1—Data supplied by the Forestry Department, Provincial Government.

Chapter Seventeen

1—Geological Survey—Memoir 205—Mineral Resources of Terrace Area.
Geological Survey—Memoir 212—Mineral Resources Usk to Cedarvale.
Additional data from the Annual Reports of the Department of Mines, Provincial Government.
2—Omineca Herald, Vol. 5, No. 29.

Chapter Nineteen

1—War Diary of the Prince Rupert Defences.
2—The original spelling of this name was Kitamaat. Present day spelling drops the third "a". The Aluminum Company have called their new City by the same name, but spell it Kitimat.

INDEX

179

SKEENA UPDATE 1981

Twenty years later, the dreams of progress have been largely realised. British Columbia during this time, has been one of the fastest
growing provinces in the Dominion, and all parts of the province
have shared in the development. Many factors have contributed to
this era of prosperity, not the least of which was the political
stability which obtained. With the same party in power for twenty
years, long range planning was possible, and orderly development
ensued.

Of first importance in a country's growth is adequate transportation and a network of first class roads thoughout the province
received immediate attention. Highway 16, from Edmonton to
Prince Rupert was given only cursory service, largely because of the
heavy demands in the southern and populous portion of the country. At the end of the Second World War, the northern highway
consisted of a narrow gravelled road, winding along the path of
least resistance, and hard-topped only in patches at the eastern
end. Only in the last ten years has the gap between Prince George
and McBride been closed.

In this same period the road west from Prince George has been
brought up to provincial standards well beyond Terrace, and down
to Kitimat. The Skeena portion was predominantly rock work, but
the Kitimat extension presented a different problem. The old road
to Lakelse Lake skirted along the lower levels of the eastern hills,
but the new highway was built down on the flats, and approached
the shore of Lakelse Lake. While construction was still proceeding,
the completed portion around the head of the lake was suddenly
destroyed. Many theories were advanced to explain the accident,
but it appears the new road interfered with the drainage off the
eastern hills. After a particularly heavy rain, the water backed up
behind the road bed, collecting in the sub-soil until a sufficient
quantity had accumulated to sweep all before it. Suddenly the
hillside slid down to the flats, carrying the road and all else before it,
and deposited the whole in the lake. The new campsite, just completed, at the head of the lake, joined the procession. Fortunately
there was little traffic on the road at the time, so that there was no
loss of life. However, road machinery was lost, and one truck
entering the area from the south, just at the crucial moment, had to
be abandoned. The driver, seeing the road heaving and cracking in
front of him, jumped from his vehicle and, springing over the

ever-widening fissures, like Eliza crossing the ice, finally scrambled to high ground, where he could watch his truck slowly sinking in the muddy sea. Alterations in the engineering of the road bed solved the problem, and the modern road over the same area has stood the test of time!

Work on the stretch from Terrace to Prince Rupert is proceeding rapidly. This piece of road presents many problems since it follows the Skeena River for seventy of its ninety-five miles, and has to share, with the railroad, the narrow bench along the river bank. It has been black-topped for the past fifteen years, and now is being straightened, rerouted and widened to meet the demands of modern traffic. Work has been proceeding from both ends and three quarters has been finished. New concrete and steel bridges have been installed, including a new crossing of the Skeena River at Terrace.

Improvements have been made in rail transportation also, although not as obviously. The Canadian National has carried out ballasting of its road bed, replaced the rail with heavier steel, and modernised its equipment. With diesel locomotives, the need for the numerous stations has disappeared, so the little red station houses have been closed and, in most cases, torn down.

The P.G.E. Railway, now called the British Columbia Railway, has pushed north and west from Prince George, and is paralleling the Canadian National as it advances west toward the upper Skeena valley. It has been suggested that a loop to unite the two railroads, should be built down the Naas valley to Terrace. This development is essential if the Canadian Cellulose Co. of Prince Rupert is going to be able to develop and harvest its timber holdings in the upper Naas valley. With the provincial government owning a controlling interest in the Canadian Cellulose Co. (see "Prince Rupert") and also the B.C. Railway, it is a logical solution.

At the end of the war, air transportation was confined to seaplanes in the Prince Rupert area, with military air fields at Terrace and Smithers. After much investigation and negotiation, an airport was constructed on Digby Island to serve the city of Prince Rupert, and the air fields at Smithers and Terrace were taken over by the Department of Transport and up-graded for civilian services. The Prince Rupert airport opened in Aguust 1961, and was connected to the city by a ferry across the harbour. The old North Vancouver Ferry No. 4 was purchased for the purpose, and gave good service until it was replaced in 1970 by one especially designed and built for the run.

Transportation by water has had its radical changes also. Northland Transportation Ltd., which replaced the old Union Steamship Co., was the only freight and passenger service left on the coast. The Canadian National and the Canadian Pacific Steamships had retired from the picture, although the Canadian Pacific still operates a cruise ship in the summer months from Vancouver to Alaska, touching at Prince Rupert on the way. Heavy freight now moves by tug and barge, and the Canadian National expanded their car barge service to Alaska in 1962, by a second route across the Gulf of Alaska to Whittier, where contact is made with the Alaska Railroad. At the end of 1972, the original barge service to Ketchikan was terminated to be replaced by a direct barge service from Bellingham.

The big development has been in ferry service in and out of Prince Rupert. The interest of the State of Alaska in the Skeena valley previously noted, and particularly in the highway, resulted in the establishment of a ferry service or "marine highway" down the panhandle to Prince Rupert. Four ships regularly connect the ports of Southeastern Alaska with the Skeena highway at Prince Rupert, the service being instituted in 1963. Almost immediately the provincial government announced that a ferry service would be operated from Vancouver Island to link up with the Alaska Ferries at Prince Rupert, and in 1966 the "Queen of Prince Rupert" made her maiden voyage from Kelsey Bay on Vancouver Island to the northern terminus at Prince Rupert. With the beginning of summer service in 1979, the point of departure on Vancouver Island was changed to Port Hardy. This was made possible by the building of a road up the island from Kelsey Bay. In the summer of 1980 a new ferry, the "Queen of the North" replaced the "Queen of Prince Rupert" on the coastal run, and after a short interval of duty out of Victoria, the "Queen of Prince Rupert" has been placed on regular service between Prince Rupert and the Queen Charlotte Islands.

While ocean shipping has existed sporadically since the construction of the railroad and the port of Prince Rupert, the development of industry in the area has resulted in a considerable expansion in this field also. Export of lumber and logs, and an addition to the grain elevator at Prince Rupert in 1963 have brought more ships into the terminal city, while the ports of Kitimat and Port Edward have numerous ships throughout the year, servicing their respective plants.

Further development in the port of Prince Rupert will be discussed later. The most recent happening in transportation was the sudden withdrawal in 1976 of the federal subsidy paid to the Northland Transportation Co., to supply regular freight and passenger service to the isolated communities of the Pacific Coast. This resulted in the withdrawal and sale of the Northland ships and loud protests from all concerned. No adequate substitute has yet been found by what appear to be indifferent governments in Ottawa and Victoria. In fact a grant has been made to the B.C. government for ferry services, and it has been left to the provincial authorities to find some way of servicing the northern ports. This may well result in Kitimat becoming a port of call for B.C. Ferries, but in the meantime heavy freight is moving up the coast on barges.

Two other utilities are essential in area development — power and communications. B.C. Hydro took over the power supply with local plants in the smaller communities, and in 1964 acquired the Northern B.C. Power Co., supplying Prince Rupert and district. In 1965, transmission lines were erected linking Kitimat, Terrace and Prince Rupert, and the following year the Kemano Power House capacity was increased to eight generators of 112,000 H.P. each. In the meantime Peace River power was being brought west on a new high tension power line. This line was carried down the Telkwa valley into the Copper River valley and so into Terrace and is now linked up with the Kitimat-Terrace-Prince Rupert grid. Plans were advanced to increase the Kemano power still further by diverting water from Morice Lake. However, this has received strong opposition, since it would inevitably decrease the water flowing into the Bulkley River and adversely affect the salmon run in the Skeena River.

In 1968 a natural gas pipe line was extended west from Prince George and this has been completed to Prince Rupert and Kitimat, bringing a new source of power to households and industry. Just outside the city of Prince Rupert, B.C. Hydro has erected a stand-by electrical plant, powered by this natural gas.

Before the last World War, communication with the outside world was by means of telegraph lines accompanying the railroad, and the early AM radiophone. During the war a microwave system was built along the coast from Vancouver to Prince Rupert, and in 1959 a radio-telephone connection from Prince Rupert to Vancouver was completed and operated by the Northwest Telephone Company. In 1962, CFTK, a television station, was established in Terrace and by means of a microwave station on McLean Mountain, the programs were beamed into Prince Rupert. This station's network has steadily expanded and extends east, north, west and south from Terrace as well as covering the neighbouring coast out of Prince Rupert. At first all programs were initiated in Terrace, but in 1967 live coverage was approved by the Canadian Broadcasting Commission and this was made possible through the completion of a micro system extending west from Prince George, and built by the B.C. Telephone Co. In Nov. 1970 colour television was instituted, and later cable television service was added, supplying rebroadcast programs from Vancouver.

FISHERIES

The economy of the Skeena District has always been dependent on its natural resources — fisheries, foresty, and, to a lesser degree, mining.

The trend to consolidation in the fishing industry, previously noted, has continued and the canning of salmon is now carried out by three companies — B.C. Packers Ltd., Canadian Fishing Co. Ltd., and the Cassiar Packing Co. — as well as the Prince Rupert Fishermen's Co-operative which has added canning to its other processing. A new co-operative has been formed in Port Simpson which will be referred to later.

B.C. Packers have centralized all their canning at Port Edward, having absorbed the Nelson Brothers' plant, and closing their Sunnyside cannery nine years ago. The Canadian Fishing Co. acquired North Pacific Cannery and Inverness on the Slough, and these were both closed. This company canned all their fish in the Oceanside cannery on the waterfront of the city of Prince Rupert. The only Cannery operating on the Skeena River now is the Cassiar Packing Co., at Cassiar or Caspaco.

In June 1972 a disastrous fire struck the Prince Rupert waterfront destroying the Ocean dock and with it the Oceanside Cannery. The loss of the cannery and the season's supply of cans three weeks before the fishing started, presented a bleak picture for the fishing company and for the large body of workers who depended on their seasonal employment in the cannery for their annual income. What followed is an amazing story of organisation and co-operation. The two other companies came to the rescue, something which could never have happened in the old "cut throat" days of salmon canning on the Skeena. The Canadian Fishing Co. reactivated the old North Pacific Cannery — no mean feat in itself — and the Cassiar and Port Edward plants operated on a twenty-four hour schedule. During the day they canned their own fish, and at night the Canadian Fishing Co. crews took over to process theirs. With this arrangement all fish caught in the Skeena-Naas area were successfully processed. The accomplishment of keeping machinery running twenty-four hours a day without major breakdowns, for a full season is a tribute to men and machinery, and undoubtedly produced many unsung heroes.

Canadian Fishing Co. have rebuilt the Oceanside Cannery and a new cold storage plant on the old drydock site in Prince Rupert harbour.

In the halibut fisheries the main development has been the building of larger and more modern vessels with improved facilities for handling and caring for the fish. In 1971 the "mercury scare" seriously curtailed the catch, as government regulations forbade the taking of fish over a hundred pounds in weight. Common sense returned in 1972 and Canadian fishermen were allowed to deliver any size of fish to a Canadian port. The astronomical prices paid for halibut during the last few years undoubtedly have made up to the fishermen for the losses of yesterday.

Government regulations are making themselves felt in the salmon fishing too. The "Davis Plan" instituted in 1971 for the restriction of fishing licences and the purchase of obsolete boats, aroused much antagonism amongst the fishermen, particularly the native Indians, who saw themselves being forced out of fishing, source of their main livelihood for uncounted generations. The object of the plan was to up-grade the boats and restrict their numbers, but inevitably this worked a hardship on many who had depended entirely on fishing for their income, and for economic reasons used old equipment and, in many cases, cannery-owned boats.

The government activity in attempting to regulate and improve the salmon runs is more commendable. By using a test net on the lower river, and counting the salmon reaching the spawning grounds, the Fisheries department is able to determine if and when adequate numbers of fish are getting up the river. The number of days allotted for fishing is set accordingly and varies from week to week, during the season. To improve the production of fry, a large artificial spawning bed has been constructed on the Fulton River, and it is evident already that this is improving the Babine Lake run.

Unfortunately similar steps cannnot be taken in the halibut fisheries and considerable concern is being felt over the diminishing catches. Drag fishing by foreign vessels is being blamed for destruction of the young halibut, but no one really knows much about the spawning grounds of the halibut. Canada has finally declared her ownership of the off-shore waters extending out for 200 miles. It is hoped that this will enable better control of conservation methods. Already it has produced a new commercial product — filletted ocean perch — which previously was being harvested by foreign vessels. Another valuable addition to fisheries has been the oriental market for fresh herring roe. This is processed in the south and in Prince Rupert, and last year, in the Rupert area amounted to over 260 tons of roe.

FORESTRY

The utilization of forest products has been responsible for the major developments in the Skeena District during the past twenty years. The building of secondary roads to make the timber accessible has resulted in an immense network throughout the area north and west of the river. Most of the roads have been constructed by the Columbia Cellulose Co., to open up the vast acreage of their Forest Management License, while the Forestry department of the provincial government has pushed a road up the Kispiox valley into the Swan Lake district, close to the Naas River. This road will ultimately connect with the Naas River road running north from Terrace.

The Columbia Cellulose road begins at Terrace, extending up the Kitsumkalum valley and across the divide into the Naas valley. It was opened in 1958 and has been extended up and down the Naas River until it reached the level of the Meziadin River. Here the provincial government built a bridge across the Naas River which was opened in the fall of 1971. A second road to the Naas holdings was opened up the Kitwancool valley, and this road joins up with the main road up the Naas. This road is now extended to link up with the Cassiar road from Stewart. All these roads are open to the general public on week-ends and holidays. At Kitwanga, Columbia Cellulose has built a combination sawmill and chipping mill to service the timber brought down this road. The unit has been in operation since 1971.

In 1964 the Cellulose announced the construction of a bleached Kraft pulp mill to share the site with their mill on Watson Island, and the provincial government extended their timber holdings to take in additional acreage up the Naas valley, extending into the Bear Lake country. At the same time forest licences were granted to MacMillan Bloedel Ltd., for a pulp mill in Kitimat, and to the Bulkley Valley Pulp & Timber Co. for a mill at Houston. In both cases the acreage involved was in the immediate area of the respective mill sites, and in the former case, also embraced the Ootsa Lake region.

The kraft mill at Port Edward was proceeded with immediately and went into production in December 1968. The project for a pulp and sawmill at Kitimat was abandoned by MacMillan Bloedel, and was subsequently undertaken by Eurocan Pulp and Paper Co., an enterprise financed by a combination of European and North American capital. They built in two stages — a sawmill, opened in 1969, and a pulp mill in 1970.

In the Houston development there was even more delay. Bowater Paper Co. announced a mill for Houston in 1966. Ultimately a modern sawmill, now referred to as a "lumber complex," was opened by Bulkley Valley Forest Industries in 1970. The plans for a pulp mill received a great deal of organised opposition, because of the threat of pollution to the Bulkley River, and to date no further steps have been taken. The "lumber complex" got into difficulties under the management of Consolidated Bathurst Co. and Bowater Pulp and Paper, and is now operated as Northern Pulp Ltd. Production is a million board feet per day. Presently a consortium of Eurocan and Weldwood of Canada is building another sawmill as the Houston Forest Products which will have a similar output.

In addition to the production of lumber and pulp, there has been a great increase in the export of logs. These have been drawn from coastal areas and chiefly exported through the port of Prince Rupert. A small industry was begun at Port Simpson in 1963 and some logs exported, but it proved uneconomical and has been closed down for some years. However the Port Simpson harbour is now being used for booming and shipping logs from an operation farther up the coast.

MINING

The Skeena valley presents a highly mineralised area, and prospecting and development work have continued throughout the region. Three properties have come into production in the interval. Granisle Copper, a wholly owned subsidiary of Granby is producing 14,000 tons of ore per day in open pit mining, and Bell Copper of Noranda, 10,000 tons, also in open pit. Both these mines are located on Babine Lake. The opening of these two mines has resulted in the building of the town of Granisle, situated on the western shore of Babine Lake, and connected by thirty miles of paved highway from Topley on Highway 16. It was incorporated as a village in June 1971, and has a present population of 1700.

The mines are located on the opposite side of the lake, and traffic is maintained by barge. To keep the lake route open in the winter, an ingenious arrangement was installed. Two plastic pipes were strung across the lake, lying on the bottom. Through small holes in the pipes compressed air is released which bubbles up to the surface and prevents the formation of ice by bringing up the warmer water of the bottom of the lake to the top. A couple of miles down the lake the same arrangement obtains for access to the Noranda property.

The town is nicely laid out, with modern accommodations and a first class hotel. Medical and hospital services are the principal lack, Burns Lake being the nearest hospital.

Equity Mines, 17 miles south of Houston is presently under construction, for copper, silver and gold. Concentrates of the Babine mines were being shipped through Prince Rupert until fire destroyed the Ocean dock. With the new facilities in operation at the Pacific port, it is hoped that the traffic will resume.

TOURISM

Only indirectly is tourism dependent on natural resources, but it has suddenly become an important part of the economy of the area. While fishing and hunting always were an attraction, the principal contributing factor has been the establishment of ferry service, north and south from Prince Rupert. The lure for Americans of their biggest state has brought a steady stream of traffic in and out of Alaska, ever since the ferry was begun in 1963. In 1971 over 14,000 vehicles embarked or disembarked on the ferries, transporting approximately 57,000 tourists. In addition the "Queen of Prince Rupert" carried about 30,000 passengers. Most of these passengers and vehicles passed along the Skeena highway, along with many more who did not use the ferries. Subsequent years have witnessed a steady increase and every community along the Skeena is feeling the impact of the tourist. Last year the total for the first nine months for the "Queen of Prince Rupert" was 50,000 passengers and 14,000 cars.

THE BULKLEY VALLEY

Little change has occurred in this area, with the notable exception of the town of Houston. With the development of lumbering and now mining, the quiet little village of Pleasant Valley has blossomed into a thriving community of 3500 souls. On a recent visit the writer picked up a copy of "Marks on the Forest Floor" which is a recently published history of the area. In it, the story of a murder in the village which occurred in Sept. 1930, casts a new light on the Sankey Trial recorded on pages 39 to 41. The murderer, who was captured, had in his possession a silver brooch which was identified as belonging to the school teacher who was killed in Port Essington in 1926. An indication of the inadequacy of communications in this vast territory, in those days, was the fact that such an important discovery never reached the press in Vancouver or Prince Rupert. Only now, fifty years later, is Joseph Sankey exonerated!

HAZELTON

Here again, at the Forks, there has been little change except for a slow growth in keeping with the general population increase. The Old Town was incorporated as a village in 1956 and boasts a mayor and alderman, but New and South Hazelton remain unincorporated. The most noteworthy development has been in the native population. Amongst the northern tribes there has been a rebirth of interest in their ancient culture and a corresponding enthusiasm for their arts and crafts. This has been stimulated by the great increase in tourist activity and the accompanying market for any products or writings pertaining to Indian culture.

In the Hazelton area this movement has been encouraged and promoted by Polly Sargent, wife of Bill Sargent who continues the family's interests in the Old Town. Through her efforts the provincial government built a model Indian village on the point of land at the junction of the Bulkley and Skeena Rivers, and nearby constructed a modern camp site for tourists. K-San Indian village originally consisted of five "long houses." Two of them contain life size dioramas of Indian culture, before the arrival of the white man, and during the trading era, respectively. A third houses a museum of native artifacts, a fourth, a shop for native arts and crafts, and the fifth, a work shop. The complex was opened by the Premier, Hon. W.A.C. Bennett, in the summer of 1970, when he was made an honorary Chief, and a totem pole was erected in his honour. The Premier entered fully into the spirit of the occasion, and in proper "potlatch" style, presented an additional twenty thousand dollars for another building, which has since been erected. A seventh long house has now been added which houses the expanded museum and is glorified with the title — "Northwestern National Exhibition Centre."

K-San Village is not the only accomplishment of Mrs. Sargent, for along with Stan Rough, late of Kitimat, and other interested individuals, she organised the Skeena Totem Pole Restoration Society. By interesting government and industry, the society raised funds and undertook the restoration of the fast disintegrating totem poles of the Skeena valley. Kitwanga, Kitwancool, Kispiox, Hazelton and Kitzeguecla, all have benefitted from the work, and the visitor to the upper Skeena may once more see these superb examples of ancient Indian art. A well earned accolade has been awarded to Polly Sargent with membership in the Order of Canada.

Hazelton was originally proposed as Route A for the road to the north. The Forestry road up the Kispiox valley, at the time of writing, is within a few miles of connecting with the Stewart — Cassiar road. It may yet become the accepted trucking route from the north to southern B.C.

TERRACE

Of all the communities on the Skeena, the growth of Terrace has been the most spectacular. As the operating centre for the woods activities of the Columbia Cellulose Company and the junction point for the branch railway line to Kitimat, as well as for the highway to the same city, it would expect to be prosperous. However, it has surpassed even the most optimistic expectations, and at the last census had a population of 15,000. Occupying a hub position with Prince Rupert on the west, the system of logging highways to the north, connecting with the Cassiar road, Highway 16 to the east, and Kitimat and pulp and paper industries in the south, Terrace is in a fortunate position.

The town has spread in all directions and with the modern highway travelling eastward has crossed the river and formed a suburb known as Thornhill. It is reported that 3500 people live there.

As mentioned elsewhere, Terrace has become the communication centre for the television for the district, and inevitably the logical centre for many of the government services. A modern shopping complex in the middle of town and a new hospital with complete facilities contribute to the amenities of life in the community.

The road constructed by the Columbia Cellulose Company, which originally extended up the Kitsumkalum valley, has now crossed over into the Naas valley and, extending up that river, connects with the Stewart-Cassiar road, thus opening up a tremendous area of the northern half of the province. The road to Lakesle Lake has been continued to the city of Kitimat and has been brought up to first class standards. This has resulted in the development of a recreational area surrounding Lakelse Lake which serves both communities. The centre of this playground is the famous Lakelse Hot Springs, a resort which has the potential to rival the well known Harrison Hot Springs in the south.

In 1970 a large vocational school was opened on the bench land to the west of town, and later a regional college was instituted. This town will continue to grow, and if the suggested link between the C.N.R. and B.C.R. goes north from Terrace, it will rival Prince Rupert for the honour of first city on the Skeena.

KITIMAT

Owing to its unit construction, the visitor to Kitimat does not appreciate the changes that have occurred during the past eighteen years. Appearances are deceptive, for this city has grown steadily, and with the addition of the Eurocan Mills, now numbers about 12000. The plant of the Aluminum Co. has 6½ pot lines and has an annual production of 268,000 tonnes. (Approx. 295,000 tons).

Mention has already been made of the large amount of electrical power which is available and being used from the Kemano power plant. Lines were extended to Terrace in 1960 and Prince Rupert in 1965-66. The Kemano installation was increased to eight 112,000 H.P. generators to meet the demand.

Altogether the city of Kitimat is a thriving community with a stable economy and well equipped with all the social amenities which make for satisfactory living in an isolated area.

PORT SIMPSON

This village, which began as a Hudson's Bay Co. fort and became the centre of government for the north coast, was superceded by the city of Prince Rupert, and sank into comparative oblivion. Today it has experienced a renewed lease on life and is steadily increasing in importance. Deserted by its white population except for a few people connected with essential services, it has still remained one of the largest Indian villages in the province. Its population has increased to well over the thousand mark.

Assisted by the provincial government, a co-operative fishing company has been formed and a modern cannery has been built. The cannery has had a number of operational problems, but has had a re-organisation of management and it appears will eventually be a successful venture. The federal government has made extensive harbour improvements which now afford ample sheltered anchorage for the large fishing fleet which operates in the immediate vicinity. In addition federal money has been made available for new housing, and the village, which was once a collection of antiquated and run down dwellings, has blossomed out into a town of neat, colourful modern homes. Much still requires to be done in demolishing old buildings, and improving the roads, before Port Simpson will once again be one of the beauty spots of the coast.

Surveys have been undertaken for a road to connect it with Prince Rupert, and it would undoubtedly become a welcome addition to that city's recreational facilities.

PRINCE RUPERT

The growth of this city from the last World War has been slow but steady and the population has doubled in that period. Last census gave about 16,000 with an additional 1000 in Port Edward, and these figures have certainly increased. Port Edward still depends entirely on the fish plant of Nelson Bros., or B.C. Packers Ltd. It has been vastly improved with new dwellings and good roads. The main road has been extended up the Skeena to Cassiar, serving the other canneries in the Slough. Except for Cassiar these canneries are no longer in operation but they serve as year round homes for a substantial native population. Port Edward incorporated as a village in 1966 and has a mayor and council. It will always be linked with Prince Rupert since it depends on that city for most of its cultural amenities as well as medical, hospital and high school facilities.

The city of Prince Rupert began as the Pacific terminus of a transcontinental railroad, but that dream faded with the Grand Trunk Pacific, and it became merely the end of a branch line of the

Canadian National Railway. As such, it received less and less attention until the Second World War, when the railroad was forced to upgrade its facilities. The war over, railroad interests flagged again; the drydock was dismantled, sold, and floated away, the C.N.R. dock torn down, and what services remained were concentrated in the Ocean dock, part of which had been built by the Americans during the war. The only positive use of the port was through the building of a car loading ramp and the establishment of a car barge service to Alaska. In 1972 a disastrous fire wiped out the Ocean dock, including the Oceanside cannery in the south end of the building. At this writing nothing now remains of the Canadian National terminus except the marshalling yards along the waterfront and a small station perched on the shore of the harbour. Uptown, the C.N.R. Telegraph occupies a building on Second Avenue.

Fortunately, the City Fathers kept up a steady pressure on the federal government to do something about the long neglected port on the north Pacific coast, and in 1970 Premier Bennett took a hand in the negotiations. Ultimately in 1972 the port of Prince Rupert was declared a National Harbour, and, as such, is now administered under the National Harbours Board. The first visit of the new officials almost coincided with the burning of the Ocean dock. Fate, having cleared out the last of the old, left a clear field upon which the National Harbours Board could build anew. A small passenger dock has been retrieved from the remains of the old Ocean dock, and a new Ocean terminal has been constructed immediately south of the Prince Rupert Fishermen's Co-operative Plant. The first ship to use the new facilities docked on Feb. 21, 1977. Its use has steadily increased and there is now a continuous flow of lumber, sulphur pellets, non-board grain and copper concentrates, with other odds and ends.

The grain elevator has been modernised and doubled in capacity. Recently it was sold to Prince Rupert Grain Ltd. which is a consortium of three grain co-operatives and three private grain operatives from the prairie provinces. It was sold by the federal government for one dollar. Part of the deal, however, was an agreement to erect an additional elevator of eight million bushels on the proposed bulk loading facility on Ridley Island.

Ridley Island is one of a group of islands lying in the mouth of the Skeena River. It is practically continuous with Kaien Island at low tide, and forms part of the entrance to Prince Rupert Harbour. It also forms the harbour of Port Edward. The island is low lying and when levelled off would supply six hundred acres for marshalling yards and bulk storage. It is being financed jointly by the provincial and federal governments. Construction of a road is underway on the back of Kaien Island as a branch of Highway 16, and is due to be completed by the fall of 1981. Clearing of land for the site of the new grain elevator is also proceeding, as well as a test causeway for the access of the railroad.

In the meantime negotiations have been proceeding with Japan for the sale of coal by Dennison Mines of Toronto, and Teck Corporation of Vancouver and an agreement was signed in February 1981 between the two companies, the provincial and federal governments and representatives of the Japanese steel industry. The source of the coal is the large deposits in the north-eastern part of the province, and access will require the building of an extension from the B.C. Railway into the Quintette Coal Fields by the Anzac route. Up-grading of the C.N.R. from Prince George to Prince Rupert with heavier steel will also be required. Target date for beginning of shipments is 1984.

During these years the city's economy has been thriving steadily due in large part to the Columbia Cellulose mill on Watson Island. In 1964 the company constructed a bleached kraft mill alongside the original mill, with a resultant increase in employees residing in the city. To ease the city in financing the increasing population which has resulted in the opening up of three new sub-divisions, the provincial government in 1966 authorised the extension of the city's boundaries to include Watson Island. This brings the company's properties on to the municipal tax roll. While the move was understandably opposed by the company, the difficulties were eventually settled and the large increase in tax revenue has enabled the city to carry out a continuing program of civic improvement. In spite of financial difficulties, the company has proved itself a good corporate citizen of Prince Rupert and has made numerous contributions to improve the recreational facilities for employees and others in the city. In 1973 the provincial government bought out Columbia Cellulose and now holds a controlling interest in the new Canadian Cellulose Company. The original acetate pulp mill became obsolete, and has been dismantled and remodelled for kraft. It went into operation again in 1978.

Without going into detail, one must record the construction of an airport on Digby Island by the Department of Transport, the building of a new hospital, opened by Her Majesty, the Queen, in 1971, a new recreational complex which includes a covered ice rink, a public library, a golf course of 18 holes, sundry motels and apartment buildings, and two modern shopping malls. In short, the city which celebrated its Diamond Jubilee in 1970 has definitely arrived, and with its many parks and paved streets presents a picture of prosperous and comfortable living.

The Government of Canada has been making much of the development of the north. British Columbia, too, has become very conscious of the potentials of its northern half. The Skeena valley has already felt the impact of that interest. The future looks promising, indeed!